HIJACKING AMERICA

In memorium CHG – cinq ans déjà

HIJACKING AMERICA

HOW THE RELIGIOUS AND SECULAR RIGHT CHANGED WHAT AMERICANS THINK

SUSAN GEORGE

polity

First published in 2008 by Polity Press

Polity Press
65 Bridge Street
Cambridge CB2 1UR, UK.

Polity Press
350 Main Street
Malden, MA 02148, USA

ISBN-13: 978-0-7456-4460-8
ISBN-13: 978-0-7456-4461-5 (pb)

A catalogue record for this book is available from the British Library.

Typeset in 10.75 on 14 pt Adobe Janson
by Servis Filmsetting Ltd, Manchester
Printed and bound in United States by Maple-Vail

The publisher has used its best endeavors to ensure that the URLs for external websites referred to in this book are correct and active at the time of going to press. However, the publisher has no responsibility for the websites and can make no guarantee that a site will remain live or that the content is or will remain appropriate.

Every effort has been made to trace all copyright holders, but if any have been inadvertently overlooked the publishers will be pleased to include any necessary credits in any subsequent reprint or edition.

For further information on Polity, visit our website: www.polity.co.uk

CONTENTS

INTRODUCTION

HOW THE SECULAR AND RELIGIOUS
RIGHT CAPTURED AMERICA

After the tragic events of September 11, 2001, nearly all Europeans felt profound sympathy for the United States. The Director of *Le Monde*, Jean-Marie Colombani, summed up the outpouring of solidarity in his editorial (leader) next day entitled: "We are all Americans." Only a tiny minority reacted to the terrorist attack with a shrug and a comment to the effect that it was horrible for the victims, but the US "had it coming." Within a few short years, however, this affection and fellow-feeling of the vast majority had transmuted like gold into lead. Dismay, distrust, and what the late journalist-novelist Hunter S. Thompson might have called "fear and loathing" of the United States government predominated.

These all-too-common sentiments relate much less to a change of heart toward the American people than to the actions of President George W. Bush and his entourage. People were naturally encouraged by the outcome of the 2006 mid-term elections that returned the Democrats to power in the Congress. As I write, the campaign for the next presidential election in 2008 is in full flow, and many await the exit of Bush and the defeat of the Republicans, when the United States will return, or so they believe, to normal.

Would it were so! I too would like to believe that the first years of the twenty-first century have been a cruel aberration that will vanish from memory as a bad dream evaporates in the morning. I fear, however, that it will be much more difficult than that and the point of this book is to explain why. *Hijacking America* is thus not about the "war against terror," the "axis of evil," or other staples of the Bush–Cheney foreign or domestic programs but rather about the political, intellectual, and cultural climate that has made them possible.

I want to argue that a long-term, successful rightward shift of American culture has been underway since at least the 1970s; that its guiding spirits have acquired lasting power over policy; that this new belief system, both secular and religious, is unlikely to change fundamentally simply because one party, or one President, is in power rather than another. "Neo-liberalism" and "neo-conservatism" are the words most frequently chosen to describe this system and these terms refer to a coherent set of principles and ideas (we will look at the nuances between them shortly). This culture has been patiently constructed; it permeates the whole of American society from the leadership to the bottom rungs of the social ladder and it is not called into question because its assumptions are usually unspoken. They have nonetheless moved the center of gravity of American politics much further to the right.

This culture is significantly based on lies and the new center of gravity has increasingly made a weird kind of politics possible. The United States can be a mystifying place even for Americans because the usual rules of Western democracies often seem not to apply. We know, of course, that all heads of State keep secrets and often lie, especially when they feel sure they can get away with it. None, however, approaches the dazzling heights of deceit scaled in recent American times. Had Congress undertaken any meaningful investigations between 2002 and 2007, President George W. Bush would almost certainly have been found guilty of "high crimes and misdemeanors" and impeached (leaving the presidency to Dick Cheney who would then have had to be impeached in his turn . . .)

In contrast, the closing years of the second millennium witnessed Republican legislators falling over themselves to impeach Bill Clinton for lying about sexual hanky-panky with a plump and eager young woman. How great a threat to the nation was that? What else was a gentleman and a roving husband to do?

Few, on the other hand, now seem to care about stolen elections, exposing one's own intelligence agents to possible assassination, and lying to the American people and to Congress on the broadest possible scale in order to trick them into supporting a costly, futile, and criminal war. Some critics argue that the American public has grown blasé about deceit in high places and may even have come to expect it, although this was surely not the case until quite recently.

Lyndon Johnson and Richard Nixon were hounded out of office because of their lies on matters foreign (Vietnam) or domestic (Watergate). Ronald Reagan, although he squeaked through in the end, had a queasy period for deceiving Americans about selling weapons to Iran and using the revenues to pay for the illegal military invasion of Nicaragua by the "Contras." As for Clinton, it is hard to say whether the public was more disgusted by his behavior or by the Republican–Roman circus of attempted impeachment, but everyone could agree that the scandal cost him precious time, better employed dealing with the country's urgent business. For Bush and Cheney, however, lying is more like a way of life.[1]

The long-term costs of these lies are incalculable both for Americans and for their victims beyond US borders. The Bush administration often combines unprecedented, disarming frankness with calculated deception. As the British journalist Michael Kinsley memorably phrased it:

> Bush II administration lies are often so laughably obvious that you wonder why they bother. Until you realize: They haven't bothered. If telling the truth were less bother, they'd try that too. The characteristic Bush II form of dishonesty is to construct an alternative reality on some topic and to regard anyone who objects to it as a snivelling dweeb obsessed with "nuance."[2]

From their point of view, the method has paid off. The Bush–Cheney (always keep a close watch on Cheney) presidency has used the Big Lie of a winnable war on terror in Iraq, not just to kill thousands of young Americans and hundreds of thousands of Iraqis, but also to reduce dramatically the civil rights of the American people established at the time of, and thanks to, the American Revolution.

This is the first regime in well over two hundred years to allow searches and seizures in people's homes without judicial warrant. New methods of broad electronic surveillance and trawling for information among ordinary Americans destroy the Fourth Amendment which forbids not only "unreasonable searches and seizures" but also requires a precise description of the "place to be searched, and the persons or things to be seized." This Presidency has even dared put an end to habeas corpus and authorize torture of anyone considered an enemy. If your aim is to throttle democracy, lies can work.

Without indulging to the slightest degree in conspiracy theory, nor even evoking the petroleum connection, anyone interested can verify that the Bush–Cheney clan

- wanted and planned to invade Iraq long before September 11, 2001;
- manipulated the intelligence community and distorted its research in order to justify this intervention;
- knew there were no weapons of mass destruction in Iraq;
- knew there was no connection between the secular Arab regime of Saddam Hussein on one hand and Osama bin Laden and the religious fanatics of Al Qaeda on the other.

Politics are debased. The hope that Keynesian policies as practiced during the New Deal and the post-war period might still be applied grows ever more faint. No critical, credible, alternative project exists on the left and there would be few progressive organizations to sustain it if it did. The Democratic Party no longer pretends that it is social-democratic or that it seeks to protect the poor and vulnerable. Anywhere but the United States, this party would be seen as a right-of-center organization, with many of its members engaged in pushing the party further rightwards. Past or present "conservative" European leaders like Angela Merkel or Jacques Chirac are probably more progressive than most Democrats, with some honorable exceptions, like the members of the Congressional Progressive Caucus.

The financing system ensures that Democrats running for election are just as beholden to big corporate money as the Republicans. The problems and the opinions of the working class no longer count for as much with the size of that class dwindling. The North American Free Trade Agreement (NAFTA) and similar free-trade pacts have wiped out many workers' jobs and for the past twenty-five years, successive administrations (including Carter's and Clinton's) have gutted the welfare system. Some parts of some American cities resemble nothing so much as the Third World, as anyone could observe when Hurricane Katrina struck New Orleans.

The two-party system nonetheless remains intact and so far no significant popular political forces of revolt are pushing politics to the left.

Since the fateful attack on the Twin Towers and the launching of its unnecessary but costly wars, the American executive has consistently ignored and downgraded the legislative branch. The executive continues, for example, to build permanent military bases in Iraq, which the Pentagon plans to use indefinitely, although Congress has specifically prohibited further spending on them.

The "War on Terror" has been a godsend to the neo-conservative leadership, for the excellent reason that it cannot be won. The country remains on a war footing, spending tens of billions of dollars, feeding enormous contracts to corporations like Cheney's Halliburton; handing over ever-greater powers to the "wartime President." Americans and Iraqis continue to die for nothing. As virtually everyone now admits, the situation in that martyred country is far worse than when the United States arrived and the US itself is less secure than it was prior to the invasion. In spite of the embargo, Iraq functioned, though no one denies either that Saddam Hussein ran a repulsive dictatorship.

It remains to be seen if the Democrats, with their recaptured majority in Congress, will investigate the many impeachable offences committed by the Bush–Cheney axis and inquire into the commission of war crimes in Iraq, Guantanamo, and elsewhere. Democrats do not now, it is true, command the necessary two-thirds majority in the Senate for impeachment, but the crucial question is that of courage. The party leadership seems already to have decided it must not "look backwards." The corporate-controlled media are bored with the whole business, explaining that the public has "moved on." Aside from a few independent journalists, websites, and citizens' groups, there is at present no public outcry for such investigations.

The economic front is no more inspiring. Most Americans are working harder for less. Inequalities have never been so deep and pervasive since the late 1920s. The top one percent of Americans has more than doubled its share of the national income since the end of the Second World War; working people's wages, however, have stagnated or declined. The definition of the "poverty line," first established in the 1950s and virtually unchanged since then, seriously underestimates (at 12.5 percent) the number of poor people in the country. One child in four is born into poverty; 45 million Americans have no health insurance. The minimum wage hardly moved in a quarter-century, although the Democrats have now acted to increase it. Poverty is endemic within significant segments of the white majority as well as the black or Latino minorities.

Still there is no popular clamor for economic reform, higher wages, retirement benefits, health coverage, greater equality – much less demonstrations and riots in the streets. With some courageous exceptions, the trade unions are weak and often concentrate – like much of the rest of the American left – on questions of gender and sexual-orientation and racial non-discrimination issues. People seem quite prepared to vote, if they vote at all, against their own interests, and they stubbornly retain their faith in the "market." At least half – especially among the least educated and worst off – do not vote at all.

Corporations continue to rake in record profits: in 2006, Exxon's were $40 billion. The government still gives flagrant tax breaks and outrageous subsidies to the corporate sector, especially the already opulent oil industry. One financial scandal after another bursts upon the country, the guilty are mostly bailed out with taxpayers' money, the occasional scapegoat goes to jail and the outcry subsides. The salaries of corporate CEOs are now well over 400 times those of their average employee. The progressive movements of the 1930s that called for greater equality and social justice are long gone.

The crusading press of yesteryear has accepted self-censorship and in any case belongs to the same sorts of corporations as the rest of the economy. Television, from which most Americans get all their news, is supine and replaces real news with the latest celebrity gossip and trivial (though not for the victims) news, endlessly repeated, about the latest storm damage or road-crash. All this provokes a collective yawn. As Gore Vidal says, "America is a quarter of a billion people totally misinformed and disinformed by their government. This is tragic, but our media is – I wouldn't even say corrupt – it's just beyond telling us anything that the government doesn't want us to know."[3]

As for popular religion, the Pulitzer Prize winner and former *New York Times* correspondent Chris Hedges sees the radical Christian right as a nascent breed of fascism, American style.[4] The poor, as well as increasing numbers of the threatened and unstable middle class, are plunged into despair, trapped in soulless communities of a numbing sameness where they feel abandoned, isolated, and lonely. They often find solace in churches that promise community, utopia, and, for many of them, revenge. Most of these church-goers are just lost souls clinging to their often bizarre beliefs; many of them are even earnest idealists or utopians and the majority are sincere believers, certainly not evil people. They are nonetheless easily manipulated.

Some Christian evangelical leaders are downright dangerous demagogs whose dream is to establish a quasi-fascist theocracy in the United States. It is not unfair to draw a comparison with the early 1930s in Germany at the beginning of Hitler's reign. The Christian right's leadership knows how to maneuver the masses and are sure that their troops will follow their lead, at least at the beginning; just as those precursors uncritically followed Hitler, Mussolini, and other dictators.

A triggering event like another terrorist attack on the scale of September 11, a devastating ecological crisis, or an economic meltdown could give them just the chance they pray for. No countervailing force stands against these leaders while the moderating influence of traditional, mainstream Christians diminishes daily. Most American intellectuals and middle or upper middle-class people do not take this threat seriously; for them, the tens of millions of religious people are just "nuts," or "Jesus-freaks," not a genuine political force.

You have heard much of this before, at least in broad outline, and except for religion, I do not intend to dwell on these issues in detail. Gross inequalities, endless war, ruling class greed, the desperate situation of increasing numbers of Americans are not my real subject here although they are necessarily the backdrop and figure in the pages that follow.

My purpose is rather to ask *how all this happened.*

How could a few decades suffice to trample into the mud American ideals, expressed in some of the most inspiring political documents ever written? How can the country whose first independent act was to declare that "all men are created equal" now be one of the most unequal societies on earth? Why were those who planned the takeover strategy – for that is what it is – so free to operate? Why have they met so little opposition? What hope is there for change? I hope to show that the battle has been above all cultural and that the strategy of the far right wing has paid. If you can get into peoples' heads, you need not worry about their hands and hearts. They will follow. Then the leadership can do as it pleases.

Many people, particularly Europeans, continue to live for the most part in a rational, well-educated world, with public services and at least some social protection. Their societies, despite many injustices, are still relatively liveable. Perhaps as a result, these people tend to believe that the present calamitous situation of the United States is entirely the doing of Bush and his neo-conservative followers. Logically, then, this situation will cease as soon as the present leadership is ousted, at the latest in 2008, and replaced by more principled officials.

Again, most Europeans who travel to the United States for work or pleasure never venture beyond the Atlantic and Pacific coasts – admittedly more attractive, more Euro-friendly and certainly more fun than the places that lie in between. They have no idea what people are thinking – or not thinking – about in the vast heartland. They do not understand how Americans can have elected the leaders they have wished upon themselves and are sure that any day now they will come to their senses. Such strange behavior is temporary and will cease when a different party or different personnel capture that leadership.

I disagree. Such an optimistic scenario strikes me as both dangerously misleading and a cruel illusion. It also reflects conscious or unconscious social or intellectual snobbery that treats common people as beneath contempt. One cannot simply laugh off the beliefs, attitudes and knee-jerk reactions of tens of millions of people, particularly when they are citizens of the most powerful and arguably the most dangerous country on earth. This is why I try to explain where these belief systems come from and how they are propagated by a reactionary and, yes, sometimes fascist cadre; and fed to ordinary people through highly effective, sophisticated, and long-term strategies that are unlikely to change.

The signs I have tried to identify, whether in the spheres of government, civil society, or religion, point to a conscious long-term effort carried out by ruthlessly efficient, well-funded, and well organized elites. They intend to continue advancing their authoritarian, anti-democratic, corporate-controlled oligarchic State, using reactionary but soul-satisfying religion as window-dressing and as an element of social control. Having a Bush-type president naturally makes their lives easier but they do not depend upon it.

New facts and fresh evidence are flooding in every day and I have constantly had to confront the temptation to return to sections of this narrative I thought completed in order to be as thorough and timely as the subject deserves. I have succumbed to this temptation more than once, but finally decided I must resist because the need is overwhelming that outsiders – as well as many incredulous Americans – understand the country. That urgency should finally be the guiding principle for a writer who considers herself a "scholar-activist" or "public scholar."* My entire effort is frustratingly incomplete but rather than trying to attain the unattainable *magnum opus*, and one too weighty to read on the bus, I have opted for getting the word, however imperfect, "out there," wherever the "there" may be.

Allow me now to take exactly the opposite tack in order to avoid possible misunderstandings. I may be wrong and would be exceedingly pleased if I were. I try to describe a state of affairs that strikes me as a clear, present, and lasting danger to civilization but this fear says nothing about the inevitability of such an outcome. Americans have more than once proven themselves to be inventive, resilient, and just plain smart.

There are dozens – hundreds – of citizens' organizations that have not given up, working under difficult conditions, goading Congress to do the right thing, informing lazy journalists, promoting citizen action around local, national, and even international issues. There are dozens – hundreds – of faith-based and church groups helping the poor, the

---

* At its 48th annual Congress in Chicago in March 2007, the International Political Economy section of the International Studies Association was kind enough to present me with its first "Outstanding Public Scholar Award" of which I'm inordinately proud as that is what I've always tried to be.

immigrants, the downtrodden, and the environment. This book is almost entirely about the right wing, but that does not mean that the right has no opposition. The country is huge and progressives may be rather thin on the ground, but they do exist and such people and organizations fighting against the dishonoring of their nation deserve all the support they can get. Perhaps, thanks to the coalescing of all these efforts, the great majority of Americans will understand in time where their real interests lie, how the right manipulates them and will turn away from false prophets.

Such an outcome is more likely, however, when one shines a spotlight on the manipulations and that is what I have tried to do here, with no pretensions to being exhaustive. It would be profoundly satisfying to find that this book inspires others to take up and complete the task. It would be even more satisfying if it helped progressives to ask themselves how the right accomplished a cultural takeover no one predicted a few decades earlier, what tools they used, what skills they deployed. Progressives could then put the answers to such questions to good use.

There is nothing especially mysterious about the takeover – those who engineered it used money, willing talent, and organization strategically to promote ideas. Progressives, too, have plenty of willing and articulate talent, they too can organize; there is even money available if funders at last recognize their responsibilities and start supporting the production and dissemination of progressive, enlightened ideas, because ideas have consequences.

1

MANUFACTURING COMMON SENSE, OR CULTURAL HEGEMONY FOR BEGINNERS

> One of the most important characteristics of any group that is developing toward dominance is its struggle to assimilate and to conquer "ideologically" the traditional intellectuals. But this assimilation and conquest is made quicker and more efficacious the more the group in question succeeds in elaborating its own organic intellectuals.
>
> Antonio Gramsci, *Prison Notebooks*

THE DOCTRINE

Capturing culture requires strategy, shrewdness, and stamina but before all these comes belief. To make the assumptions and main ideas of present-day American "common sense" explicit, the first step is to start with the doctrine. Because it is a belief system, we can compare it to a religion, and as with other religions, it is rarely practiced in its purest form. If it were, it would adhere to principles much like these:

- The market solution is always preferable to State regulation and intervention;
- Private enterprise outperforms the public sector on criteria of efficiency, quality, availability, and price;
- Free trade may have temporary drawbacks for some but will ultimately serve the entire population of any country better than protectionism;
- It is normal and desirable that activities like health care and education be profit-making activities;
- Lower taxes, particularly for the rich, will guarantee greater investment and thereby prosperity;
- Inequality is inbuilt in any society and is probably genetic if not racial;
- If people are poor, they have only themselves to blame because hard work is always rewarded;
- A truly free society cannot exist in the absence of a free market; it follows that capitalism and democracy are mutually supportive;
- Higher defense spending and a strong military will guarantee national security;
- The United States, by virtue of its history, its ideals, and its superior democratic system, should use its economic, political and military might to intervene in the affairs of other nations in order to promote free markets and democracy;
- People in other countries will welcome such interventions because they will rid the world of undesirable and disruptive elements in the international community and will ultimately prove to be for the good of all.

I've stated these principles in their most pared-down, extreme form. Naturally, trade unions often reject free-trade agreements; other interest groups or minorities may dispute one or another of these principles; but strip away the rhetoric that often makes them appear less harsh, most American citizens have come to agree, at least tacitly, with most of these statements. The last two regarding foreign intervention have been once more horrendously negated in Iraq (for those who had forgotten Vietnam, Cambodia, Chile, Nicaragua, or any number of other American interventions) where the legacy is again one of turmoil, massacre, and ultimately defeat. The majority of Americans have turned against the war in Iraq. This does not necessarily mean that they have rejected the notion of American exceptionalism and the interventionist principle itself. Perhaps many have simply turned against the fact that the US is losing.

Ordinary Americans are not encouraged to examine the place of their country in the international order, about which they are often spectacularly ill-informed; much less to acknowledge the rights, the interests and the place of others. Nor are they encouraged to ask such basic questions as "What is the economy for? Should it provide huge gains to some? Should it instead aim to satisfy the needs of my own and everyone else's family?" "What is the proper role of government? Should it do more for the people? Is it responsible for health, education, and general well-being, or not?" If citizens do not ask such questions, it is not their fault. Everything in the culture – from the media to most of the schools to widespread religious practice – discourages critical thinking.

Americans do not lack, however, for vigorous debate and firmly held views, generally on subjects I think of as "body politics" – abortion, homosexuality, gay marriage, stem-cell research, euthanasia – and with the definition of fundamental rights. Do these include the right to carry a gun, to pray in the public schools, to teach sex education against the parents' will? They are often hugely preoccupied as well with their personal salvation and their fate in the afterlife in which the majority say they are fervent believers (at least if you believe the frequent opinion surveys) as we shall see in subsequent chapters. Plenty of Americans may be poorly educated and they are often misled, but they are not stupid. They know exactly, for example, what they think of George W. Bush. Twice a year, the Pew Research Center asks a representative sample to supply one word that for them best describes the President. In February 2005, the top two words were "honest" and "good." Two years later, in February 2007, they were "incompetent" and "arrogant."

Why have the doctrinal principles I listed at the beginning, uncritical attitudes, and peculiar beliefs triumphed over the past three decades? Does this trend reflect a natural evolution and simple acquiescence to reality, or are deeper and more explicit forces at work?

This chapter will examine the secular side of what America, or much of it, now thinks. Despite significant overlap, we will save the religious aspects for later. Here we will encounter the ideology-makers and shakers and examine their increasing – if not fully accomplished – attainment of "cultural hegemony," as the path-breaking Italian Marxist thinker Antonio Gramsci called it. He brought to light this concept that encapsulates the ability of the dominant class to occupy the ideological high ground. The neo-liberal elite in the United States in particular, but often in Europe and many other places on the planet, has managed to penetrate our public and private institutions one after another. These elites now enjoy a virtual monopoly over ordinary Americans' minds and thus over political power.

Their success reflects a long-term strategy that progressives have barely noticed, much less counteracted. An activist, wealthy far-right minority has consciously put this strategy into play, carefully cultivating its advantage from seedlings planted in the 1940s and 1950s. By the early twenty-first century, the seedlings had grown into towering trees. Our itinerary now is to trace the progress of this ideological transformation from its philosophical roots to its full fruition in our own time, identifying the major actors, their motivations, and their methods.

Some will say in essence "Not to worry. Everything will fall back into place once George Bush and his minions have vacated the seats of power." Such optimism strikes me as dangerously misplaced. Just as it took years to build the present cultural hegemony, so it will take years to bring it down – if indeed it ever is.

PETER'S FRIENDS: ALL THATCHERITES NOW

Peter Mandelson, an intimate friend and advisor to Tony Blair, is with Anthony Giddens, the inventor of the British Labour Party's "Third Way." Since 2004 he has been European Commissioner for Trade and remains a power in the Labour Party. Thus it may come as a surprise that in June 2002, he declared before an audience including the cream of British Labour and various visiting luminaries like Bill Clinton, "We are all Thatcherites now."[1]

Was Mandelson consciously mimicking a famous *Time Magazine* cover which had proclaimed at the end of 1965, "We are all Keynesians now"? The iconic all-American weekly had told its readers, "Some twenty years after his death [John Maynard Keynes'] theories are a prime influence on the world's free economies, especially on America's, the richest and most expansionist . . . [His ideas have led to] the most sizeable, prolonged and widely distributed prosperity in history."[2] *Time* had it right: in 1965: virtually everyone in the country who mattered was a Keynesian or some other stripe of social democrat. The idea of being a "Thatcherite" was laughable, yet a mere fifteen years after that *Time* cover appeared, the Iron Lady was in Downing Street and her more affable counterpart Ronald Reagan was sitting in the White House.

Whether or not Mandelson recalled *Time*, he surely deserves praise for his forthrightness. Not even forty years after *Time*'s unstinting praise for Keynes, the "left" was officially giving the poor man a second burial and consigning him to limbo. The reasoning behind Mandelson's astonishing statement goes like this: In April 2002, Lionel Jospin, the socialist candidate for the French presidency, suffered a humiliating defeat, coming in third and reducing the run-off vote to a choice between the right (Chirac) and the far right (Le Pen). That same year various other European social-democratic leaders were similarly knocked off their perches. In the United States, George Bush had already defeated Clinton's natural successor, Al Gore – or at least, with the help of his brother, Governor of Florida, had bent the rules and managed, with the help of the Supreme Court, to get himself declared the victor.

It seems not to have occurred to Mandelson that such defeats might have been protest votes against the rightward shift of these purportedly progressive governments. He concluded, rather, that the electorate was clamoring for anti-Keynesian "reform" along the lines of those Margaret Thatcher had earlier forced upon a reluctant Britain; including wholesale privatization of public services and "flexibility" for markets in goods, services, capital and especially labor. The United States, under Bill Clinton, had already perfected such a program with particular success in reducing welfare rolls while increasing the prison population several fold.

Third Way ideology rests on the proposition that it is fruitless to fight against market forces, nor should one even want to. Capitalist globalization is a simple fact, not a problem in need of a solution; nor is it a state of affairs to be criticized, much less overthrown. Since market forces cannot be countered and will prevail, intelligent people and social-democratic politicians can only accept reality and echo Saint Margaret's battle cry: "TINA: There Is No Alternative."

NEO-LIBERALISM'S PHILOSOPHICAL ROOTS

What, then, is Thatcherism and who are the "Thatcherites" – including the Reaganites, the Bushites, etc. if all Peter's friends have now joined their ranks? What is the content of their doctrine and what lies behind their thinking? Why has this doctrine become mainstream, not just among the followers of the traditional or extreme right wing but inside the US Democratic Party and among many European social democrats as well? These deep changes call for explanation.

Nearly everyone now knows the answer to the first question. Thatcherism is the doctrine that tells us to put our faith in market freedom, monetarist economics, high defense spending, privatization of public services, tax cuts for the higher brackets, curbs on trade unions, general opposition to the Welfare State, general friendliness toward the corporate sector and, as the defunct European Constitution and its twin-sister replacement, the so-called "Reform Treaty," repeatedly state, "free and undistorted competition."

The concept of Thatcherism still requires a bit more archeological digging to uncover its foundations. Margaret Thatcher did not emerge fully armed from the head of a market-friendly Zeus and she was not herself, strictly speaking, a Thatcherite, but a "Hayekian." The story goes that one day in the House of Commons, she retrieved a book from her briefcase, thumped it vigorously and announced to the assembled MPs "*This* is what we believe." The book in question was Friedrich von Hayek's *The Constitution of Liberty*.

Hayek was an Austrian economist, jurist, and philosopher with an astonishing output. From Austria, he had observed the beginnings of National Socialism and self-exiled himself to

England as early as 1932. He taught at the London School of Economics until his departure for the University of Chicago where he was to enjoy a long and highly influential career. Since he wrote some two dozen books, innumerable articles and influenced generations of students, I can attempt only the briefest and most inadequate summary of his thought and action here.

According to the generally received wisdom among economic historians, Hayek lost the great theoretical battle against John Maynard Keynes in the 1930s. Consequently, Keynesian economic policies were to dominate not just theory but practice over the coming decades, starting with Franklin D. Roosevelt's New Deal and its determined government interventions to overcome the Great Depression. Following his intellectual defeat, Hayek virtually ceased to write on the economic subjects that would win him a belated Nobel Prize in 1974.*

Instead of economics papers, he began producing an abundance of political articles and gained fame in 1944 with the best-selling *The Road to Serfdom*. The *Readers Digest* excerpted the book, which thus reached millions of American homes and is still a classic among neo-liberals. Thomas Sowell, a black Fellow of the right-wing Hoover Institution at Stanford University says "Hayek was the central pioneering figure in changing the course of thought in the twentieth century." Progressives had always thought it was Keynes . . .

In *The Road to Serfdom*, Hayek develops the following arguments. In any large system, knowledge is by nature fragmented and widely dispersed; it depends in particular on too many factors and too many actors for any central authority ever to

---

* The Nobel Prize in Economics does not strictly speaking exist. In 1969, the Royal Bank of Sweden decided to award an annual prize "in memory of Alfred Nobel;" most of them have gone to neo-liberal economists. Amartya Sen and Joseph Stiglitz are exceptions.

become omniscient enough to plan a national economy. Any State intervention in the economy will be arbitrary, pernicious, and tend necessarily toward tyranny. One must have confidence in the market, as order will emerge spontaneously from the expression of millions of individual preferences.

Adam Smith had been the first to make this point in the *Wealth of Nations.* Recall the famous quote pointing out that we do not expect to get our dinners thanks to the benevolence of the butcher, the baker, and the brewer but from their selfish pursuit of their own interests. Hayek stresses that individual self-interest is a better guide to satisfying human wants than any kind of economic planning or interference by a centralized authority, no matter how benign and well-intentioned. Prices will give us all the information we need concerning what the public desires. The government has no business deciding in the place of the public.

Hayek takes Adam Smith further, underscoring the importance of law in a free society, but only in so far as *negative* law is concerned. The role of the law is to state what is forbidden, period. It should not give anyone the positive power to carry out any interventionist action. Freedom consists in the absence of coercion. To be free is to be free of anyone else's will, including the will of the legislator, except when the legislator decrees that certain acts are illegal.

The human consequences of this doctrine are immediately apparent. The doctrine of negative freedom says, for example, "I can eat, you can eat" because no law forbids it, thus we are free to eat. It says nothing whatever about the tangible presence of food on the table, which alone could make the "right" to eat effective. Positive law (and progressive politics) says that, contrary to Hayek's assertions, the "freedom" to eat is both meaningless and worthless without practical, concrete access to food. The task of government and the purpose of society is to create a framework within which everyone has the

power to eat, not merely the theoretical possibility. In this
light, the entire body of human rights law can be seen as a kind
of anti-Hayekian manifesto.[3]

Pursuing Hayek's theory to its logical conclusion, one
can better understand Mrs Thatcher's meaning when she
exclaimed, "There is no such thing as society." This is also
how Hayek sees his ideal world – not as a society in which
people have common interests, common goals and seek
through their institutions to attain the common good; but
rather as a collection of atomized individuals, all choosing
what they consider best for themselves, subject to no con-
straining framework except for a small body of legally prohibited actions.

Lest I give the wrong impression, it is important to say that
Hayek was not some sort of moral monster. He saw his philosophy as entirely compatible with a State which would
ensure that everyone had sufficient food, shelter, and clothing
so as not to perish from hunger or exposure. He did not
accept, however, that a government might, say, tax rich people
in order to provide schools and hospitals for poor ones. It is
not the State's business to decide that one group should pay so
that another group can enjoy certain benefits. According to
Hayek, social justice is a pernicious illusion. One should stand
against redistributive measures – the hallmark of the Welfare
State – because they are bound to be purely arbitrary, and
whatever is arbitrary eventually and inevitably leads to
tyranny; the "serfdom" of his most famous title.

Hayek's reasoning has influenced generations of neo-
liberals, never more so than today. The solidity of his doctrine
depends, however, on a conflation of several different concepts of freedom which Western, particularly Anglo-Saxon,
philosophy has tried to keep separate for at least three centuries. The first of these is the concept of *political freedom*,
which is the basis of democracy because it allows citizens to be

actively involved in deciding how society and government are to be organized. Second come *intellectual and religious freedom* and *freedom of expression* (including a free press) which are necessary corollaries to political freedom. These freedoms allow everyone to think, state opinions, however unpopular, and worship freely; so long as these expressions do not impinge upon the freedom of others and thereby harm society.[4] A third category of freedom, usually defined as *personal or individual freedom*, underlies the right to hold property and concerns the protection of the family and the right to keep one's private life private.

Most thinkers consider that a fourth category, *economic freedom*, is of a different nature from political, intellectual or personal freedom. Hayekians (or Thatcherites or Reaganians) refuse, however, to make this distinction. They believe that an individual's right to dispose of his or her income and property is inviolable and that no public or private authority, including the State, has the right to interfere.

Here we arrive at the core of the ideological opposition between progressives and neo-liberals. The former believe that democratic governance and the survival of society itself depend on limits imposed on economic freedom. Only the "sovereign" can determine those limits (most thinkers from Hobbes onwards give this role to the State, which can be benevolent, popular and democratic, or authoritarian, coercive, even tyrannical. This is why Constitutions from the American and French Revolutions onwards have made clear that the *people* are sovereign.*

Ideally, popular sovereignty arbitrates between conflicting interests in order to arrive at the common good. In any case,

---

* Neither the European Constitutional Treaty which French and Dutch voters rejected in referenda in 2005, nor the 2007 "Reform Treaty" which replaces and is nearly identical to the dead Constitution has anything to say about popular sovereignty.

in a democracy, the people must be free to choose the nature of the State under which they will live. This is also why an American Founding Father like James Madison was so attached to the separation of powers and Constitutional government so that no branch whether executive, legislative, or judicial could acquire too much power and thus deprive the people of theirs.

If, however, the sovereign is neither a more-or-less benevolent State, nor the people but the *market*; then society and government will be organized in such a way that economic freedom overrides all the other kinds of freedom. Society will eventually be reduced to an aggregate of unlinked individuals, or, if one prefers, "consumers." Little by little, the erosion and, finally, the breakdown of social cohesion will make life scarcely worth living, even for the rich.[5]

In practice, of course, the balance struck will be the result of pressures coming from the social forces present at a given moment: that is what politics is about. Marx was the foremost and most radical exponent of this theory, defining history itself as the outcome of constant struggle between social classes.

By accepting economic freedom as paramount, however, Peter Mandelson and those who are "all Thatcherites now" have chosen a slippery slope – more slippery even than the one Hayek saw leading from State intervention in the economy to political tyranny and "serfdom." They have taken the path that leads to the concentration of rights in the hands of the only people actually able to enjoy their "freedom," which is to say the minority of the rich, who are thereby also the powerful. Their "right" to eat (or to own a yacht and a private jet) is not just a theoretical possibility but also a practical reality. In a system of negative law, wealth necessarily equals power – the power to express one's own desires, to command others, to prevail. Perhaps the "All-Thatcherites-now" crowd present at the New Labour-fest in 2002 were unaware of this drastic shift due to intellectual laziness – that is the most charitable explanation. Perhaps Mandelson simply chose to appeal to naked self-interest.

Whatever road "New Labour" and its equivalents elsewhere may have chosen, this concept of society and of law is the doctrinal adversary that progressives should seek to overturn. As the great nineteenth-century reformer and French Dominican priest Henri Lacordaire declared, "Between the strong and the weak, between the rich and the poor, between the master and the slave, it is freedom that oppresses and the law that frees." Market freedom does indeed oppress the weak; the task of progressives is thus to strive for a framework of positive law at both the national and the international levels ensuring respect for the rights and the dignity of all human beings.

WHO ARE THE NEO-LIBERALS? THE NEO-CONSERVATIVES? WHAT'S THE DIFFERENCE? WHO CARES?

As Butch Cassidy and the Sundance Kid said as they were pursued by a mysterious posse, "Who are these guys anyway?" The answer as regards neo-liberals and neo-conservatives is not a simple one and requires a bit of historical grounding. It could involve endless distinctions, which I will not attempt. But the question "Who cares?" is easily answered: the whole world cares, or ought to, because no part of the globe has been left unscathed by the doctrines these people champion. This is borne out by one public opinion survey after another.

The tale of how they gained the power to put their beliefs into practice is our main concern here. Their broad domestic agenda visibly and demonstrably deepens and reinforces inequalities and serves the needs of the better-off.

Consequently, elites everywhere have enthusiastically seized upon these policies made in USA. The foreign affairs agenda of these same policy architects continues to cause untold suffering abroad and, at home, to place dangerous people who care nothing about the Constitution or the separation of powers in positions of great influence. We shall be adding to their collective portrait throughout the book.

When we ask "Who are these guys anyway?" we encounter various problems of vocabulary. I will be using the terms "neo-liberal" and "neo-conservative," or "neo-con," almost without distinction. There are nuances, however. The term "neo-liberal" in particular, can create confusion. In the United States, but not in Europe, to be "liberal" means to be at least mildly progressive. Democrats are supposed, rightly or wrongly, to be more "liberal" than Republicans and the American right always pretends to be victimized by the "liberal media." This explains why the designation "neo-liberal" is in less common usage in the US than in Europe, including Great Britain, and elsewhere, though US academics know perfectly well what it means.

Beyond US borders, "neo-liberal" unequivocally designates people who are "all Thatcherites now" in their political and economic views – although, just to confuse the picture further, some would call themselves "libertarians," particularly in the United States. These more pure-bred Hayekians take economic freedom to its conceptual limits and have their own think tank in Washington, DC, the Cato Institute.

Whatever their names, both sorts of "neos" seek to reduce taxes and State intervention devoted to providing citizens with social benefits. They want to rescind protective labor laws, assistance in the cases of unemployment, serious illness, homelessness, and other personal mishaps or disasters. In their view, any remaining "public" services should be contracted out to private companies, just as private schools and health care facilities should largely replace public ones. The United States is the only rich developed country to offer its citizens such minimal not to say non-existent public health care. On this score, citizens have started to complain vociferously and presidential candidates have duly begun paying attention. As for schools, the right calls for a voucher system allowing parents to choose among various educational facilities on offer in the marketplace.*

In the United States, neo-conservatives defend the same political and economic agenda, but they are also extremely preoccupied by what I call "body politics," often revolving around issues of sexuality. Who can have sex with whom, at what age, of what gender, of what color, under what conditions and with what prior education regarding reproduction and sexually transmitted diseases? What civil rights if any, including the right to marry, should apply to people whose sexuality is (in their view) "deviant"? What rights have women to control their own reproductive organs and to terminate unwanted pregnancies? What is the status of the human embryo with regard to scientific research? At what moment is a human life finished? Can one legitimately hasten that moment? All these basic cultural questions are grist to the neo-con mill.

Such questions also attract far more attention in American society and are far more hotly debated than abroad. Neo-cons are also extremely sensitive, in the negative sense, to issues of racial equality and women's rights. Many of them have never digested the achievements of the civil rights and the women's movements during the 1960s and 1970s.

Issues which are *not* hotly debated include capital punishment – whose abolition is a requirement for membership in

---

* The voucher represents a set federal government or state payment per child; parents can settle for the local public school or choose to pay more for higher quality schools, a religious-based curriculum, etc.

the European Union. In the thirty-eight out of fifty US states where it exists, the death penalty attracts little controversy. Regular Gallup polls consistently show at least two-thirds of Americans in favor of it (with peaks at 74 percent approval in May 2003 and again in May 2005). Similar polls between 2002 and 2006 showed between 47 and 53 percent of respondents saying the death penalty should be applied more frequently than it is now. Since 1976, more than a thousand people, 99 percent male and 34 percent black, have been executed – over a third of them in Texas alone. As of 2008, 3,263 convicted murderers remained on "Death Row."

The impact of the gun lobby is well known and its narrow interpretation of the Second Amendment to the Constitution shows few signs of wear and tear.* The National Rifle Association's slogan "Guns don't kill people. People do" seems generally accepted, at least in the American heartland. Even after massacres carried out by clearly deranged individuals, the lobby successfully manages to assuage public opinion and no Congressional representative who wants to be re-elected is likely to cross the NRA.

So some neo-cons are on a cultural, moralistic and frequently religious trip as well as a political one. For most of them, culture and politics are inseparable. This category often takes in the "born-again Christians" and includes George W. Bush and plenty of officials in Washington. Their action is blurring ever further the separation between Church and State, evident, for example, in the concerted efforts to teach creationism or its more presentable replacement "intelligent design" in the public schools. As we shall see in detail later, some seventy million Americans would include themselves in the born-again group and although they do not all

---

* "A well regulated Militia, being necessary to the security of a free State, the right of the people to keep and bear Arms, shall not be infringed."

support a strictly conservative agenda, they do make up a size-able portion of the ground troops of many neo-con organi-zations.[6]

In the area of foreign policy, the Americans who now call themselves neo-cons were stalwart anti-Communists during the Cold War and they are steadfast supporters of the global war on terror now. Both neo-liberals and neo-conservatives tend to support US foreign interventionist policies, including military ones, although the American isolationist tradition is still alive as the huge recent drop in President Bush's popular-ity ratings has made clear (although some would say they are not against intervention, just against losing). Neo-liberals support the extension of NATO and give the United Nations short shrift. They mostly agree with the principles we laid out in capsule form at the beginning of this chapter but the neo-cons would not support international financial institutions like the World Bank and International Monetary Fund which they see as too progressive; whereas real progressives view these institutions as purveyors of right-wing policies world-wide. Neo-liberals and neo-cons ardently back the State of Israel and see it as a kind of outpost for supporting US policy and democracy in the Middle East. These aspects are central and the following chapter is devoted to them.

Are "these guys" Hayckians? Yes and no. Yes, because Hayek's philosophy is definitely relevant to global, as well as to national, politics and ideology if only because the doctrine of market supremacy he advocated has gone global; it lies at the very heart of what many now call "neo-liberal globaliza-tion." The World Bank and the IMF, working hand in hand with the US Treasury Department, have been busy for decades applying privatization, market-friendly, and State-weakening policies around the world. The thousands of pages of World Trade Organization Agreements are painstakingly explicit about the rights of corporations that do the trading but contain not a word referring to the protection of workers or the environment. Neo-liberals everywhere (including those who inhabit nominally "communist" countries like China) are trying to reduce citizenship to consumer-hood, with sweeping disregard for human rights.

But "these guys" are not Hayekians in so far as Hayek's philosophy does not suffice to illuminate entirely the latest phase in American and world history. It does not explain the propensity to war, to armed intervention, to ever-increasing defense budgets that are also a hallmark of the elites in power; although many would say these policies are more due to the neo-conservatives than to neo-liberals. Some acerbic commentators have pointed out that these defense and security policies constitute the American version of socialism, requiring a strong, interventionist State and heavy public spending in certain well-defined and limited areas of little or no direct benefit to citizens. The jobs the military-industrial complex and the military provide would exist elsewhere given similar investment. Unadulterated Hayekians – libertarians mostly – want to reduce the size of the State, including the militarized State. In present-day America, however, the supremacy of the market and State-directed expansionist, expensive interventionism go together.

This strong American State now also plays its designated role in imposing market law on unwilling victims outside the US. American transnational corporations have had a defining influence on many of the agreements that together make up the law of the World Trade Organization.[7] In another recent example, one of the first acts of Paul Bremer as de facto governor of Iraq* was to abrogate the existing foreign investment code and instate a new one, entirely favorable to (mostly American) business interests. Hayek would doubtless have rejected the notion

* President George W. Bush named Ambassador L. Paul Bremer III as his "Presidential Envoy" to Iraq in May 2003; his formal title was Administrator of the Coalition Provisional Authority.

that one State should intervene in the affairs of another in order to "export democracy." We shall have more to say about this aspect in the following chapter.

The right-wing in the United States pulls together many strands – political and economic, rich and poor, religious and secular, outward- and inward-looking, masculine-feminine, black-white, Republican and Democrat. Americans themselves tend to lump the lot under the term "neo-conservatives' or "neo-cons." Europeans would not necessarily go along with that usage and would make more social and cultural distinctions, saving "neo-liberal" for the political and economic aspects. I will not try too hard to differentiate in what follows. Generalizations are hazardous; perhaps one can still attempt a modest one. Although the groups clearly overlap and the vocabulary may differ from one side of the Atlantic to the other (and from there to the rest of the world); whereas all neo-cons are neo-liberals, all neo-liberals are not neo-cons. Further than that I fear to tread.

FROM LEFT TO RIGHT IN NOT-SO-EASY STAGES

Whether neo-liberals or neo-cons, they have pushed their ideas relentlessly and used every available instrument to do so. These ideas, however, needed fertile soil in which to grow and prosper and here the "liberals" and the Democratic Party often played into their hands. Sheer demographics also weighed heavily. The "continental drift" of the United States in both the geographic and social sense has been away from the more left-leaning East and North and toward the more traditionally right-wing South and libertarian West. Two smart Oxford graduates, both of them US correspondents and editors for *The Economist* have written an outsiders' insider report on these transformations of the American scene, dissecting the population trends that have led to present power configurations. John Micklethwait and Adrian Wooldridge (M&W) explain the context clearly.[8]

The country is moving, literally. The US Census Bureau measures the population push southwards and westwards at three feet an hour, or five miles a year. Sheer numbers give the South and West more members in the lower House of Congress and fewer to the East. Whereas Europeans are used to politics grounded mostly in social classes and class interests, American politics revolve far more around values. The South is the haven of social conservatives who hate abortion and gays and want their government to "do the Lord's work;" their Western counterparts are more anti-government conservatives who love guns, hate taxes, and want the government to get off their backs.

Whatever their geographical habitat, they are now all united in the Republican Party. This shift constitutes a revolution. From the end of the Civil War onwards, the Democrats literally owned the "solid South," where Republicans – the party of Abraham Lincoln who freed the slaves – were anathema. The Civil Rights and the Voting Rights acts of 1964–5 put an end to this Democratic dominance. As Lyndon Johnson, a Democrat and native Texan, accurately predicted when he signed the Civil Rights Act, he was "signing away the South for 50 years."[9]

President Johnson, triumphantly re-elected in 1964, was determined to carry through his Great Society project and the country was prosperous enough to pay for it. The Supreme Court started handing down decisions granting new rights thick and fast to groups previously excluded – blacks, women, homosexuals, the handicapped, prisoners, criminal defendants, the mentally ill . . . New bureaucracies were set up to run special programs for early-childhood education and older people's health-care; for the Humanities and the Arts, for minority communities; for just about everyone and everything except, as many saw it, for ordinary American white people. Their cup of resentment overflowed with the federal "busing" decree, which required children to travel long distances on school buses to attend classes outside their districts, all in the name of "achieving racial balance."

Meanwhile, the great Keynesian moment had passed. The Vietnam War was escalating, costing the earth and causing inflation; the counterculture was taking over the college campuses; serious crime was on the rise. Petty street crime was also rife. Every "long hot summer" of Johnson's term, major cities like Philadelphia, Los Angeles, Cleveland, Detroit, Newark, and dozens of others witnessed explosive race riots that left hundreds dead and millions of dollars in property damage. None of this was to the taste of vast middle-America.

The year 1968 was a truly terrible vintage. Lyndon Johnson, who in 1964 carried forty-four states and earned the greatest plurality of popular votes in American history (23 percent more than his arch-Conservative rival Barry Goldwater), in March announced that he would not run again in 1968. Two weeks later, Robert Francis "Bobby" Kennedy declared his availability and seemed likely to become the Democratic presidential candidate. In early April, Martin Luther King was assassinated in Memphis; just a month later "Bobby" was gunned down in Los Angeles a few hours after winning the California Democratic Primary election. Neither assassination was ever truly elucidated. Senator Hubert Humphrey from the far northern state of Minnesota stepped into the breach but refused to distance himself from the Vietnam War. The Democratic Party was in total disarray, riven with factionalism. Vietnam, race relations, crime, and the culture wars were tearing the country apart.

The Republican candidate, Richard Nixon, had a field day

running on the campaign theme of "Law and Order" and easily outdistanced the patrician, traditional "liberal" Republican Nelson Rockefeller. The populist, segregationist Southerner George Wallace, former governor of Alabama, knew what "the folks" down South liked and didn't like and jumped into the race as an independent. His vice-presidential running-mate was General Curtis LeMay, best known for wanting to "bomb Vietnam back into the Stone Age."

The election results in November 1968 were close, with each of the major parties winning 31 million-plus votes, but Nixon got 500,000 more votes than Humphrey. One surprise was Wallace's showing: he attracted nearly ten million votes, for 13.5 percent of the total. Between the five states that went for Wallace and the 32 for Nixon, the real shocker was the way the Republicans now covered the map of the country from sea to sea. Texas may still have voted for the Democrats, but otherwise, Humphrey won only the Northeast coast and three states in the far North. Forty years later, this is how the country still tends to look.

But in 1968, the right had not yet hit its stride. Despite being triumphantly re-elected in 1972 (his opponent George McGovern carried only poor little Massachusetts) Nixon was forced to resign over the Watergate scandal and, thanks to him, the Republicans had gained little but a reputation for dirty tricks. The little known Democrat Jimmy Carter won a close election in 1976 over Nixon's former Vice-President Gerald Ford but lost in 1980, when the Ronald Reagan supernova lit up the Republicans' firmament. Reagan's election brought with it the bonus of Republican control of the Senate for the first time in twenty-eight years. With Reagan, we have finally arrived in true neo-liberal-neo-conservative territory and from now on in these pages we will remain there.

FROM NETWORK TO GALAXY

Now let us look at the systematic dissemination of neo-liberal economic and social policies inside the United States. They have affected not only the lives of Americans but have also exercised a pernicious influence well beyond US borders. The first thing one notices about the neo-liberal hijacking of economic and social thought is that progressive social forces, even moderate ones, inside or outside the US, failed to pay it much attention. A quiet revolution was taking place under their noses but they did not even smell a rat, much less try to set a trap for it. The right was able to go about its ideological business unobserved, unchecked, and unmolested.

The premonitory tremors of this revolution occurred at the University of Chicago where Hayek became a professor in 1950. He gathered around himself a small coterie of devoted followers who came to be known as the Chicago School and later, more ominously, in Chile and elsewhere, as the Chicago Boys. Even earlier, in 1947, with the help of the young Milton Friedman, Hayek had already founded the Mont Pèlerin Society, a secretive community of true-believer neo-liberal economists of which Margaret Thatcher has remained a member to this day.

Despite slow beginnings, these embryonic institutions have endured and played an important if largely occult role at home and abroad. Between 1985 and 2002, Mont Pèlerin received over $500,000 from various conservative foundations and recruited top-drawer neo-liberal thinkers – it now counts over 500 members from forty countries. Mount Pèlerin's best-known past presidents, apart from Hayek and Friedman, are Nobel Prize Laureates George Stigler, James Buchanan, and Gary Becker.

One member of the conservative Chicago circle, Richard Weaver, had titled his 1948 book *Ideas Have Consequences*. This title could serve as a kind of motto for the neo-cons. Right-wing family foundations took that statement literally and decided to put what we now call "neo-liberal" or "neo-con" theory and practice on the national and international map. They used their money strategically and their "freedom to choose," to misquote the title of one of Milton Friedman's most successful books. They bought and paid for a huge cadre of scholars and skilled communicators in a network of academic and non-academic institutions and think-tanks. They created virtually out of nothing an entire ideological climate under which we live today, as dangerous in its own way for the social world as global warming is for the natural world.

Progressives, doubtless sure of the force and rightness of their own ideas, were incredibly slow to recognize the threat; they scarcely deigned even to argue until the culture wars were over and had already been won by the neo-cons. One of the earliest progressive critiques of neo-liberal ideology was a well-researched analysis by James Allen Smith, published in 1991, fully a decade after Ronald Reagan first occupied the White House and had already overseen the transformation of dozens of neo-con proposals into legislation. A short piece by Jon Wiener had appeared a year earlier in *The Nation* weekly magazine and a handful of academics had written about the conservative foundations; for far too long, however, the people, the planning, and the institutions behind Reaganism and Thatcherism attracted scant attention.[10]

Other contributions to the literature emerged during the 1990s, including a short one of my own, in 1997 in *Le Monde Diplomatique* and *Dissent*. In this piece I attempted not only to trace the history of the right's successful intellectual gravity shift, but also to point out to potential progressive donors the folly of supporting projects but not ideas like those produced by my own colleagues at the Transnational Institute (TNI) and like-minded institutions. Such efforts elicited little response, at least not in the quarters that mattered. To quote my article:

> Today, few would deny that we live under the virtually undisputed rule of the market-dominated, ultra-competitive, globalized society with its cortege of manifold iniquities and everyday violence. Have we got the hegemony we deserve? I think we have, and by "we," I mean the progressive movement, or what's left of it . . . the "war of ideas" has been tragically neglected by the side of the angels. Many public and private institutions that genuinely believe they are working for a more equitable world have in fact actively contributed to the triumph of neo-liberalism or have passively allowed this triumph to occur . . . [But] if we recognize that a market-dominated, iniquitous world is neither natural nor inevitable, then it should be possible to build a counter-project for a different kind of world . . . The now-dominant economic doctrine did not descend from heaven. It has, rather, been carefully nurtured over decades, through thought, action and propaganda, bought and paid for by a closely knit fraternity . . ."[11]

The buying and paying were always crucial. In his book, James Allen Smith introduces the key *dramatis personae* who shaped and continue to shape the neo-con movement. He describes the institutions in which they work and the intricate money machine that funds them. He shows how these founding fathers (few mothers make an appearance) departed from the American empirical tradition in the social sciences and journalism to place their message in an overtly ideological framework.

They also developed formidable outreach and PR skills, understanding that mainstream print, radio, and television journalists would use their work, if it was properly crafted, in the name of "balance" – as well as out of laziness. The stock in trade of any number of neo-con outfits includes the preparation of myriad press briefings, communiqués, and ready-to-use commentaries; and the supplying of articulate experts to appear on talk shows and news networks like CNN or National Public Radio on a broad range of topics. The left has nothing like the machinery, the money, the communications savvy and the personnel the neo-cons can mobilize. This is one way they have shifted the "balance" further and further to the right.

Irving Kristol, a godfather figure to this movement who once famously said that a neo-con was a liberal who had been mugged by reality, identified the neo-con target as the "New Class." According to his analysis, this class was not only hostile to the private sector but had successfully taken over the bastions of ideas – the universities, the think tanks and foundations that acted as "idea legitimizers." Kristol's answer to what he saw as "liberal" ideological hegemony (in the American, moderately leftish sense of the word) was to build the right's own rival institutions, supported by philanthropy from corporations and conservative foundations. Kristol's aim of creating a network of neo-con institutions and scholars was explicit from the start; his strategy focused on the capacity to influence national policy debates, inside and outside Washington. The concept was brilliant and the success of the strategy has been breathtaking.

What began as a loose network is now more like a galaxy. As far as one can judge from the outside, the cohesion between the various nodes in the hugely enlarged network – funders, think tanks, universities, single-issue policy development centers, grass-roots organizations, publications, individual intellectuals, and activists – is remarkable. The best way to study them would be to find an enormous piece of blank paper and write on it the names of all the donors and recipients. It would cover all the relevant sub-categories (for instance individual scholars in specific research centers in particular universities, all three of which are receiving financial grants) and draw the connecting lines between them. Similar lines in different colors might represent not money but affinities – between organizations, publications, media and so on that work together, for example. The most lines leading to a node would give some idea of the power, reach, and influence of each actor.

One could then make a reasonably accurate map of the galaxy, locating the individual "stars," the "suns" around which the most "planets" orbit; the "moons" that in turn orbit those planets and the gravitational fields between them. Such a process would also illustrate Gramsci's concept of the march toward a new cultural hegemony and of developing one's own "organic intellectuals." In the past quarter-century, these actors have brought about genuine ideological climate change, although many of them continue falsely to pretend that the media, the universities and other institutions are still dominated by "liberals," still their code-word for "left-ists."

NEO-FOUNDING FATHERS AND FUNDERS

At the heart of the map of the galaxy we would find the funders, because without them the rest of the infrastructure would collapse. They were quick to seize upon the importance of ideas and to embrace enthusiastically the "Kristol program" of building alternative right-wing intellectual elites and institutions capable of changing the national policy debate. The most important neo-conservative foundations are Bradley, Olin, Smith-Richardson, Charles Koch, and Scaife-Mellon (the last comprising four separate foundations based on the same family steel fortune). Some smaller foundations pursue identical goals, including Eli Lilly, JM, Earhart, Castle Rock, David Koch. The so-called "four sisters" – Bradley, Olin, Smith-Richardson, and Scaife – often join forces in funding the same recipients. Large or small, all these foundations are intensely aware that together they are "building a movement." Individual private donors and corporations tend to follow their lead (we shall look at the specifically corporate side of the cultural project in the final chapter).

How do these foundations use their money strategically to "build a movement"? The short answer is that they do everything progressive donors nearly always refuse to do. Neo-cons understand that producing sharp and well-packaged ideas may take time. They give large, predictable, multi-year grants; some of their protégés have received funding literally for decades. Recipients know they can undertake long-term work; they know that their donors are prepared to wait for their ideological payoff.

And progressive donors? They like the short term; they usually start with a one-year grant, sometimes renewable. In extreme cases they may go as far as three years, but then, even if the work has been successfully completed, they may drop the recipient because it's time to move to something – and someone – new. Neo-cons identify their future stars and nurture their grantees, helping them move from youth to maturity. As the President of the Bradley Foundation said about his funding policy and scholarship program for younger conservative scholars, "It's like building a wine collection."

Progressive donors are usually uncomfortable making grants to individual scholars – no fine vintage wine collections for them. At most, they may fund a project which the individual scholar may be allowed to define, but will also be required to manage and coordinate, rather than doing his or her own research, thinking, and writing full time.

Not only do right-wing foundations fund individual scholars lavishly, they also give generous "core operating support" to neo-con institutions because without a decent infrastructure, nothing works. Progressive donors hate to give money to "core" budgets; that is, to boring things like secretariats and computers. They will only fund projects that include a small "overhead," usually no more than ten percent, that the recipient is authorized to contribute to the "core."

The most remarkable difference between the two sorts of donors is the tragic contrast in their objectives. Few progressive donors are prepared to contribute anything at all to the production and dissemination of ideas. At the heart of their strategy is the "project" – a well-described objective involving something, somewhere that needs fixing – with clearly measurable results. The project may be a good one – but the donors do not realize that in the wrong ideological climate, it will rarely become self-sustaining and that, when the funding stops, it will collapse like a beach-house washed away by a tsunami.

Furthermore, economic incentives built into foundation practice are counter-productive for the spread of progressive ideas. Personnel employed by foundations must necessarily justify their own existence, so they must make work for their grantees that they can then discuss with colleagues, criticize, and evaluate. They are never going simply to hand over money and say "get on with it," even to people and organizations that have consistently proven their capacity to spend it effectively. They will not do this because such an approach would take about five minutes. Consequently, institutions and individuals hoping to gain or renew their standing with funders must spend inordinate amounts of time writing proposals and reports, filling in forms, answering questionnaires and courting their "benefactors" when they should be sticking to their own "core business" of producing and disseminating ideas. The right, on the other hand, trusts its people, keeps bureaucracy to a minimum and does say, in effect, "get on with it."

One former program director with one of the largest mainstream US foundations has explained to me (requesting anonymity) that the foundation he worked for had no overall institutional policy whatsoever; nor did it set any Foundation-wide goals. Each program director was able to build his/her own unit without regard for what any of the others were doing. The capacity to fund progressive work therefore depended greatly on the individual preferences and politics of program directors. The large, potentially progressive or at least even-handed Foundations are also, he says, extremely timorous and susceptible to criticism. They tend to stampede into "safer" areas at the slightest alert (which neo-liberals will always be happy to supply) in order to avoid anything in the least smacking of controversy. Under the circumstances, it is amazing that any left scholarship gets done at all; that any progressive ideas ever reach the public or the policy agenda. The universities provide much of it and they have their own constraints.

In other words, whether they realize it or not, progressive, or potentially progressive donors frequently do everything in their considerable power to limit if not halt entirely the production and diffusion of progressive analysis, proposals, and action. They make it difficult for good individual scholars and institutions to survive, whereas the funding strategy of the right allows reactionary ones to prosper and endure.[12] As the right gains ground, with its media and communications professionals shifting the "balance" further and further in the neo-con direction; progressive thought, constantly on the defensive, begins to seem truly eccentric, beyond the pale, and grows ever more marginalized.

THE BRIGHTEST STARS IN THE GALAXY

Although it is impossible here to examine in detail all the neo-con financial powerhouses, it is useful to underline the importance of a few, beginning with the Bradley Foundation. The Bradley brothers of Milwaukee, Wisconsin, were members of the ultra-right John Birch Society from its inception in the 1950s. They made their money in high-tech, precision-guided machinery, paid women less than men to operate the same machines (their women workers won a lawsuit against them in 1966), and sold out to the military-industrial giant Rockwell in 1985 for $1.65 billion. Their foundation suddenly became one of the largest in America.

Bradley found its influential director, Michael Joyce, in another neo-con organization, the Olin Foundation (this one founded on chemical and munitions money, about which more in a moment). Joyce died at only 63 in 2006, having definitively changed conservative philanthropy and the intellectual landscape of America. In 2004, Bradley's Annual Report celebrated "20 years of strategic philanthropy" totalling $527 million. It still has more than $700 million in assets.[13]

The upscale magazine *Atlantic Monthly* quickly named Joyce one of the three people most responsible for the success of the American conservative movement. He consistently funded conservative intellectuals, but also encouraged pilot programs in Bradley's home city of Milwaukee and in Wisconsin where the Foundation maintained its headquarters. He worked with the Republican Governor of the state to push through welfare reform measures that later served as a template for Congress and President Clinton to overhaul welfare at the national level in 1996. He encouraged school voucher systems allowing poor children to attend private schools at state government, that is, taxpayer's expense – a program that has not yet become national but which is frequently copied.

In the late 1970s Joyce also set up the Philanthropy Roundtable and played a key role in shaping its political direction. The Roundtable has grown into an organization that brings together over 600 smaller foundations and corporate and individual donors, virtually all of them rightward-leaning. Its Board comes from that world as well; Joyce served as its Board chair until 2003. The Roundtable's organizational budget of about $4 million a year is itself funded by donations from conservative foundation and allow it to host national and regional meetings for its members where they can listen to neo-con experts and intellectuals. It puts out a bi-monthly magazine and publishes guides for conservative giving. One of its brochures is called "Strategic Investment in Ideas: How Two Foundations Reshaped America" about the Bradley and Olin Foundations.

Bradley exemplifies the philosophy of "discover, recruit, and reward" for supporting individual scholars, not just through its generous scholarship programs or its regular grants to established authors and research centers; but also through four handsome yearly awards of $250,000 each for "outstanding intellectual achievement." One recent winner is Ward Connerly, the head of the American Civil Rights Institute. Connerly, who is black, successfully led the California ballot initiative ("proposition 209") to *end* affirmative action in the State's colleges and universities. Affirmative action, the practice of giving preference to racial minorities for admission to educational institutions, sometimes at the risk of excluding better-qualified white candidates, is dismissed by prize-winner Connerly who says "Race has no place in American life or law." He calls for "color-blind" policies with no admissions goals set for purposes of "diversity." This approach perfectly suits the wealthy white majority.

Although some disgruntled white candidates have taken successful legal action against the academic authorities for excluding them, affirmative action has been on the whole a tool to reduce somewhat America's ever-present and endemic racism. Unless and until public primary and secondary schools in poor neighborhoods allow minority students a reasonable degree of scholarly attainment, affirmative action can ensure that at least some poorer young people of color can jump the hurdles.

Other Bradley $250,000 laureates are Charles Krauthammer, who got an MD from Harvard before turning to journalism. Now a syndicated conservative columnist writing on foreign affairs in the *Washington Post* and a frequent commentator on Rupert Murdoch's Fox News; Krauthammer has said of the United States' foreign policy, "We run a uniquely benign imperium."[14] George Will, also a conservative syndicated columnist, won another Bradley award for outstanding intellectual achievement, as did Thomas Sowell, a black economist who did his doctoral work at Chicago and is now "Rose and Milton Friedman Senior Fellow" at the Hoover Institution, a venerable conservative think tank situated at Stanford, also generously funded by the neo-cons.

Charles Murray, whose home base is the American Enterprise Institute (founded in 1943, consistently supported by the four sisters and other right-wing foundations) has received since 1988 at least nineteen grants, all but one from Bradley, for a startling total of nearly $2.8 million. Murray's two best known works are *Losing Ground : American Social Policy 1950–80* (1985) which attempts to demonstrate that giving people welfare payments causes poverty; and *The Bell Curve: Intelligence and Class Structure in American Life* (1994) whose thesis is that blacks have inherently (hereditary) lower mental ability than whites. Both these books caused great controversy but the point was that they became best-sellers, were discussed and argued over on radio and television, and that Murray became an "expert authority" on these questions. His views on the damage done by welfare have been particularly influential in shaping policies, including those of Bill Clinton and the Democrats.

The "Sisters" have also given unstinting support to Dinesh D'Souza, a still youngish neo-con of Indian origin who first made his mark as a militant anti-affirmative action student at Dartmouth College. He now fights against social welfare and feminism as well and, like Ward Connerly, rejects the notion that institutional racism can exist in the United States. In foreign affairs, he denies the existence of US imperialism and believes in hard-core, laissez-faire economics. Dinesh D'Souza appears so often on current events and commentary programs that his adversaries refer to him as "Distort D'Newsa"; he has nonetheless received over $1.5 million in twenty-one separate grants from the Bradley, Scaife, and Olin foundations and like many other prominent neo-cons routinely receives $10,000 for delivering a speech at corporate venues. Other well-known recipients of smaller sums from the Sisters include Samuel ("Clash of Civilizations") Huntington and Francis ("The End of History") Fukuyama (who has more recently strayed somewhat from the neo-con path).

The Olin Foundation, which closed its doors in September 2005 after half a century and $370 million worth of grants, was particularly precocious in supporting right-wing institutions and individuals. Said its director: "We invested at the top of society . . . in Washington think tanks and the best universities. The idea is this would have a much larger impact because they were influential places."

As early as 1988, the Olin Foundation's annual report showed grants of $55 million to underwrite university programs "intended to strengthen the economic, political and cultural institutions upon which . . . private enterprise is based." Olin president William Simon was a power in the Reagan administration and convinced corporations to stop "financing their own destruction." "Why," asked Simon, "should businessmen be financing left-wing intellectuals and institutions which espouse the exact opposite of what they believe in?"[15] He encouraged them to jump on the neo-con funding bandwagon.

Olin Foundation grants to selected conservative scholars include the hefty $3.6 million awarded to Allan Bloom to head the University of Chicago's John M. Olin Center for Inquiry into the Theory and Practice of Democracy. Irving Kristol, who designed the blueprint for the conservative intellectual movement was rewarded with $376,000 as distinguished professor at New York University's graduate school of business administration; earning a similar stipend later when he joined the American Enterprise Institute as an Olin Fellow. Over fifteen years, beginning in the late 1980s, Kristol received a total of $1.4 million in sixteen Olin grants.

"TRADITIONAL VALUES"

The donors support a predictable set of values. Bradley explicitly states that it is "devoted to strengthening American democratic capitalism," and seeks to help "public policy research supporting free enterprise, traditional values and a strong national defense." The Foundation believes in "moving toward personal responsibility" and away from "centralized, bureaucratic, 'service-providing' institutions" (i.e. welfare) which it sees as "disenfranchizing citizens" who thereby become either "victims or clients." It wants "choice" for people. This emphatically does *not* mean abortion, as in the expression "pro-choice" legislation, supported by the left.

Examples of providing people with more personal responsibility include school vouchers which parents can use to educate their children in the schools of their choice, including religious ones, or at home. Parents could take the public school on offer or voluntarily supplement the vouchers to pay for better educational establishments. The Foundation also calls for social security "reform," emphasizing private accounts. The point is to shift all public institutions toward the ethic of individual "freedom of choice" à la Hayek. Bradley also appreciates the ideological value of traditional religion and gives dozens of grants directly to churches and to "faith-based organizations," most, but not all of them local.

Bradley's strategy (which could as easily apply to any of the neo-con galaxy) was summed up on the excellent Media Transparency site. "Bradley funded the authors and writers who could set the terms for national debate on key issues of public policy, the think tanks that could develop specific programs, the activist organizations that could implement those programs, and the legal offices that could defend those programs in court, as well as carry out legal offensives against other targets."[16]

In order to, in its own words, "defend and advance freedom" (i.e. support US defense and security policy, including the "war on terrorism") Bradley gives large sums to the American Enterprise Institute in Washington, the Hoover Institution at Stanford and the School for Advanced International Studies (SAIS) at Johns Hopkins University in Washington. The SAIS was Paul Wolfowitz's place of refuge when in exile from government and before assuming the presidency of the World Bank; Fukuyama and Zbigniew Brzezinski both teach there.

In a general way, the neo-con right supports the rollback of progressive legislation but displays a certain genius and contrarian logic in naming its institutions so that they sound not just innocuous but incredibly progressive. For example, the Independent Women's Forum is anti-choice, anti-feminist, and encourages women's subservience to their husbands. The American Civil Rights Institute (Ward Connerly's outfit already mentioned) was "created to educate the public about racial and gender preferences." In fact it fights against preferences for minorities or women. The Center for Equal Opportunity and the Center for Individual Rights are also Bradley grant recipients with similar aims and similar feel-good names. The Citizens for a Sound Economy are the foot-soldier activists fighting for tax cuts.

Whenever neo-cons talk about "reform" – of taxes, welfare, the judiciary, social security, minority rights, whatever – they invariably mean abolition, abrogation, dismantling or privatization. A good example is Grover Norquist, who runs a shop called Americans for Tax Reform. Norquist doesn't so much want "reform" as to realize his goal which is to "reduce government to the size where we can drown it in the bathtub." This program does not include the Pentagon.

Not content to defend far right-wing policies, right-wingers want the policy field entirely to themselves. Norquist further promises to "hunt (progressive or liberal groups) down one by one and extinguish their funding sources." He is also a formidable organizer, famous in neo-con circles for his Washington Wednesday breakfast meetings at which a hundred or more representatives of conservative groups, along with Congressional staff people, journalists, and government functionaries – sometimes including White House staff – gather for a briefing and receive their marching orders for the week. The *Wall Street Journal* refers to Norquist as "the V. I. Lenin of the anti-tax movement" and "the Grand Central Station of the right because all the trains run through his office." His donors include the usual suspects among conservative foundations but he also receives money from corporations like Microsoft or AOL-Time-Warner.

THINK-TANKS

Neo-con foundations unsurprisingly fund neo-con think-tanks – the Four Sisters concentrating on what one might call the Six Brothers: the Heritage Foundation, the American Enterprise Institute, the Hoover Institution at Stanford, and the Manhattan, Cato and Hudson Institutes. There are dozens of smaller think-tanks, many of them regional; these are useful for adding "balance" in media across the country. The journalists who quote the "experts" from these think-tanks rarely mention where the money comes from and what color it is.

Take the example of the Heritage Foundation, founded in 1973. It is not a foundation in the sense of Bradley or Olin, but rather a recipient of their grants, although it fundraises well beyond the neo-con foundations and calls upon thousands of individual donors as well. As of 2004 it boasted over $150 million in assets, 205 employees, 200,000 donor members and an annual budget of about $40 million. Heritage prepared the book of legislative proposals for Ronald Reagan's first term, nearly all of which became law. Later it recommended 200 people who got top jobs in the Bush administration.

Heritage stresses the "Four Ms: Mission, Money, Management, and Marketing" and judging from its results is particularly strong in the final category. The Foundation boasts that its communications and marketing department averages "6.5 media interviews every working day." Ninety percent of their TV time is on national and international networks. Heritage runs its own talk radio network and has two TV studios on its own premises. It designs educational programs for Congressional staff members and provides a free "confidential, high-quality service" for job placement of neo-cons in "Congressional offices, trade associations, polling groups, faith-based organizations, and, more recently, colleges and universities."

Based on some of its more recent output, one can verify that in international affairs, Heritage is pro-Paul Wolfowitz, anti-United Nations and a supporter of the counter-terrorism bill called the US PATRIOT Act. Domestically, it works to privatize social security, further weaken Medicare and welfare, reduce taxes and cut government budgets. In 2004, six members of President Bush's Cabinet spoke at various Heritage functions. It hopes one day to overturn Supreme Court decisions like *Roe* v. *Wade*, which in 1973 made abortion legal.

The American Enterprise Institute (AEI), the oldest (1943) and some say most powerful think-tank in the United States is the perfect "revolving door" institution – it's where Administration people come from when the Republican Party is in power and it's where they go when it isn't. The two-way flow began when President Ford lost the 1976 election to Jimmy Carter and went to AEI, taking a dozen of his top staff people with him. Ronald Reagan practically emptied the Institute to fill his administration, unwittingly exposing it to a serious organizational and financial crisis. When President Bush spoke at AEI in 2003 at a celebration of Irving Kristol's life and work, he commended the Institute for having "some of the finest minds in our nation." He added, "You do such good work that my administration has borrowed 20 such minds."

In the other direction, Newt Gingrich went to AEI when he had to step down as Speaker of the House of Representatives; John Bolton, ex-Bush Ambassador to the United Nations, is there now, along with Vice-President Cheney's wife Lynne, former Bush speechwriter David Frum, former Assistant Defense Secretary Richard "Prince of Darkness" Perle and a host of others. It was at AEI that Federal Reserve Chairman Alan Greenspan made his celebrated "irrational exhuberance" speech in 1996. If the next President is a Republican, it is likely he will already have close ties to the AEI – this is the case for Senator John McCain, for example. Another Senator with strong links to this think-tank is Joseph Lieberman, Al Gore's running mate in the 2000 elections, who keeps moving rightward and kept his Senate seat in 2006 as an independent.

AEI people are, like those from Heritage, media fixtures but they are more serious intellectuals as well, following their institutional slogan "At the intersection of scholarship and policy." Their books and position papers on both domestic and foreign policy are forces to be reckoned with and cannot be dismissed as mere propaganda.

THE PEN IS (SOMETIMES) MIGHTIER THAN THE SWORD

Publications, both scholarly and popular, are another tool for building neo-con success and the conservative foundations consistently fund everything from campus newspapers to more elite journals like *Commentary* or *The Public Interest*. Norman Podhoretz, editor of *Commentary*, has received thirteen "research fellowships" from neo-con foundations for a total of nearly $800,000. News laced with ideology is provided by the *Weekly Standard*, owned by Rupert Murdoch, where Irving Kristol's son Bill is editor; the *New Criterion* or the *American Spectator* also figure on the foundations funding list. The *Standard* is said to lose about a million dollars a year, which Rupert Murdoch can afford, particularly since it is influential and much quoted.

Donors contribute as well to specific book projects or television programs, for example those sponsored by the Hoover Institution (a TV series on Reagan received $120,000 in 2002). Lots of articles written by Olin grantees or other neo-con-backed scholars appear in such mainstream publications as the *New York Times*, the *Washington Post* and *Time Magazine*. Fox News, part of the Murdoch media empire, is a 24 hour/seven days a week neo-con presentation of the news. It is widely rumored that when a neo-con scholar produces a book, the foundations provide enough cash to buy several thousand copies so that the books go straight onto the best-seller lists and are thus automatically reviewed and discussed. It sounds plausible but I have not found proof.

THE LEGAL NEO-LIBERAL EAGLES

The American legal establishment and the judiciary have been particular Olin targets. An early innovator, Olin invented a new university discipline called "Law and Economics," in the 1960s and endowed the first chair at – where else? – the University of Chicago. The idea is to teach "free market economics" as it applies to law, emphasizing "economic efficiency and wealth maximization as the conceptual corner-stones" for judicial opinions. Ultimately, Olin and similar institutions seek to change the American legal system in order to make corporate profits and private wealth secure and untouchable, while downgrading social justice and individual rights. Longer-term goals include a nationwide ban on gay marriage and on abortion and the elimination of Social Security in favor of private schemes for survival in old age.* These are centralized Four Sisters efforts, receiving hundreds of thousands of dollars yearly.

Other "Law and Economics" centers and scholarship pro-grams exist at the most prestigious universities in the United States: Yale, Harvard, Johns Hopkins, New York University,

* "Social Security" in the US means retirement payments, not health care as in Europe.

Georgetown, Princeton, Stanford, and the Massachusetts Institute of Technology. This is truly investing in the "top of society." Only the University of California in Los Angeles – UCLA – has turned down an Olin program in Law and Economics after a year's trial run, complaining that it was "taking advantage of students' financial need to indoctrinate them with a particular ideology."[17]

For their vision to become law, the neo-cons need their own law professors, lawyers and judges in strategic positions. The outstanding vehicle for the propagation of neo-liberal doctrine in legal circles is The Federalist Society. It was established in 1982 and although its website is singularly uninformative, it does admit to having at least 25,000 members (other sources say 35,000) who are legal professionals, 5,000 law students in 150 of the 182 US law schools, including all the highest ranking ones, and chapters in sixty cities. It does not say how many law school faculty and deans are members. Between 1985 and 2002, the Society received 122 grants for a total of $9 million. The Director of the Federalist Society admits that without Olin, it would never have existed.

Well-known Federalist Society members include Robert Bork (also the recipient of large grants as an Olin Fellow in the Olin-funded American Enterprise Institute); Clinton's nemesis, the Federal Prosecutor Kenneth Starr, and Supreme Court Justices Antonin Scalia and Clarence Thomas. Along with the American Enterprise Institute, the Society also runs a program called "NGO Watch" whose aim is to challenge "liberal" non-governmental organizations.

Legal cases to test policies are an American specialty and the neo-cons understand that their final victory will not be secure until the courts have made it so. Their judicial strategy thus concentrates on indoctrinating and recommending judges for Federal Court openings. It is still too early to tell, but Bush's choice of the young and personable John Roberts as Chief Justice of the Supreme Court may utterly change the judicial picture in the United States. Although it is hard to prove that the Federalist Society piloted Roberts' appointment, there is no doubt that it was behind that of Samuel Alito, named to the Supreme Court in February 2006. The Bush Justice Department is also riddled with Society members, including its former top man, Alberto Gonzalez.

The two Bush appointees, Roberts and Alito, are likely to reinforce the trend toward reversing certain long-standing Supreme Court decisions. Heritage, for example, estimates that it may take another decade fully to privatize social security and to overthrow *Roe* v. *Wade*, both typical neo-con goals which the Federalist Society naturally shares. Its longer-term agenda is to rescind a huge body of legislation passed since the 1950s, particularly in the areas of civil and individual rights; as well as get rid of a slew of regulatory or environmental health and safety measures covering a broad range of industries

Other grantees of neo-con foundations specializing in legal issues include Norquist's Americans for Tax Reform, Union Watch (which fights against worker rights), the Center for Equal Opportunity, the Center for Individual Rights, Public Interest Law and Legal Reform. A larger ancillary organization called the Institute for Justice, received between 1985 and 2002 eighty grants for a total of $6.65 million; it concentrates on fighting "the intrusive presence of government in economic and private affairs" and carries out strategic litigation against regulatory measures and the "Welfare State."

The Koch Foundation (based on oil) has been active in funding "friends of the court" ("*amicus*") briefs, open to interested parties. It has spent $600,000 in an attempt to get rid of the Clean Air Act, an effort to which corporations like Daimler-Chrysler and General Electric have also contributed. The Fund for Research on Economics and the Environment, another Koch project, invites judges to its ranch in Montana where they may attend a seminar or two but also enjoy the scenery, the cuisine, and the sports activities. In 2000, six percent of all US Federal judges attended one of these all-expenses-paid junkets.

This may presumably help the Kochs as well, because their oil businesses find themselves in frequent legal trouble. They have been fined many times for faulty pipelines and oil spills and they drill on federal and tribal lands. Prior to 2000, the Clinton justice department had come up with 97 separate violations by Koch companies of the Clean Air and Hazardous Waste laws. The Bush administration conveniently dropped all charges and the court settled for a $20 million fine and no jail term instead of the $350 million and jail terms previously called for. David Koch gave $500,000 to Republican campaigns in the 2000 elections. Since both he and his brother Charles figure on the list of the fifty richest Americans, they can also afford to support, as they do, the Federalist Society.

SHREDDING THE CONSTITUTION: "THE MOST POWERFUL MAN YOU'VE NEVER HEARD OF"

That is how the magazine *US News and World Report* described David Addington.[18] If you want to know how the Constitution of the United States is being cut to pieces, you need look no further. The secretive, ultra-discreet Addington has for two decades served as Vice-President Dick Cheney's hit man (he is as of 2007 Cheney's chief of staff, replacing the disgraced Scooter Libby). Addington is well worth getting to know. He also confirms the maxim of many Washington insiders: "Don't bother watching Bush; keep your eye on Cheney." Widely recognized as a brilliant and ruthless workaholic lawyer, he is also the acknowledged master of national security law that he indisputably knows better than anyone else in Washington.

This knowledge is a particular advantage in an administration where none of the top people are lawyers. Addington has thus enjoyed a virtually free hand to shape law as he wishes and he has not wasted his time.

His agenda consists in one over-riding, easily described and brutal objective: broaden the executive power of the President and reduce the legislative branch to impotence. Addington drafted many of the memos signed by Attorney General Gonzales, including the notorious one of January 2002 calling the Geneva Conventions "obsolete" and justifying torture. He bases his action on the so-called "Unitary Executive Theory" of Constitutional interpretation. This theory, championed by Cheney, claims that any attempt by Congress to divest the President of control must be beaten back. A war-time President has even more latitude as Commander in Chief – this is one reason that the "Global War on Terror (or on Terrorism)" must be prolonged indefinitely. Addington has crafted what he calls the "New Paradigm," the legal strategy to accompany this unending war.[19]

Immediately after September 11 he consolidated his position which, according to a distinguished law professor who chairs the New York Bar Association's International Law Committee, consists in "trying to overturn two centuries of jurisprudence defining the limits of the executive branch. They've made war a matter of dictatorial power."[20] So if the President wants to collect intelligence without a court order, wiretap American (and foreign) citizens, open their mail, break into their homes, take their papers and computers, declare anyone an "illegal combatant," keep prisoners in Guantanamo forever without trial, or commit torture, then he can. The Addington attitude is "the courts can't stop us and neither can the Congress."

He operates thorough secrecy and tight control of the information flow, keeping even the Secretary of State and the chief Pentagon lawyer out of the picture when necessary. Addington has also made massive use of a little known legal tool called the "signing statement." Normally, when the President receives a piece of legislation voted by the Congress, he either signs it, or, if he disapproves, vetoes it. In his first six years, Bush never vetoed a single bill. He preferred a much more underhanded method, repeatedly appending "signing statements" to legislation. A signing statement sets out how the executive branch will interpret the law, and historically most have been innocuous, in the delighted to sign vein.

American Presidents from Monroe (1817) to Carter (1981) appended a total of 75 signing statements to legislation; Reagan (1981) to Clinton (2000) accelerated the pace, adding a further 247, for a grand total of 322 signing statements in 183 years. Midway through his second term, in 2006, Bush had already appended 750 signing statements to legislation, most, perhaps all of them drafted by Addington. Although Bush enjoyed a Congressional majority, and one therefore assumes that Congress did not pass much legislation to which the President would be hostile, virtually all his signing statements changed the intent of Congress when it voted the law in the first place. Plenty of historical texts show how wary the Founders of the Republic were of excessive Presidential power. How right they were.

Further reason to make the poor Founders turn in their graves was another Addington brain child: the creation in 2002 of military commissions with the right to try any non-American the President designated as having "engaged in," or "abetted," or "conspired to commit" terrorism. According to the text creating these commissions, the customary rights of the defense could be waived, and the court could accept hearsay evidence or evidence obtained by "physical coercion" (read "torture"). Addington considers every prisoner in Guantanamo including the old and the ill as an "enemy combatant," although even the CIA has reported otherwise.

But there is good news! The military hated the military commissions because they tarnished their proud traditions and the Uniform Code of Military Justice. In June 2006, the Supreme Court also found them illegal. The Court ruled five to three that these commissions violated both the Uniform Code and the Geneva Conventions.

The bad news is that the three ultra-conservative Supreme Court justices (Scalia, Thomas and the new Bush appointee Alito) dissented and voted to retain them. The new Chief Justice, also Bush's choice, did not take part in the decision because he had earlier ruled on the same case when he was an Appeals Court Judge in Washington – and at the earlier trial he had found the military commissions perfectly legal. Further decisions on similar subjects may well be decided five to four. If the next old and ailing justice steps down while Bush is still in the White House, the President can name another young, ultra-conservative judge who will remain on the bench for a period approaching forever.

Cheney and his second in command Addington have made the Vice-President's office the strongest in American history. Until now, the Vice-President has been virtually powerless, though handy for laying wreathes, cornerstones and attending the funerals of foreign leaders. Infrequently, as in the case of Al Gore, the President has handed his VP the occasional substantive dossier. Cheney, however, has deftly merged the offices of President and Vice-President into a single executive: to use a business metaphor, he plays Chief Executive Officer to Bush's Chairman of the Board.

Bush has said about himself, "I'm the decider" but Cheney executes the decisions that he often dictates as well. No matter what the decider decides, it is by definition legal. Addington works out the legal details: he is Cheney's CEO, just as

Cheney is Bush's. And as one perspicacious observer notes, "If the executive branch needed a war to justify its claim to absolute power, then Iraq (as Rumsfeld was heard to say on September 12, 2001) had the targets."[21]

NOW WHAT?

In the final analysis, what do the right-wingers want? Their goal is, roughly, to undo all the progressive political, social or environment legislation enacted since the Second World War (and sometimes before that). They are relentless, but they make haste slowly, readily admitting in public that "these sorts of things take decades," as they told the progressive magazine editor Robert Kuttner who shared a panel discussion with them.[22]

Kuttner, calling himself the "token liberal," participated in an event aptly titled "Philanthropy, Think Tanks and the Importance of Ideas," featuring the heads of Heritage and the Cato, Manhattan, and American Enterprise Institutes, which together receive at least $70 million a year from rightwing foundation donors. The latter agreed that over the previous twenty years – from the beginning of the 1980s – well over a billion dollars had been spent on ideological production and dissemination (they naturally called it something else), assuring the audience that "you get a huge leverage for your dollars."

That leverage is what I hope to have shown in this chapter.

2

FOREIGN AFFAIRS

The nation prompted by ill will and resentment sometimes impels to war the government contrary to the best calculations of policy. The government sometimes . . . adopts through passion what reason would reject. At other times, it makes the animosity of the nation subservient to projects of hostility, instigated by pride, ambition, and other sinister and pernicious motives. The peace often, sometimes perhaps the liberty, of nations has been the victim.

President George Washington, *Farewell Address*,
1796

PRELUDE

Imagine for a moment that you are an American neo-conservative official or think-tanker. You are charged with foreign affairs; gauging America's place in the world, examining long-term threats to its security and well-being, thinking about its vulnerabilities. You must not only try to define the most appropriate policies; you must also know how to defend them in front of officialdom and the American people. One of your problems is that you are working in the post-Cold War world. "Fighting Communism" can no longer serve as the public justification for virtually any policy. While you hope to maintain alliances, the concerns of other countries are not yours; you subscribe to Charles de Gaulle's observation that "No nation has friends, only interests." The point of your work is to keep the United States Number One and your job is to give policy advice to people in a position to use it.

If you were such an official or think-tanker, would you not be prodigiously worried about China, which has by now amassed enough dollars to buy the Empire State Building plus a controlling interest in various strategically placed American corporations? If China decided instead to sell off its dollar reserves it could provoke a huge devaluation and wreak havoc with the economy. You would be praying for China to remain a responsible player in the global system and you would do well to think about ways to reduce its potential hold over your government and your economy.

Moving to the other great emerging Asian power, instead of subscribing blindly to the views of the *New York Times* columnist Thomas Friedman in his best-selling paean to neo-liberal globalization *The World is Flat*, you might also decide to look more closely at the Indian subcontinent. The novelist and political critic Arundhati Roy does not hesitate to describe it as bordering on revolution. What if she is right when she compares India to pre-revolutionary France, and claims that it is poised "on the edge of violence?" As Roy sees it, the country of her birth is not coming together but falling apart – convulsed by "corporate globalization" at an unprecedented velocity. "The inequalities become untenable." What effect might untenable inequalities in India have on the United States? How fragile is the rest of Asia?

Like huge glaciers splitting off from the polar ice-caps, a great part of the industrial base has been breaking away from your country and floating off to Asia and elsewhere. Your economy is now overwhelmingly one of information and services, not manufacturing. You know of course that your own transnational corporations still control these migrant firms, but they pay little into the US treasury in the way of taxes. As these companies take an increasing percentage of their profits in tax havens like Bermuda, the American tax burden shifts significantly to individuals and purely domestic companies. How will this trend affect the longer-term health of the US economy? How will the country continue to pay for the policies it wants to practice?[1]

Perhaps you are more a Western than an Eastern hemisphere specialist. You are reflecting on the historic importance of Latin America to your country. In 1822, the United States recognized newly liberated countries like Argentina, Chile, Peru, Colombia, and Mexico and shortly afterwards issued one of the first-ever independent American foreign policy proclamations, the Monroe Doctrine of 1823. In this document, the US told the European powers to keep their hands off the independent nations of South America that many Old World statesmen were eyeing greedily at the time. Just as the United States would refrain, said the Doctrine, from interfering in European wars and internal affairs, so Europeans were expected to leave the Americas alone. They have done so ever since. But now, the Latinos themselves are showing dangerous signs of independence.

You would be thinking about the more recent past, remembering how the US initiated its own version of colonialism in Latin America and supported a broad spectrum of fascist military regimes. From the 1950s to the 1980s, it helped to devastate Central America in small, martyred countries like Guatemala, El Salvador, and Nicaragua. Dictators you aided and abetted, your protégés like Pinochet in Chile and the generals in Brazil, Argentina and elsewhere left a heritage of mistrust, bitterness, and hatred.

In early 2007, your ultimate boss, President Bush made a whistle-stop tour in Latin America, greeted everywhere by angry crowds. You might ask, as did *La Jornada* of Mexico, why he bothered to come at all since he had nothing to propose; you might wonder what the US might usefully propose in future.

In particular, you would be watching Hugo Chavez warily as he gradually organizes the resistance of countries in your "backyard." You would observe him mounting independent, alternative energy and industrial policies for the continent and a Southern Bank in a position to counter the International Monetary Fund in the region. You would be thinking, in short, about the future of hemispheric relations and US interests in Latin America.

You might also meditate on the 1992 document by Paul Wolfowitz's team called *Defense Planning Guidance* that posed an over-riding goal for the United States: to prevent the emergence of any rival power, even a regional one. This "dominant consideration" meant that "we endeavor to prevent any hostile power from dominating a region whose resources would, under consolidated control, be sufficient to generate global power." The US must convince "potential competitors that they need not aspire to a greater role or pursue a more aggressive posture to protect their legitimate interests." At the same time, in non-defense areas, the US must take into account the "interests of the advanced industrial nations to discourage them from challenging our leadership or seeking to overturn the established political and economic order." Finally, said the document, "we must maintain the mechanisms for deterring potential competitors from even aspiring to a larger regional or global role." Such potential rivals are identified as Western

Europe, East Asia, the territory of the former Soviet Union, and Southwest Asia. What major changes have occurred in all these places since 1992? What policies are still relevant to deal with these possible competitors?

There are many other delicate and difficult issues confronting you around the globe, yet you, the hypothetical conservative official or think-tanker, are looking in none of these directions because you are completely mesmerized by the Middle East. And it is not even sure you can think straight about this key area even though you are a well-informed pillar of the policy-making Establishment. Ideology weighs too heavily even on your well-trained mind. The "Global War on Terror" may be a convenient all-purpose replacement for the Cold War – a bone you can throw to the media and the public – but it doesn't work as an analytical tool. Do you claim victory, admit defeat, or just blindly plunge ahead?

THE MESMERIZING MIDDLE EAST

A single, short word has frequently served to justify concentration on this region and we all know it: "oil." This all-important resource played a large part in the decision to invade Iraq even if it was not alone. Control over oil cuts both ways – insuring supply to your own economy and your military, which also runs on oil; and diverting it if necessary from your rivals. Is this what Wolfowitz meant in 1992 when he wrote about preventing rivals from "dominating a region whose resources would, under consolidated control, be sufficient to generate global power?" This seems unlikely, for even there, "resources" is in the plural – he can't have meant only petroleum. There must be some other explanation for the fascination the region exerts.

If policy experts are unable to think clearly about the challenges of foreign policy, what can one say about ordinary citizens? The American people have been excluded from any discussion of the world at large because prejudice and propaganda have too often replaced information and reasoned argument. In the context of the Iraq War, it is understandable that the Middle East now superimposes itself on both popular preoccupations and official American policy. But it does so almost as if no other place on earth existed – well, perhaps North Korea and the odd "rogue State," but little else. There must be functionaries deep inside State Department burrows developing policy for other areas, but you would hardly know it from the general American "conversation." And given their past record, this may be just as well . . .

The Middle East suffers no such lack of attention and in this area one particular set of neo-cons has been especially visible. Let us call them the "reincarnated radicals" because they have had more than one political life. Irving Kristol, the neo-con godfather, the man who identified them as "liberals who've been mugged by reality" used to be a leftist. So did plenty of others. These intellectuals were internationalist in outlook, often dabbled in Trotskyism or Communism; they wrote in publications like the *Partisan Review*, a lot of them lived in New York and they all knew each other. Many were Jewish radicals and they were interested not only in internal American politics but deeply concerned as well by international political movements and by America's place in the world. Now their focus is the US relationship with the Middle East, the war in Iraq, Islamic terrorism, Iran, and Israel.

Traditionally, the Jewish community, particularly on the East Coast and in New York City, was unfailingly left wing and voted solidly Democratic. The older ones sometimes called themselves the "red diaper [nappy] babies" – they absorbed left politics with their mothers' milk. Many now side with Bush and his followers and their former comrades on the left heartily dislike them for it. One such critic says about Norman

Podhoretz, another neo-con "godfather" figure, that he always "knew just when to jump on the latest liberal-left hobby-horse – and, more importantly, when to jump off."[2]

Podhoretz himself, criticizing the critics of the Iraq war, has remarked,

> At first the framers and early spreaders of this defamatory charge [that a cabal of Jewish officials in the first George W. Bush administration had promoted the interests not of the United States but of Israel] considered it the better part of prudence to identify the conspirators not as Jews but as "neo-conservatives." It was a clever tactic, in that Jews did in fact constitute a large proportion of the repentant liberals and leftists who, having some two or three decades earlier broken ranks with the Left and moved rightward, came to be identified as neo-conservatives.[3]

Other recruits to this particular neo-con cause came from at least nominally Democratic Party politics. One group that moved collectively to the right were known as "Scoop Jackson Democrats." Senator Henry "Scoop" Jackson, representing the state of Washington, was also called (although perhaps not to his face) the "Senator from Boeing"; he was a hawk's hawk and defense build-up advocate who persuaded the *New York Times* among many others to accept and spread his views.

One brilliant example of a younger former left neo-con recruit is Joshua Muravchik, now a scholar at the top neo-con think-tank American Enterprise Institute. He began his political life as a Young Socialist, moved to the left of the Democratic Party, then to the entourage of Scoop Jackson and finally to outspoken – not to say scary – neo-conservatism. Muravchik's line as of late 2006 was "We must bomb Iran."

Writing in *Foreign Policy*, he defends his fellow neo-cons and makes their basic worldview clear: "Our intellectual contributions helped to defeat communism in the last century and, God willing, they will help to defeat jihadism in this one." For him, the only way to win that war is to "transform the political culture of the Middle East from one of absolutism and violence to one of tolerance and compromise" – a large order by any standards and one that places military intervention firmly on the agenda. The mantle of "absolutism and violence" thus passes from Middle Eastern rulers to the United States making a unilateral decision to use armed force but Muravchik does not seem conscious of this irony. One wonders also if he believes that such US allies as, say, Saudi Arabia practice "tolerance and compromise." It is intriguing that in Muravchik's piece, there is not one word about oil.

Given the ambitious neo-con goal – wholesale transformation of the political culture of an entire region – Muravchik warns that a nuclear-armed Iran is intolerable. "World peace is indivisible, ideas are powerful, freedom and democracy are universally valid, evil exists and must be confronted." So even if the neo-cons made a mistake about the Iraqi welcome for American forces, the answer to the problem is not to withdraw from the Middle East but rather to apply the same forceful policies, longer and harder. [4]

Therefore, Muravchik says (this time in the *Los Angeles Times*)

> The reality is that we cannot live safely with a nuclear-armed Iran. One reason is terrorism, of which Iran has long been the world's premier state sponsor, through groups such as Hamas and Hezbollah. Now, according to a report last week in London's *Daily Telegraph*, Iran is trying to take over Al Qaeda by positioning its own man, Saif Adel, to become the successor to the ailing Osama bin Laden. How could we possibly trust Iran not to slip nuclear material to terrorists?[5]

Like Norman Podhoretz, Joshua Muravchik confronts head-on the "relentless obloquy" to which he finds the neo-cons subjected and he too links it to the fact that many neo-cons are Jewish: " 'Neo-con,'" he claims, "is now widely synonymous with 'ultraconservative' or, for some, 'dirty Jew.'" He attributes these views to conspiracy theorists like Lyndon La Rouche or former Stalinists but does not bring up the subject of Israel or the Palestinians.

An enduring problem in American political discourse is the difficulty of holding a rational discussion about Middle East policy in general and about Israel and Palestine in particular. Deep sensitivities and raw nerves on both sides tend to place criticism or even mention of the Israel–Palestine conflict off-limits. Some defenders of Israel are quick to label even the mildest critics "anti-Semites." If the critics happen themselves to be Jewish, they may be called "self-hating Jews" as has happened, for example, not only to Noam Chomsky but to my friend and TNI colleague Phyllis Bennis, a peace activist and expert on the Middle East.

Politicians are mostly scared witless of being blasted by such criticism and either try to avoid the subject or meekly submit to the law of silence. In Israel itself, the government's policies are subject to vigorous, not to say vitriolic debate (try the newspaper *Ha'aretz*, for instance) but not in Washington. In early 2007, Prime Minister Ehud Olmert boasted a two percent – that is not a misprint – two percent approval rating in his own country but you would never know it inside the Beltway, as the locals call Washington's ring road.

Such extreme reactions on the part of the neo-cons are linked to their perception, articulated by Muravchik, that the "political culture of the Middle East is one of absolutism and violence" and Israel is the only outpost of democracy in the region. For the neo-cons, this is the bottom line: Israel unlike all the other nations of the region is democratic so they have no problem offering whatever Israeli government may be in office unconditional support. In this they are scarcely alone: they have unswerving allies (although for other reasons) among the right-wing Evangelical Christians, as we shall see in the next chapter.

Many Jewish as well as many non-Jewish neo-con intellectuals are active in the influential Washington think-tank JINSA – the Jewish Institute for National Security Affairs. Its work is supported by 20,000 members and led by a Board of fifty-five defense policy hawks. They lobby for higher US military spending and consistently support Israeli policies. Their basic claim is that there is no difference between the security interests of the US and those of Israel because Israeli policies "bolster" the interests of the United States.

Senator Joseph Lieberman also argues the case for ever-closer US-Israeli ties. Lieberman, the center-right Democrat from the East-coast state of Connecticut who ran for Vice-President on Al Gore's ticket in 2000, narrowly kept his Senate seat in 2006 in a close election fought on the issue of the war in Iraq, which he staunchly continues to defend. Here are some quotes from his speech to "America's leading pro-Israel lobby," as the American Israel Public Affairs Committee (AIPAC) describes itself. This speech encapsulates many aspects of present American foreign policy thinking on the right. Lieberman cogently presents the arguments for supporting Israel, he understands the political mood in the US, and he is genuinely fearful not just for Israel but for his own country's security. Said Lieberman to his AIPAC audience:

> I do not need to tell you about . . . the regime in Iran – its determination to acquire nuclear weapons, its sponsorship of terrorism, its repression of its own citizens . . . about Al Qaeda and Hezbollah and Hamas – their addiction to violence, their pathological hatred of America and Israel, their ambitions for conquest . . . about the fanatical ideology that links these dif-

ferent groups – the ideology of Islamist extremism, a totalitarian ideology as violent and vicious as . . . fascism and communism . . . Unfortunately, many in our country today do not seem to share that critical understanding of the threats we face.

He sees the President at the center of the storm, polarizing the nation. When Bush says Yes, his opponents reflexively say No and vice-versa. This knee-jerk reaction greatly worries Lieberman. Although he says he understands the country's anger over Iraq, he sees appeasement of dangerous enemies as the real problem.

> The feelings of animosity that many people have for President Bush, have begun to affect the way we talk and think about what is happening in the world beyond Iraq and America's role in it. There is something profoundly wrong when opposition to the war in Iraq seems to inspire greater passion than opposition to Islamist extremism . . . when there is so much distrust of our intelligence community that some Americans doubt the plain and ominous facts about the threat to us posed by Iran . . . when, in the face of attacks by radical Islam, we think we can find safety and stability by pulling back, by talking to and accommodating our enemies, and abandoning our friends and allies.[6]

Neo-con intellectuals like Muravchik; pro-defense, pro-Israel lobbies like JINSA and AIPAC; defenders of the Iraq war like Lieberman see themselves playing Cassandra, trying to convey a grim but necessary message to Americans, who increasingly refuse to listen. Or they see themselves in something of a Winston Churchill role, faced with their opponents' appeasement à la Neville Chamberlain. They see little that separates a President Ahmadinejad of Iran from a Hitler (Ahmadinejad's Holocaust denial conference could only confirm this view) and they are frantically trying to get their fellow Americans to remember the lessons of September 11, whose effects are beginning to wear off.

In other words, they recognize that the United States has genuine and determined enemies out there – prominent among them the configuration some neo-cons now call HISH, for Hamas, Iran, Syria, and Hezbollah. One can disagree with their position, and I do, but it is not fair to accuse them of neglecting US interests, at least according to their own lights – they are extremely worried about what its foes can do to the United States. What does seem dangerous in a complex world is their dualistic, black and white, good and evil view of international politics.

The other worrying aspect is that they are not looking at these interests in traditional "realist" terms; for example the often perceived need for the United States to maintain control over the price, distribution and direction of oil-flows. If they were talking about straight power projections, an honest confrontation of views would be easier, but they almost never mention them so the real questions tend not to be confronted. Is their attitude something like the "curious incident of the dog in the night?"* Do neo-cons not talk about power because in some strange way they are actually starry-eyed idealists?

THE MEARSHEIMER–WALT AFFAIR

Passionately held beliefs on both sides of the argument help to explain the extraordinary case of John Mearsheimer and Stephen Walt, distinguished scholars and professors of international relations at the University of Chicago and the

---

* In the Conan Doyle "Sherlock Holmes" story "Silver Blaze," the "curious incident" is the fact that the dog didn't bark. If the murderer had been a stranger, the dog would have barked, but he wasn't – he was quite familiar to the dog. Needless to say, Holmes solves the mystery in short order.

Kennedy School of Government at Harvard respectively. In March 2006 they published an essay entitled "The Israel Lobby" in the *London Review of Books* and simultaneously posted a much longer documented version of the article on the "Working Paper" website of the Kennedy School so that anyone interested could examine their sources and the evidence for their conclusions.

As the two scholars report, "The response . . . was dramatic. As of mid-July 2006, there had been over 275,000 downloads of the KSG Working Paper version, and a lively (albeit not always civilized) debate was underway." For a scholar – indeed for almost any non-fiction author – figures like that are undreamed of – rather the equivalent of writing a scholarly *Da Vinci Code* or *Harry Potter*.

The bi-monthly magazine *Foreign Policy* immediately picked up the debate, featured it on the cover of its July–August 2006 issue and introduced it with the comment that the authors had "sparked a firestorm when they raised questions about the power the Israel lobby wields over US foreign policy."

The magazine gave space to Mearsheimer–Walt to summarize their argument, to three of their critics to refute it and to Zbigniew Brzezinski to explain that as Jimmy Carter's National Security Advisor he had dealt with equally assertive Cuban-American, Armenian-American, and several other What-Have-You-American lobbies, so why should the Israel-American one alone be immune from criticism? At this point, the scholarly quarterly journal *Middle East Policy* jumped into the fray, asking the authors for an expanded version including replies to the comments and criticisms their work had provoked. In September 2007, they had expanded the expansion into a book whose publisher clearly had best-sellerdom in mind.[7]

Before we go to the substance of the M&W (as I shall now call Mearsheimer and Walt) argument, the reader should first understand that lobbying is a standard and long-standing feature of US politics. The up-front nature of this activity in America stands in stark contrast to Europe, where thousands of lobbyists go about their business as furtively as possible. The European Commission averts its eyes, though it has now reluctantly proposed a laughable solution: a voluntary register where lobbyists may, if they feel like it, disclose who they work for and where their money comes from.*

American lobbyists, in contrast, are required to register with Congress and they are perfectly candid about their work, which is generally seen as a normal part of the democratic process. They may call themselves "advocates" rather than "lobbyists," but everyone understands the two are identical. An American lobbyist is therefore about as far away from a conspirator as one can get – anyone who wants to know who pays them can find out, they often seek out supporters and ask for donations from the public, publish documents with their name on them; they publicize their goals and brag about their accomplishments.

Thus the American Israel Public Affairs Committee (AIPAC), which is M&W's chief target in what they call the "Israel lobby," lists its achievements on its website, including "securing critical foreign [and] military aid to Israel . . . keeping world pressure on Hamas" and eleven other successful initiatives. Lobbyist-advocates like AIPAC tell their supporters which issues they should act on, indicate the best ways to influence their elected representatives and they do it very effectively. Three surveys between 1997 and 2005 asking members of Congress to rank the power of various lobbies put AIPAC among the top two, three, or four. Only the American

---

* See the work of the Corporate Europe Observatory, a partner of my own Institute TNI, in exposing lobbying practices in the EU. The activists pushing this issue are not satisfied with the Commission's timid proposal, nor should they be, and promise to continue the fight to force the horde of EU lobbyists to be more transparent: www.alter-eu.org

Association of Retired People, the National Rifle Association and the labour confederation AFL-CIO were sometimes ranked higher in terms of their clout with Congress.[8]

My purpose here is not to retrace and reiterate all of M&W's arguments, their critics' rebuttals and their counter-rebuttals – this would involve writing the book M&W have already published and would be in any case well beyond my competence as I am no expert on the Middle East. I merely want to illustrate my previous points: the intellectual, scholarly and policy community as well as a large slice of the general public in the United States is mesmerized by this discussion, which is certainly important but should be conducted soberly and not lead to the dangerous exclusion of many other equally important debates.

This is where M&W come in – whatever their conclusions, we should be grateful to them, in the atmosphere of deafening silence that reigns in Washington, for raising the subject of Israel's influence, for taking a cooler and more factual approach to a sensitive issue, and for trying to promote an objective assessment of an explosive dossier. Their long article includes twenty-four pages devoted to 227 notes in microscopic print providing sources (many of them quoting Israeli media and scholars) and further elaboration of their various points. Their paper has elicited the full range of positive and negative reactions, including accusations of shoddy scholarship – looking at the notes, however, the non-specialist wonders what more research M&W could have done to fulfil their duty as academics.

Among the facts M&W present, from official sources beyond dispute, are the large amounts of aid garnered by Israel. It certainly does not rank among the world's needy countries and it is not subject to the usual conditions requiring that US aid money be spent on previously agreed and stated purposes. So if Israel wants to use American funds for building settlements in the Occupied Territories (which the

US says it opposes) it can do so. Since the Second World War, Israel has received (in 2003 dollars) $140 billion worth of American aid, an average of $3 billion a year, about 20 percent of total annual US foreign aid. Put another way, the US gives about $500 a year to every Israeli, that is, to the people of a country that has nearly the same per capita income as Spain.*

Furthermore, in exchange for American largesse, Israel does not always behave like a loyal ally: for example, it has transferred US military technology to China, a potential rival, causing the US State Department's Inspector General to call attention to a "systematic and growing pattern of unauthorized transfers" on Israel's part. According to the US General Accounting Office, Israel "conducts the most aggressive espionage operations against the US of any ally." The contrarian French may be pleased to learn the opinion of veteran journalist Jim Hoagland: "With the possible exception of Charles de Gaulle, no friendly foreign leader has complicated modern American diplomacy more consistently or gravely than Ariel Sharon."[9]

M&W also argue that Israel is not, as JINSA or AIPAC claim, a strategic asset for America but rather a "strategic liability" and a "burden." Whereas Palestinian terrorism targets Israel alone and does not directly threaten the United States, Israel's treatment of the Palestinians inflames Arab and Islamic opinion and this does severely jeopardize US security. In their view, Israel's actions provide a permanent grievance and make recruitment, harboring, and funding of terrorists that much easier.

Even if Iran were to acquire nuclear weapons, say M&W, it would not be a "strategic disaster" for America. The US man-

---

* According to the *CIA Factbook*, Israel enjoys one of the lowest infant mortality rates (6.9/1000 live births) and highest life expectancies (79.5 years) in the world; the Israeli population is over 95 percent literate. We are definitely not in the "Third World" and probably US aid is responsible for part of this success.

ages to live with Chinese, Indian, Pakistani, and even North Korean nukes, so why not Iranian ones? Iran would not itself use nukes against the US nor would it give them to terrorists to use because in either case it knows that US nuclear retaliation would be swift and terrible. On the contrary, argue M&W, other States in the region want nuclear weapons because Israel has them, but the US has "turned a blind eye" to Israel's own arsenal.

There is a lot more along these lines, but this sample is enough to show that M&W could scarcely stand farther away from the views of, say, Lieberman or Muravchik. Hence the "firestorm" their work has caused. M&W share the view of the fifty-two British diplomats they quote who wrote to Tony Blair to say that the Israel–Palestine situation has "poisoned relations between the West and the Arab and Islamic worlds" and that Bush's policies are "one-sided and illegal." If these diplomats and M&W are right, the US special relationship with Israel jeopardizes America's real interests.

And if they are right, who is responsible for endangering these interests? M&W take pains to affirm that they support Israel's right to exist and they "do not believe that Americans who lobby on Israel's behalf are in any way disloyal" to their own country. Still, according to these authors, the overwhelming support the United States gives to Israel itself and to the views of the Israeli government concerning the entire region is directly attributable to the power of the "Israel lobby" in the US, a term they use to designate a loose collection of organizations, individuals, networks, and so on.

How does "the lobby" operate? According to M&W, it has "an unchallenged hold on the US Congress." They quote former Senator Ernest Hollings who left office saying "Around here, you can't have an Israeli policy other than what AIPAC gives you." The Israeli leadership itself certainly seems to appreciate the organization: Ariel Sharon said that when people asked him what they could do for Israel, he always replied "If you want to help Israel, help AIPAC." His successor, Ehud Olmert concurs, saying "Thank God we have AIPAC, the greatest supporter and friend we have in the whole world."

In an electoral system like that of the US which depends entirely on private money for campaigns, one of AIPAC's great strengths is its capacity to channel political donations toward candidates who have a good voting record on its issues and away from those who don't. An example of AIPAC's "hold on the Congress" dates from 2002 when Bush started putting pressure on Ariel Sharon to withdraw from the Occupied Territories. The lobby swung into action, obtaining strong pro-Israel, anti-withdrawal resolutions that passed the House by 352 to 21 and the Senate by 94 to 2. Bush caved in. Without the lobby, M&W believe the US would also have been "far less likely to have gone to war (in Iraq) in March 2003."

AIPAC has considerable impact as well with the media – M&W give many examples – but less in academia where its action is more limited. It does send speakers to college campuses and it mobilizes students to monitor and counter what professors write and teach – this action seems to be having an effect. Whereas two-thirds of professors of international relations surveyed by *Foreign Policy* agreed "strongly" or "somewhat" with the statement that "the Israel lobby has too much influence over US foreign policy," their students didn't agree, and seemed little influenced by their professors' views. *Foreign Policy* also surveyed 700 students in introductory international relations courses at a dozen universities and found that "students were *less* likely to believe that "the Israel lobby exerts too much influence over US foreign policy" after taking the course than before."[10]

Still according to M&W, the most powerful weapon the lobby wields is the one they call "the great silencer," the charge of anti-Semitism. "In effect, the lobby boasts of its own power and then attacks anyone who calls attention to it . . . Anti-Semitism is loathsome and no responsible person wants to be accused of it," so they often prefer to keep quiet. Israeli media, on the other hand, are less punctilious, frequently referring to "America's Jewish lobby."

M&W's position is that the United States should use its power

> to achieve a just peace between Israel and the Palestinians (which) would help to advance the broader goals of fighting extremism and promoting democracy in the Middle East. But that is not going to happen anytime soon.

The lobby's influence increases the probability of terrorism for America as well as for its allies but it also endangers Israel itself. The authors claim that AIPAC and its followers have discouraged Israel from "seizing opportunities . . . that would have saved Israeli lives and shrunk the ranks of Palestinian extremists . . . Ironically, Israel itself would be better off if the lobby were less powerful." On this pessimistic note, Mearsheimer and Walt rest their case.

Their critics do not lack for counter-arguments. One, Aaron Friedberg, a professor at Princeton and former assistant to Dick Cheney for national security affairs, centers his critique on the consequences of appeasement. He asks rhetorically what would happen if the US cut off support to Israel, as M&W would apparently like it to do. Such a move would not "make Israel more pliant" – to the contrary – and would "certainly embolden Israel's enemies and empower the more radical among them." Jihadis would not be placated or renounce their war against Israel and the Great Satan but would rather claim victory and rally more followers.

Another critic, Dennis Ross, a US negotiator during the Clinton presidency, says that neither the lobby nor the neo-cons convinced Bush to go to war – September 11 did that. Furthermore, the lobby does not necessarily get its way: it has failed to prevent several major arms sales to Arab countries and has opposed various peace initiatives that were put on the table against its wishes. "Never in the time that I led the American negotiations on the Middle East peace process did we take a step because 'the lobby' wanted us to," writes Ross. "Nor did we shy away from one because 'the lobby' opposed it."

A third, Shlomo Ben-Ami, a former Israeli foreign minister, calls M&W's account of the lobby's influence "grossly overblown" and gives details of several instances (like Reagan's official recognition of the PLO) where the lobby's views made no difference to US presidents. He adds that

> The United States should do more to end the humiliation of the Palestinians. But it is preposterous to claim that Israel or the lobby is responsible . . . for America's terror problem . . . Mearsheimer and Walt display an abstruse indifference to the complex fabric of America's interests in the Middle East . . . the current Iraq war may benefit Israel, but it benefits Iran as much or more. Certainly no one would say that it was waged at Iran's bidding? . . . Suggesting that the United States would be unconcerned about threatening states such as Iran, Iraq, or Syria were it not closely tied with Israel is absurd.[11]

He might have added that the Iraq War benefits China, OPEC oil producers and Al Qaeda too but they had zero influence in causing it.[12]

THE PUBLIC RELATIONS BLITZ: AMERICA THE BRAND

Ammunition against the "power of the lobby" thesis also comes from an unexpected quarter, the media experts and opponents of the Iraq War Sheldon Rampton and John Stauber. In their book *Weapons of Mass Deception: The Uses of Propaganda in Bush's War on Iraq*, these authors give a fascinating account of the ideological build-up to the invasion of 2003.[13]

However many neo-cons may have come along for the ride, and plenty of them did, the government itself was fully in charge of the invasion strategy and did not call on AIPAC or indeed any other lobby to prepare the country for war. For that, they relied on professional mind-manipulators.

The Bush–Cheney machine began public relations operations right after September 11, at first with the objective of improving the US image in the Arab world, a purpose for which Congress allocated tens of millions of dollars. The problem, as the administration saw it, was selling America just as one would sell soft-drinks, shampoo or any other mass-market product. As Secretary of State Colin Powell explained, "it was an attempt . . . to really brand foreign policy."

America would be Brand Freedom. The administration hired a successful female advertising executive who explained, "With any great brand, the (most valuable) asset is the emotional underpinning." Unfortunately, the "emotional underpinning" for most people in the Arab world consisted of fear, distrust, and rage. They didn't care how happy Muslim-American women were in their fancy kitchens in New Jersey; they were angry because of American policies, particularly the way it bombed civilians in Afghanistan, backed authoritarian regimes in their own countries, and did nothing to alleviate the plight of the Palestinians.

As an Egyptian merchant remarked to a *New York Times* reporter, pointing out the obvious, "No matter how much the US tries to change its image in the Arab world, what we are seeing with our own eyes is much stronger." A fortnight before the invasion of Iraq, after a series of abject failures, the advertising executive resigned. This shambles had been predicted from the outset by people like Osama Siblani, publisher of the *Arab-American News*. "The United States lost the public relations war in the Muslim world a long time ago," said Siblani. "They could have the Prophet Muhammad doing public relations and it wouldn't help."[14]

These setbacks did not, however, prevent the government from sinking further hundreds of millions into other PR operations. They established the new White House "Office of Global Communications," the "Iraq Public Diplomacy Group", and front organizations such as the "Iraqi National Congress" to showcase their choices for leadership of the opposition to Saddam Hussein; often quite dodgy people like Ahmad Chalabi. They hired various PR pros to counsel a clutch of government inter-agency task forces whose activities the industry trade paper *PR Week* regularly chronicled.

PR Week also took the view that from the Bush–Cheney camp's perspective, the taxpayers' millions had been well spent – not in the Arab world but on the home front. "The Bush administration has succeeded in making the question '*Should we attack Iraq?*' the most considered political question in the US today." Corporate crime (Enron et alia), the faltering economy, the threat to civil liberties – even the whereabouts of Osama bin Laden – all these questions had been pushed off the stage and faded from the front pages of the nation.[15] The Democrats were furious because they could not get any of their own issues onto the political agenda in time for the 2002 mid-term elections, which Bush duly won.

In the midst of all this, the "Israel lobby" was nowhere to be seen. As one would expect, with or without AIPAC, a good many neo-con policy people were cheering the government on and, for those of them in office, helping to shape its policies. Especially prominent among the advocates of the Iraq War were members of the PNAC.

POLITICS AS WAR BY OTHER MEANS: THE
PROJECT FOR A NEW AMERICAN CENTURY

First the good news: before describing the dire decade of the Project for a New American Century (PNAC), we can be almost sure that PNAC is a lame duck and perhaps by now a dead one. As of early 2007, it still had its website but reportedly (by the BBC) a single person remained on staff, apparently to wrap up its affairs and close down the shop. Without meaning to tempt fate, let us speak of it in the past tense.

The name chosen was no accident and deserves explanation. The founders of the Project for a New American Century were paying tribute to Henry Luce, influential publisher of the mass-circulation magazines *Time*, *Life*, and *Fortune*, who coined the term "The American Century" in a celebrated editorial published in *Life* in February 1941, ten months before Pearl Harbor.

Luce was part of the East Coast Establishment, but he argued against the many Republican isolationists who wanted to keep the US out of the war. He was alarmed by the Nazis' victories and farsighted enough to tell his compatriots that even if Britain managed to stop Hitler, the war would leave her too exhausted to play the great world power any longer. Americans had to accept the "inevitable": first armed intervention to save Europe; then a post-war world order dominated by the United States. The twentieth century was destined to be the American Century.

In 1944, well before the disintegration of the United States–Soviet alliance, Luce already mistrusted the Soviet Union and its post-war designs on the world. Soon his influential magazines left millions of readers in no doubt that they would also have to fight this new enemy. He never wavered from the belief he stated before a Senate Committee over a decade later: "I do not think there can be

a peaceful co-existence between the Communist Empire
and the free world." Until his death in 1967, Luce continued to call for American hegemony, maintaining his anti-
communist stance up to and including the Vietnam War,
which he supported.

American post-war foreign and defense policy had always
rested on the bedrock of anti-communism, support for "anti-
communist" foreign leaders no matter how despotic, high
levels of armaments, and tried-and-true imperial strategies of
resource capture, particularly of oil. In many respects, Iraq is
only the most recent example of traditional US intervention
but the context has changed. Once communism disappeared
as a geo-political force, the neo-cons were obliged to find new
pretexts for penetrating any region of the globe in which they
took an interest. Whenever useful, the American policy-
defining Establishment can invent a new security concept
such as preventive war, rogue States, the duty to spread
democracy, and the hands-down favorite, the Global War on
Terrorism.

In this new context, the PNAC rationale and project would
become the most successful initiative in the creation and dissemination of a bellicose and hegemonic ideology. In 1997,
some two dozen seasoned neo-con policy experts came
together to design the future and America's place in it. The
Project had a profound influence on government; if only
because so many of its founders *became* the government from
the day George W. Bush took office.

Fifty-six years after Henry Luce framed his project, the
PNAC's "Statement of Principles" echoes him. Here is part of
it:

> [We need] a military that is strong and ready to meet both
> present and future challenges; a foreign policy that boldly
> and purposefully promotes American principles abroad; and

national leadership that accepts the United States' global responsibilities . . . America has a vital role in maintaining peace and security in Europe, Asia, and the Middle East. If we shirk our responsibilities, we invite challenges to our fundamental interests . . . it is important to shape circumstances before crises emerge, and to meet threats before they become dire. The history of the past century should have taught us to embrace the cause of American leadership.

A more eloquent apology for American uniqueness and intervention would be hard to conceive. To accomplish the goals the PNAC set, the nation had to be proactive and daring. Thus on 20 September, 2001, a mere nine days after the attack on the World Trade Center, PNAC leaders wrote to President George W. Bush exhorting him to punish Saddam Hussein. Their logic may appear tortured, but their intentions were clear:

> It may be that the Iraqi government provided assistance in some form to the recent attack on the United States. But even if evidence does not link Iraq directly to the attack, any strategy aiming at the eradication of terrorism and its sponsors must include a determined effort to remove Saddam Hussein from power in Iraq. Failure to undertake such an effort will constitute an early and perhaps decisive surrender in the war on international terrorism.

This passage is bizarre. On the one hand, PNAC's membership is a hotbed of foreign policy experts. On the other, opinion is unanimous that the terrorist acts perpetrated on September 11 had an undeniably Islamic, that is, religious, jihadist dimension with strong Saudi participation. Why, then, go after one of the very few Moslem countries where the State was entirely secular with a nationalist Ba'athist party in charge? Osama bin Laden and Saddam Hussein had about as much brotherly love for each other as the Pope and Martin Luther – bin Laden in fact saw Saddam as an "infidel."

Furthermore, as PNAC experts must surely have known, there were no "weapons of mass destruction" waiting to be discovered in Iraq – the regime had got rid of them in the early to mid-1990s.

PNAC's obsession with Iraq was not, however, unprecedented. Paul Wolfowitz, one of its co-founders, had already recommended attacking Iraq in his notorious *Defense Planning Guidance* paper of 1992, which was leaked to the *New York Times* and caused a huge row. Early in 1998, PNAC members wrote to President Clinton recommending "removal of Saddam Hussein from power." When nothing happened, they wrote to Republican minority leaders Congressman Newt Gingrich and Senator Trent Lott urging them to act decisively in the "absence of Presidential leadership." What did PNAC want Gingrich and Lott to do, given that President Clinton was not leading the nation as it ought to be led? "US policy," said PNAC, "should have as its explicit goal removing Saddam Hussein's regime from power and establishing a peaceful and democratic Iraq in its place."

Was the PNAC influential? Plenty of its people were or still are in high government positions and its members still intervene regularly on the media circuit and in other opinion-shaping institutions. The signatories of the PNAC "Statement of Principles" and its many letters were the likes of the Vice-President and a former Vice-President (Dick Cheney, Dan Quayle) plus Cheney's then Chief of Staff (Lewis Libby); the two top men in the Defense Department (Donald Rumsfeld, Paul Wolfowitz). Add to them the President's brother and governor of Florida (Jeb Bush); the US Special Trade Representative (Robert Zoellick); the Permanent

Representative to the United Nations (John Bolton) and his replacement (Zalmay Khalilzad).

These top people were joined by a rich assortment of special advisors and assistant or deputy secretaries of this and that – Paula Dobriansky at State, Elliott Abrams in the White House, Peter Rodman at Defense; Aaron Friedberg in Cheney's office. Not to leave out prominent and influential academics like Francis Fukuyama, Donald Kagan, or Eliot Cohen; intellectuals like Norman Podhoretz and his wife Midge Decter; the Chair of the National Endowment for Democracy (Vin Weber) and a couple of men with great influence in right-wing religious circles (Gary Bauer for the Evangelicals and George Weigel for the Catholics). The members of this group undoubtedly counted for a great deal in the decision to invade Iraq.[16]

In September 2000, PNAC called for "Rebuilding America's Defenses" and set the benchmark for a proper Pentagon budget at 3.8 percent of GNP. When, shortly afterwards, Bush took office, he pushed the defense budget up to $379 billion, exactly 3.8 percent of GNP . . . This budget has climbed steadily ever since, amounting in 2007 to about $513 billion (still 3.8 percent of GNP).

In the same document, PNAC signatories admitted that their goals would be difficult to realize "*absent some catastrophic catalytic event – like a new Pearl Harbor*" (shades of Henry Luce again, emphasis added), a role which September 11 later miraculously and conveniently fulfilled. These words were both prescient and troubling.

As the 9/11 Commission *Staff Report* recorded, between April and September 2001, the Federal Aviation Agency received 52 reports concerning possible attacks against the United States. Many observers have concluded that such a great number of potential threats should have prodded the authorities into action; some have seen conspiratorial intent in the fact that they did nothing, although massive bureaucratic rivalry and failure remain a distinct possibility. By their own premonitory admission, PNAC members saw the need for – whether or not they welcomed – Al Qaeda's daring and "catastrophic catalytic" attacks on the World Trade Center and the Pentagon. These events indeed produced an effect similar to Pearl Harbor.

PNAC also articulated early on the need for permanent military bases in Iraq. Condoleezza Rice, who was not a member of PNAC, later assured Congress that US engagement in the Middle East was no less than a "generational commitment." While it is certainly impossible to pretend that PNAC people were in any way complicit in the events of September 11, they still knew exactly how to take advantage of them. PNAC often appeared as a kind of back-up or shadow government, setting targets for the nation and then, from various strategic positions in the Administration, helping to hit them.

THE WEIGHT OF HISTORY

The same institutions that have promoted neo-liberalism inside the United States have always defended American State power, especially its military power, abroad. As the earlier quote from Joshua Muravchik shows, they believe that the country has a right to intervene when and where it sees fit on the world scene. For neo-cons, the civilian State should be weak and defer to market forces; the military State should be strong and defer to no one.

Neo-con ideological energies have been devoted domestically to anchoring their social and economic doctrine in national institutions, in the media and the minds of the public so that it attains the status of a moral philosophy. In foreign affairs, patriotism, national security, America's "exceptionalism" and its absolute independence and right to unilateralism have always stood in the forefront. "My country right or wrong" is not an idle phrase.*

But how new is this attitude? Long before the advent of the new right, the United States was famous for standing alone and refusing to sign international agreements. It has never signed the major ILO labor conventions and has rejected the Kyoto Protocol on grounds that it would be detrimental to the American economy. Even the Convention on the Rights of the Child remains unratified by only two countries, the United States and Somalia.

The US also has its own definitions of international law or ignores it altogether. In the dispute (United States et al. v. the European Union) concerning Genetically Modified Organisms (GMOs), the World Trade Organization's Dispute Resolution Body delivered an initial judgment against the six European countries that imposed bans on imports of GMOs. Part of the European defense invoked the Precautionary Principle and the Biosafety, or "Cartagena," Protocol. According to one of the lawyers (speaking at a Greenpeace conference) the United States retorted that it does not recognize the Precautionary

---

* Curious to know where this oft-cited phrase, "My country right or wrong," came from, I learned that in 1872, Senator Carl Schurz was actually contradicting another Senator who had used the expression. Schurz said instead, "My country right or wrong, if right to be kept right and if wrong to be set right." Much later, he expanded on this theme at the Anti-Imperialistic Conference held in Chicago in October 1899. He declared to fellow anti-imperialists that he was sure that the American people would not heed this "deceptive cry of mock patriotism," but would rather see their country "kept right or set right." Schurz was wrong. Americans mostly supported the Spanish-American War (1898) through which the US acquired Puerto Rico, Guam, and the Philippines. They also mostly supported the bloody American repression against the Philippine liberation movement that began in 1899 and dragged on for over a decade. The US military committed various atrocities ("Kill everyone over ten," ordered one general) and appear to have invented the concentration camp. This war left over 4,300 American soldiers and 16,000 Filipino soldiers dead, as well as 250,000 to a million Filipino civilians who died from the war, famine, or cholera. Sound familiar?

Principle (nor, generally, does the neo-liberal WTO); and the Biosafety Protocol does not constitute international law for the excellent reason that the US has not signed it.

The International Criminal Court (ICC) provokes neo-con rage, particularly inside the Bush Justice Department. The Heritage Foundation has declared that the United States should inform countries that ratify the ICC that they have committed a "hostile act" against the United States. They must reject it or be ineligible for foreign aid. In this context, it is not surprising that the Bush administration immediately revoked President Clinton's signature of the Rome Statute creating the ICC.

As pointed out in the preceding chapter, Friedrich von Hayek's philosophy intrinsically rejects positive law and the observance of human rights whether in the domestic or the international sphere. This is coherent because respecting human rights means not universal competition and survival of the fittest but sharing wealth and satisfying everyone's needs. In the international arena, neo-liberal economic policy goes by many names, often depending on where it is applied and who applies it. In the poorer countries, it is known as "structural adjustment" or the "Washington Consensus" and is implemented by international institutions like the World Bank and the International Monetary Fund, in perfect harmony with the United States Government, particularly the Treasury Department. Together they have subjected at least 100 countries throughout the South and the East to this economic shock treatment.[17]

This constant pressure guarantees debt repayments, including those to private banks. Neo-liberal economic theory collapses, however, when public intervention is needed to ensure private profits. Stupid borrowers are punished, but stupid lenders are rewarded. The full set of structural adjustment policies includes high interest rates, wholesale privatization of public services, "export-led growth" and open borders for imports and foreign investment. These policies have had the predictable result of increasing inequalities, both within and between countries and, having stripped them of all means of defense, opening them to economic assault by more powerful nations and enterprises.

A vast literature exists on these subjects, some of it by the present author, who alas cannot claim that it has done much good, at least not yet. No matter how many socio-economic disasters occur because of neo-liberal policies, they are unlikely to disappear in the poorest and weakest countries, certainly not under the current American presidency. After many years of studying debt and the heart-rending human consequences of structural adjustment policies, I had to conclude that no level of human suffering, in and of itself, would cause policy to change. An administration that could name Paul Wolfowitz to the Presidency of the World Bank and John Bolton Ambassador to the United Nations speaks for itself.

President Bush's choice of the prominent neo-con Bolton for the UN blatantly embodied American unilateralist doctrine. Ordinary Americans are famously indifferent to their country's actions abroad, except when these may involve the loss of American lives. A campaign to defame the United Nations has been going on for decades, including – although this is very marginal – the invention of its ominous "black helicopters" heading off on unspeakable missions. More serious are the views of right-wingers like Phyllis Schlafly who, among other accomplishments, contributed significantly to the defeat of the Equal Rights for Women amendment. She delicately remarked that Bolton's appointment was a golden opportunity for the United States to say "bug off" to other nations.

Although Bolton is now gone, replaced by the former US Ambassador to Afghanistan and Iraq, Zalmay Khalilzad, a sampling of his views is indicative of neo-con foreign policy views, more forcefully expressed than by others:[18]

> There is no such thing as the United Nations. There is an international community that occasionally can be led by the only real power left in the world and that is the US when it suits our interest and we can get others to go along.

> [The International Criminal Court] is a product of fuzzy-minded romanticism that is not just naïve but dangerous.

> [The UN vote against invading Iraq is] further evidence why nothing should be paid to the UN.

> If I were redoing the Security Council, I'd have one permanent member because that's the real reflection of the distribution of power in the world.

> It is a big mistake for us to grant any validity to international law even when it may be in our short-term interest to do so; because, over the long term, those who think that international law really means anything are those who want to constrict the US.

Such considerations were enough to goad fifty-nine former United States diplomats into action. They jointly addressed a letter to the Chair of the Senate Foreign Relations Committee, Senator Richard Lugar, to point out that "given [Bolton's] past actions and statements, [he] cannot be an effective promoter of the US national interest at the UN;" they hoped that the Senate would block his appointment.

To no avail: Bush used a procedural manoeuvre unknown since the eighteenth century and made a "recess [of the Senate] appointment" – that is how Bolton slipped through the normal Senate confirmation procedure.[19]

Bolton, like Donald Rumsfeld, was a casualty of the 2006 mid-term elections. His replacement as Ambassador to the United Nations is an altogether smoother gentleman. Zalmay Khalilzad, born in Afghanistan, speaks Pashto, Dari, Arabic, and French but he has the perfect American political profile. Ever since he arrived in the US in his twenties, he has done exactly the right jobs for exactly the right politically influential superiors.

Straight out of his Ph.D. at the University of Chicago, he became a junior academic at Columbia, working closely with Zbigniew Brzezinski. At thirty-three, he was appointed a Fellow of the Council on Foreign Relations and moved closer to the neo-con Establishment, working under Wolfowitz at the State Department. Still at State, he became special advisor to President Reagan on the Soviet War in Afghanistan and on the Iran–Iraq War. In 1992, during the Bush senior presidency, he moved to Defense, again under Wolfowitz. Some say he was the man who actually drafted the notorious *Defense Planning Guidance* report that sparked a major controversy.

When the Republicans lost power, Khalilzad moved to the national security think-tank, the RAND Corporation; when they returned to power, he went to the National Security Council and became the closest advisor on the Middle East to Bush Junior. Then he was special envoy and later Ambassador to Afghanistan and finally Ambassador to Iraq. Using such a highly qualified official at the UN may signal a renewed interest in this institution on the part of the Republicans – others say that even a prodigy like Khalilzad can't bring that off.

Khalilzad leaves behind the American Embassy in the world's most unfortunate country (not counting Palestine), Iraq. Before public opinion began to sour, the invasion of Iraq had appealed to patriotism and cemented a huge majority of the American public against "Old Europeans" who dared to oppose Bush. A popular bumper sticker in the US at the time read "First Iraq, Then France." Ms. Phyllis Schlafly took pains to criticize the US's "so-called European allies," claiming that they "deserve a prize for impertinence."[20]

Once involved in Afghanistan and Iraq, the Bush government used many pseudo-legal means for doing as it pleased, with the "Global War on Terror" serving as a convenient fig-leaf. In a series of memos, White House counsel (later Attorney General) Alberto Gonzales, argued that the provisions of the Geneva Convention were "obsolete"; that terrorism had made them "quaint." In 2002, he declared that Afghan prisoners in particular were not covered by the Geneva Convention.[21]

Gonzales' then-Assistant Attorney General opined that all interrogation methods were legitimate, except for those "specifically intended" to produce severe pain equivalent to that of "serious physical injury, such as organ failure, impairment of bodily functions or even death." Any methods that fall short of causing such pain do not qualify as torture and may therefore be used, according to these authorities, on prisoners in Guantanamo and/or in Abu Ghraib Prison.[22] But was Gonzales (or White House lawyer John Yu, also involved) really the force behind this memo? Many say David Addington, Cheney's right-hand man, drafted it.

PALEO IS GREEK FOR "OLD" AND AMERICAN FOR "POWERLESS"

Although the neo-cons are in favor of interventionism abroad, this is not the case for all conservatives. Traditional American conservatism always opposed US entry into war and wanted to avoid involvement in what the Founding Fathers called "foreign entanglements." Even the occasional modern Army officer, writing in the pages of the *American Conservative*, has denounced George W. Bush's interventionism and the concept of "preventive war."[23]According to Seymour Hersh's account of US planning to intervene in Iran, several high-ranking officers have threatened to resign if a bombing campaign – especially a nuclear one – is launched.[24]

These classic Americans belong to the group sometimes labelled the "paleo-conservatives" – ancient or old, as opposed to neo or new. The paleo-cons are the sort who opposed America's entry into the First and Second World Wars and Franklin Roosevelt's New Deal in the 1930s. They are trade protectionists and isolationists; they stress tradition and feel strongly about their identity, whether local, regional, national, Christian, white, Western or all of the above. In addition to the *American Conservative*, they still have their own little-known magazine called *Chronicles* and their own think-tank at the Rockford Institute (which has lost a lot of right-wing funding over the past decade) but they are political nonentities; they have been completely marginalized and excluded from political power since the days of Ronald Reagan. None of them have served in the Bush administration, so we shall elaborate no further here on their beliefs and their doings.

NEO-IMPERIAL TRADE

All countries try to promote their national interests and those of their corporations – that is the whole point of having a modern State – but the United States seems to do it more thoroughly and often more skilfully than others through trade. Sometimes this is due to sheer weight of numbers. At the bi-annual Ministerial Meeting of the World Trade Organization in Cancun in 2003, the US delegation counted well over 600 people, more delegates than those representing the entire continent of Africa. A French negotiator in charge of the fisheries dossier – a very minor one in Cancun – told me that he had attended a meeting that day with one advisor. The Americans turned up with twenty-seven people.

No market is too small, no trading rival too insignificant to capture US government attention. America subsidizes its cotton producers – about 30,000 large farmers – to the amount of three billion dollars a year. Assuming each receives $100,000 annually, this is equivalent to about 265 years of income for a Malian farmer if he is receiving the same amount as the Malian GNP per capita. Subsidies allow the Americans to sell on world markets under their costs of production – depriving poor African farmers of cotton-producing countries of a fair return for their labor. Too bad for them. They don't vote, whereas US cotton farmers do. And so much for the neo-liberal theory of free trade.

US transnational corporations have had great influence over the various WTO agreements (on agriculture, services, intellectual property and so on) as officials of the organization have admitted. The former Director of the Services Trade Division at the WTO said in 1997, "Without the enormous pressures exerted by the American financial sector, particularly companies like American Express and Citicorp, there would have been no GATS [the General Agreement on Trade in Services] and therefore perhaps no Uruguay Round and no WTO. The US fought to get services on the agenda and they were right."[25] "Big Pharma" and big cinema were especially active in drafting a leonine intellectual property agreement guaranteeing them fat royalties for twenty years. These lobbies continue to exert strong pressure against trade barriers in the South, but erect them when their own industries are challenged, as in the case of the American steel tariffs or agricultural export subsidies.

Whatever direction negotiations at the WTO may take (at the end of 2007 they are stalled), the Americans are concentrating on bilateral and regional trade agreements in which they are invariably the stronger partner. These agreements are tools for prying open markets but they also serve broader political objectives. The US Africa Growth and Opportunity Act, for example, extends trade benefits to African countries (now 37) but only if they practice neo-liberal policies and refrain from engaging in "any act that undermines US national security and foreign policy interests" broadly defined. As a result of this Act, passed in 2000, US trade with Africa has increased, yes, but oil alone represents 87 percent of total imports from this continent and the great majority of benefits have flowed to only a few countries (Nigeria, South Africa, Angola, Gabon . . .) Just as with Bank–IMF structural adjustment, Washington Consensus-type conditionality, American trade legislation is designed to further its ideologically driven, market-oriented objectives.[26]

The Middle East aside, it often seems as if the US Special Trade Representative has more foreign policy-making responsibility than the Secretary of State. This may be why Condoleezza Rice, recognizing his usefulness, immediately brought the former USTR, Robert Zoellick, to the State Department as her second in command.* "Trade" no longer stops at borders. It is the privileged tool for obliging other nations to support US policies (no "hostile acts"). All bilateral and regional trade agreements come with provisions like those of the Africa Growth and Opportunity Act. They also include strict rules for opening up to American transnational corporate investment. Under these agreements, countries are not allowed to limit the number of investors nor the amount of

---

* Zoellick replaced Paul Wolfowitz at the World Bank after the latter was forced to resign.

their investments. Some countries used to have limits of 49 percent on foreign investment overall or in strategic sectors. If they want a trade agreement with the US today, they can forget about such limits. Local authorities cannot insist that foreigners take a local partner, employ a certain number of local personnel or include a proportion of "local content" in their production.

During the Cold War, no place on earth was totally without interest to the superpower because any point on the globe could serve as a base or a stronghold for the Soviet rival. Today, in the neo-liberal world, a kind of planetary apartheid is under construction. Some places are interesting, others, definitively, are not. Those that are not, like, say, Mali, have little recourse unless they band together. In the WTO at least, there are positive signs that they understand this, which may be one reason trade talks are stalled at the global level.

"Globalization" is a weasel word, coined to make us believe that all will share in future benefits. Nothing could be more false. Perhaps even the mighty but myopic United States will one day discover that while the real world was changing, it was looking in the wrong direction and losing the power that not even the planet's greatest arsenal can insure. Depending on how other nations use the opening, and who fills the vacuum, this can lead to a safer or a more dangerous world.

3

THE AMERICAN RELIGIOUS RIGHT AND ITS LONG MARCH THROUGH THE INSTITUTIONS

When church and state are separate, the effects are happy, and they do not at all interfere with each other: but where they have been confounded together, no tongue or pen can fully describe the mischiefs that have ensued.

Isaac Backus, New England preacher and delegate
to the First Continental Congress; a major figure in
the "pulpit of the American Revolution," 1773

I'm completely in favor of the separation of Church and State. My idea is that these two institutions screw us up enough on their own, so both of them together is certain death.

George Carlin, American comedian and author,
b. 1937

Any examination of American culture today must face a basic question: Is it still possible for outsiders to understand the United States at all, much less carry out a constructive dialog with a view to solving the global problems we all face? This chapter will not attempt to answer that question with a straightforward Yes or No, but it will try to explain the role that religious faith plays today in American politics and describe some of the more irrational, sometimes downright bizarre, forces that now hold considerable sway over a respectable portion of the American people and their government. Those who ignore these forces do so at their peril, at least in so far as they hope to make sense of the current American scene.

In the first chapter, we had a brief encounter with Antonio Gramsci's concept of cultural hegemony. The Italian Marxist thinker used the term to contrast the exercise of power using traditional, often blatantly repressive methods with more subtle means of getting one's way. Any would-be ruling class must wield both kinds of power; it must exercise both coercion and less noticeable social control, but how are they to arrive at that power in the first place? Gramsci provides the answer. Haste and brutality are useless: to achieve cultural hegemony and thereby lasting political power, the potential rulers must submit to the discipline of the "long march through the institutions."

The road these marchers must travel may be arduous, but the prize at the end is the capture of the cinema, newspapers, radio, and television; the schools and universities, the courts and the churches – even the family and the language itself. When the social institutions are secure, the political ones will follow; even – perhaps especially – in a democracy. From that point on, the political, social, and cultural institutions will reinforce each other's influence over the population. In time, without even being aware of it, the people, like fish unaware they are swimming in water, will have lost a substantial part of their freedom of thought and action.

I fear – while hoping I am wrong – that despite the electoral victory of the Democratic Party in 2006, the United States has reached this point. The American right has with great perseverance and daring carried out just such a "gramscian" offensive and is now reaping its reward. The present American century has witnessed the triumph of the right because it has largely infiltrated the culture, to the point that it scarcely matters which political party is in power.

The conservative scholar Kevin Phillips has defined the present hegemony as a coalition of "Wall Street, Big Energy, Multinational Corporations, the Military–Industrial Complex, the Religious Right, the Market-Extremist Think-Tanks and the Rush Limbaugh Axis.* Here we will try to make sense of the Religious Right and argue that it has been the coalition partner that has recruited the most resolute and resilient footsoldiers in the "long march," changing American society in depth.

WHO'S RELIGIOUS? HOW MANY BELIEVERS?

From earliest times, Americans have been a religious people. Today they are uniquely so among Westerners, certainly far more so than Europeans, who in the past hundred years have undergone rapid and quite spectacular "de-christianization" and deserted their churches. The North American continent was largely settled by religious dissidents. In the Southern "proprietary" colonies which the King of England sometimes handed out to settle his debts, settlers often remained within the fold of the Established (Anglican) Church and a few were Catholics; but most early Americans were breakaway, dissident WASPs – White Anglo-Saxon Protestants. In

---

* Rush Limbaugh has been for nearly twenty years the host of a reactionary, hugely popular talk-radio show that attracts over thirteen million listeners a week.

Massachusetts, they established a Puritan theocracy;* elsewhere they adhered to more-or-less Calvinist, Wesleyan, or Pietistic doctrines as Congregationalists, Presbyterians, Methodists, and Quakers. Later came Lutherans and other Northern European Protestants. These various Churches, along with the Episcopalians (the Anglicans or Church of England in the United States) are now collectively known as the "mainstream" Protestant denominations (although Quakers themselves might not accept that label).

These early settlers were often ahead of most other people in Europe; they were in many cases precursors of the Enlightenment and included champions of freedom of conscience and social justice. The Anglican-turned-Baptist, Roger Williams quarrelled with the authorities of the Massachusetts Bay Colony because they confiscated Indian lands without payment. Williams split from the congregation, headed South, paid the Indians for land in what is now Rhode Island and founded his colony there on the principle of the separation of Church and State.†

The Quaker William Penn, who gave his name to Pennsylvania, also treated the Indians fairly, supported equal rights for women and declared that "No man hath power and authority to rule over Men's Consciences in religious matters." The Catholic Lord Calvert, second Baron Baltimore, to whom the King had awarded the entire colony of Maryland, also issued a Law of Toleration requiring Protestants and

---

* This theocracy was not, however, totally undemocratic. Some of my own ancestors arrived in 1632 and settled in the Massachusetts Bay Colony where each congregation was supposed to be able to elect its own two ministers. When one of them died and the surviving minister wanted to appoint the successor rather than allow his election, the revolt was such that twenty-two families, including mine, hitched their wagons and took themselves off through forests where wolves still roamed, to Connecticut.
† Rhode Island was also later the site of the first Jewish Synagogue on the American continent (1763).

Catholics to live together peaceably. Unfortunately, this law also specified the death penalty for anyone who refused to declare belief in the Holy Trinity. Nobody's perfect.

Throughout American history, religion frequently inspired political struggles. Patriotic preachers like Isaac Backus, cited at the beginning of this chapter, were instrumental in gaining popular support for the American Revolution. Fiery sermons, including those of the famous John Brown, helped to launch the abolitionist movement to rid the country of slavery. Soldiers in the Civil War marched to the beat of stirring hymns. The battles for women's suffrage, prison reform, and the prohibition of alcohol were often cast in religious terms.*

Although the earliest Catholic arrivals were the Marylanders, large Catholic populations emigrated in the nineteenth century, first from Ireland, then from Italy. Many Jews who came to America, mostly from Central and Eastern Europe, were also deeply religious. The so-called "evangelicals" or "born-again" Christians, including the Southern Baptists, were until relatively recently confined mostly to what Americans call the "Bible Belt," stretching across Appalachia and much of the South.

The picture now is infinitely more complex, but here is the best stab one can make at defining who is, and isn't, "religious" in the United States today. It is based on the latest official figures available from the Bureau of the Census' *Statistical Abstract*.†

The total adult population of the US in 2001 was 208 million. Of these adults, 159 million or 76.4 percent described themselves as Christians, 27.5 million said they had no

---

* Prohibition was introduced by the eighteenth amendment to the Constitution in 1919 and repealed by the twenty-first amendment in 1933.
† Since the law forbids that people be required to answer questions concerning their religion, data on religious preference from the Census Bureau is all acquired on "a voluntary basis."

religion (13.2 percent); 11 million refused to answer the question (five percent); 7.7 million said they were Jewish (3.7 percent) and 2.8 million Moslem (1.3 percent). The rest, a mere four-tenths of one percent, were something else – anything from Buddhists to Hindus to Druids.

Of the 159 million self-described Christians, nearly a third (31.9 percent) said they were Roman Catholics and 21 percent Baptists. Of the many varieties of Protestants that figure in the statistical table, I have added up the number of members in the mainstream denominations and subtracted them, along with the Roman Catholics, from the total Christian population. The rough total of "other" Christians thus obtained comes to something like 70 million people who can be defined as evangelical or "born-again" Christians – among whom figure George Bush and many members of his government, plus Democrats and Republicans, including the former Speaker of the House of Representatives and Senate Majority Leader in Congress elected in 2004. This rough-and-ready counting method is on the low side, as it excludes all self-described Catholics, many of whom are culturally as intransigent on some moral issues as the most reactionary "born-again" Christians.

Journalist Bill Moyers, whose frightening article concerning the relationship between these believers and the environment I will cite further along,[2] also estimates the number of evangelical Christians at about 70 million. So does the fundamentalist preacher and founder of the *Moral Majority*, the late Jerry Falwell, who stated categorically "There are 70 million of us." Another authoritative source, the Pew Center on Religion and Public Life says that "white Evangelical Christians comprise 24 percent of the population," which would put their number between 70 and 75 million.[3]

The late author and political analyst Arthur Schlesinger went further, saying "Perhaps a third of Americans are born-again Evangelical Christians." These people are widely spread geographically and no longer confined to what he calls the "disdained Bible-belt minority." Schlesinger believed they make up at least 40 percent of the electorate. If that is correct, the number of these believers is well above 70 million, indeed somewhere between 82 and 90 million.*[4] So it would seem that a figure of 70 million is safe, conservative and, if anything, errs on the side of caution.

Another table included in the *Statistical Abstract* gives the number of regular participants in religious worship, reported this time not by the individuals concerned, as above, but by the churches and other places of worship they attend. The churches, temples, synagogues, mosques, and so on, surveyed claim 133 million Americans as "regular participants." This means that almost two-thirds of the entire adult population (64 percent), including the "no religion" and "none of your business" groups, practice some faith. If we are to believe the reporting institutions, almost 79 percent of those who declared themselves believers regularly go to their place of worship. Half of all the fifty American states report regular participation at 50 percent or more of their total populations; eleven states stand between 40 and 50 percent; in fifteen states (mostly those with quite small populations) churches report less than 40 percent regular religious participation.

However imperfect these figures, they give a fair basis for

---

* It is strangely difficult to define the American "electorate." In 2006, the voting-age population (VAP) was 226 million, but non-citizens, citizens residing abroad, and over 7 million people in various stages of difficulty with the criminal justice system are ineligible – so the voting eligible population (VEP) is 206 million. Depending on the base he used, Schlesinger's "40%" would thus represent a figure between 82 and 90 million people. See the many articles on the subject of VAPs and VEPs by Professor Michael McDonald, Dept. of Public and International Affairs, George Mason University, for example http://elections.gmu.edu/voter_turnout.htm.

estimating the strength of the troops on the religious right. These people have a high rate of participation – indeed religion is often at the center of their lives – and they are militant Christians, nearly always intimately involved not only in the life of the churches themselves but in many church-related organizations like Focus on the Family, the Christian Coalition, or Concerned Women of America whose objectives are openly political.

Just as the rightward move of the Republican Party has pulled the Democrats to the right as well, so this religious right wing has displaced the center of gravity of mainstream Protestant denominations, as well as the Roman Catholics, politically toward the right. Furthermore, the new alliance between the religious right and substantial portions of the Jewish community to be examined shortly is another part of religious right-wing dominance of the political climate.

RELIGION AND RULE: ON THE ROAD TO THEOCRACY?

No doubt a great many United States politicians and officials – not to mention millions of ordinary Americans – remain hard-headed, feet-on-the-ground realists, open to rational argument, apparently untouched by heavenly considerations – at least on weekdays. This is not necessarily the case for many of their elected representatives. Politicians find they must increasingly heed the voice of the religious right – indeed belong to it themselves – or risk losing elections. According to the Pew Center surveys, even atheists don't want to vote for other atheists. The Bush White House sponsors a Bible study group for its employees which those who hope for advancement are well-advised to attend. Perhaps government "*real-politik*-ers" are still to be found in the ranks of foreign policy expertise, but even here (notably in policies toward

Israel and the Middle East) the Christian right wing simply cannot be ignored. Although the fact may have no bearing on her conduct, the Secretary of State, Condoleezza Rice is herself the daughter of a Minister.

The elections of 2004 transformed the United States Congress into an entirely Republican fiefdom. Before the 2006 mid-term elections swung the pendulum back toward the Democrats, the Senate numbered 55 Republicans to 45 Democrats – the strongest Republican majority since 1929. The seven Republican newcomers to the Senate all favored the key political demands of the religious right; they, like many others, will remain in office until at least 2010.

The House of Representatives in 2004 boasted the largest Republican majority since 1949. The House is entirely renewed every two years and in 2006 the balance shifted. The Democrats enjoyed their largest numerical win since 1974 by gaining thirty seats, sending among other newcomers, two Buddhists and the first Muslim ever to Washington. The press largely attributed the shift to the quagmire in Iraq. It is true that people's disgust or fatigue with this war was a major factor in the Republican defeat. However, 42 percent of people questioned in exit-polls said that their vote had been heavily weighted by ethical questions. Several Republican downfalls could be directly traced to corruption, particularly the cosiness between the defeated Congressmen and the convicted lobbyist Jack Abramoff.

Just before the 2006 mid-term elections, the President of the thirty-million-strong National Association of Evangelicals, famous mega-church Pastor and Republican Party supporter Ted Haggard, was discovered to have used sex-enhancement drugs and enlisted the services of a male prostitute. One Congressional Representative who got the boot in 2006, Mark Foley, was stupid enough to send unsolicited erotic e-mails to an under-age Congressional page-boy, a penchant none too welcome in the Republican culture. In the brief summaries provided by Wikipedia of the victories and defeats, I counted thirteen Republicans who bit the dust because of scandals involving personal behavior (including one case of wife-beating) or money. Lots of voters simply rejected sleaze.

Perhaps the best bit of news from the 2006 mid-term elections was the defeat of Rick Santorum of Pennsylvania, a rabid-religious-right Senator. The worst news was that only 36.8 percent of the electorate bothered to go to the polls.* In the 2008 elections, the Democrats will be in a better position than the Republicans because they will only have to defend twelve Senate seats up for re-election to the Republicans' twenty-two.

What sorts of policies will the remaining Republicans and their Democratic sympathizers vote for – that is, what do their religious-right constituents want? The "Christian reconstructionists," to whom George Bush is considered close, have an overtly political program. Ideologically, the people who are part of the right-wing religious galaxy claim that "liberals" and "secular humanists" have undermined the bases of society and allowed feminists, gays, and atheists to attack the bases of the family, the nation, and the values they hold dear. These godless people call for abortion, stem-cell research, gay and women's rights, and same-sex marriage while refusing God's will in general and Bible-based law in particular.

Evangelicals have made a notable *rapprochement* with traditionalist Catholics who are also adamant on such subjects. Historically speaking, this alliance is recent: in 1960, for

---

* Here is the scoreboard: House of Representatives 2004, 202 Democrats, 232 Republicans; in 2006 these numbers were exactly reversed: 232 Democrats to 202 Republicans. Senate: 2004 : 44 Democrats, 55 Republicans, one Independent; in 2006, 49 Democrats, 49 Republicans, and two Independents. Just a shade over one-third of the eligible voters changed the balance.

example, the big question was whether Protestants would ever vote for a Roman Catholic in the person of John F. Kennedy. In 2004, John Kerry's Catholicism was hardly mentioned as such, except for the bishop who said he would refuse Kerry Holy Communion so long as he supported abortion.

Despite the far-reaching influence of Christian radio and television and any amount of proof to the contrary, evangelical Christians and their conservative allies from other denominations see, or pretend to see, the media as belonging to the liberal-secular humanist camp, where godless journalists and broadcasters promote the same satanic agenda as left-wing Democrats. The courts are supposedly peopled with unmoveable left-wing judges who rule in favor of all manner of abominations. One major goal of evangelicals is to get their own people placed on the judicial bench. The Christian right is furious, for example, that in the name of separation between Church and State, a recent court decision banned the posting of the Ten Commandments in courthouses and courtrooms.

Members of the religious right also want to reduce taxes, especially for families, and limit the size and the powers of the Federal government and its capacity to intervene in people's affairs. Most of them further believe that churches rather than government should take responsibility for health, education, and welfare. The government's role should be limited to providing families with school vouchers they can use as payment to the religious schools of their choice. The government should not regulate business or industry, much less pass laws to protect workers or the environment.

The religious right's scenario is not a fantasy, nor are their demands a distant goal. Already $40 billion yearly in State and Federal public funds is channelled through religious charities, while secular charities under the Bush regime have suffered comparable funding cuts. The border between Church and State grows constantly more blurred.*

Indeed, evidence published by the Catholic scholar and historian Garry Wills, a professor at Northwestern University, shows that this Church–State merger is well advanced. Instead of targeting only the politicians, the right has gone after higher ranking Federal administration bureaucrats, particularly in the areas of health, education, and social services. In each government department, even before Bush came to power, they knew exactly who they wanted to get rid of and with whom they would replace those evicted. Although it is common knowledge that lobbyists help to draft economic or regulatory legislation, Wills says "it is less known that for social services, evangelical organizations were given the same right to draft bills and install the officials to implement them."[5]

The filling of the higher echelons of the administration with born-again bureaucrats was further enhanced by the placement of an evangelical at the head of the White House Office of Personnel (which decides on personnel well beyond the White House). Agencies like the Centers for Disease Control, the Food and Drug Administration, and Health and Human Services administrations were particularly affected by the purges.

Individual born-again Christian pastors or agencies have also received large government grants to provide "faith-based" social services, such as sex-education for teen-agers based on the rule of "abstinence only." These grants, provided from public money, were justified on grounds that sex educa-

* The Constitution of the United States does not appear to figure among the Christian right's cherished institutions. Although the First Amendment does not refer to the "separation of Church and State" in those words, it has always been interpreted as meaning exactly that, beginning with Thomas Jefferson who declared that it established a "wall of separation between church and State." Supreme Court jurisprudence has also consistently upheld this principle.

tion was a secular matter, even though only religious groups were promoting the abstinence-only line.

Black and Hispanic ministers like Luis Cortes, credited with bringing many Hispanics to the Bush camp, also received well-targeted support. In 2004, one influential black preacher sent black voters a message urging them to vote for Bush because he "shares our values." This preacher, who previously had always supported the Democrats, did not choose to inform these black voters that Bush had shared not only his values but also $1.5 million in taxpayer funds, to pay for the preacher's "faith-based initiatives."[6]

BORN-AGAIN THEOLOGY AND FUNDAMENTALISM

The Christian right in the United States is easily as complex as the Islamic right in Muslim countries, where, for outsiders, distinctions between Sunnites and Shiites, secular nationalists and religious ones, Salafistes (revolutionary or not), Muslim Brothers, Wahhabites, and so on, are difficult to understand – in fact, in the West, the field is open only to specialists. This complexity and the consequent lack of nuance make it easier for American leaders to lump all Muslims together. We can safely assume that a similar difficulty besets people of other cultures trying to make sense of religious forces in the contemporary United States (not to mention Americans themselves).

Let us make clear that while all fundamentalists are evangelicals (or "born-again") Christians, the opposite is not the case. Several million evangelicals voted for Al Gore or John Kerry over George Bush in 2000 and 2004. In 2006, according to exit polls, fully a third of evangelicals voted for Democrats. A great many of them are trying to include social justice issues in the evangelical political agenda. Some pastors preach that it is definitely not enough to be against abortion, gay marriage, and stem cell research – their parishioners should also try to behave more like Jesus himself with regard to the poor. They have recently taken a far greater interest in the environment, conceiving their mission as one of "stewardship" rather than "dominion" over the earth. We are not dealing with a 70-million-member monolith.

Still it is the so-called "fundamentalist," ultra-conservative hard-core within the Christian right which remains the most mysterious to ordinary onlookers and requires explicating. Take the term "fundamentalist" itself, of which few know the origins. In the early years of the twentieth century, the American Christian "revivalist" movement with its huge tent meetings and firebrand preachers was losing ground. The slow trickling-down to a mass audience of scholarly biblical criticism, plus the influence of Darwinian theories, were eroding belief in the Bible as a literal document.

Conservative churchmen reacted vigorously, publishing and distributing widely a series of pamphlets called "The Fundamentals: a Testimony to the Truth." In 1920, a Baptist journalist named Curtis Lee Laws coined the word "fundamentalist," defined as someone prepared to go out and do battle for these biblical fundamentals. The word caught on and now applies to any literalist, whatever his or her religious persuasion or ideology. The fundamentalist Christian believes that because it is the Word of God, every word of the Bible is literally true and that he or she is on earth to act as a guardian and a propagator of that truth.

There are many names for Christian fundamentalists and many nuances between them: they are mostly and hastily classed as evangelicals, but they can also be reconstructionists, charismatics, pentecostalists, millennialists, dominionists, and what have you. And there are combinations and several varieties of each.[7]

They don't necessarily believe in the same things or worship in the same ways. Some, for example, but by no means all "speak in tongues" or practice faith-healing. They do share the belief that the Bible, both Old and New Testaments, is the Word of God, but some have a more metaphorical approach than others. All of them believe that Christianity is the only true religion. God has a plan for everyone and those who do not fulfill that plan can expect eternal torment in hell, just as those who do the will of God will be blessed and abundantly rewarded in the afterlife. The doctrinal bottom line is that Jesus is the Lord and Savior of every individual on earth, no matter what religion that person may have been born into. The acceptance of Jesus' personal and immediate role in one's life – often through an unmistakeable sense of calling or a mystical experience – marks the born-again.

What Jesus actually wants from his followers is another matter, hotly disputed among the born-again. The more extreme fundamentalist theologians call for the extension of the death penalty to crimes not now covered. They want a Constitutional amendment (so long as we have to keep the Constitution) banning same-sex marriage; Bush has called for one as well. A few want to establish complete male-over-female domination, meaning no votes, public offices, or other civil rights for women. Abortion is to be outlawed as soon as feasible with a Supreme Court decision reversing the landmark 1973 case *Roe* v. *Wade*, followed by another Constitutional amendment. They would deny religious freedom to the "enemies of God" (as they define them) and erect a social, political, and religious order entirely based upon the Bible (as they interpret it).

THE RECONSTRUCTIONIST CONSTRUCTION

So-called "hard reconstructionists" are also referred to as "dominionists," from God's command, recorded in Genesis, that Man should hold "dominion" over "all the earth" (Gen. 1:26–30). In the biblical text, God gives man dominion over the fish of the sea, the fowl of the air, the beasts of the earth – in other words over natural creatures. Present-day American dominionists, however, know better than the author of Genesis what God actually had in mind.

According to them, his command was meant to include all secular institutions, or what they call "civil structures." The godly must move in and occupy these structures until Christ returns to earth, just as it is their job, while waiting, to "reclaim the land (and not just the United States) for Jesus." They make quite clear that they do not want merely to have a "voice" or greater influence or equal time with secularists in deciding the affairs of the nation and the world. They are not talking about lobbying but about a complete takeover, through political or other means, in order to carry out God's plan.

Perhaps the scariest of the "reconstructionists" are the followers of the late Pastor R. J. Rushdoony, the son of a Lebanese immigrant turned hard-line follower of John Calvin (1509–64) who cluster around the Chalcedon (pronounced kalCEEdun) Foundation. Chalcedon's motto is "History has never been dominated by majorities but only by dedicated minorities who stand unconditionally on their faith." Rushdoony's son-in-law Gary North is even more frightening. He holds a Ph.D. in history from the University of California (Riverside), runs the Institute for Christian Economics and is the political leader of reconstructionism As he wrote in *The Journal of Christian Reconstruction* in 1981, "Christians must begin to organize politically within the present party structure and they must begin to infiltrate the existing institutional order."[8]

The way to infiltrate is to take advantage of America's low voter turnout particularly for local and primary elections so that those who go to every meeting, stay until the last chair is folded and vote (or run) in every election, will get into the party structures. Once they are insiders they can recruit other conservative Christians to fill vacant seats. Crucially, "You keep your personal views to yourself until the Christian community is ready to rise up . . ." Stealth is the word until the great takeover day comes.

What, then, is the political doctrine? Rushdoony, although he died in 2001, continues to speak from beyond the grave via the "Chalcedon Position Papers" and to expound the doctrine he first elaborated in his major work called the *Institutes of Biblical Law* published in 1973. Biblical law must replace civil law and "nothing is exempt from Christ's dominion," which is why "the state, the schools, the arts and sciences, law, economics and every other sphere is to be under Christ the King."

Rushdoony is notably the father of the growing home-schooling movement which we will look at more fully in the following chapter. For the moment, let us visit the contemporary early sixteenth-century mind. The following quotes come from the paper "What Chalcedon Believes" or from the earlier works of Rushdoony. "Biblical law should govern every area of man's life and thought." God gave Moses the law, which, some dietary and health prescriptions aside, remains valid – all 613 of the provisions recorded in the Pentateuch, the first five books of the Bible. "The Christian state should enforce biblical civil law and it is the responsibility of Christians to exercise dominion in the earth for God's glory." Elsewhere Rushdoony specifically cites Hayek, and one hears him echoed in "What Chalcedon Believes:" "Biblically, the role of the state is to suppress external evil: murder, theft, rape, and so forth. Its role is not to redistribute wealth, furnish medical care or educate its citizens' children . . . Our objective therefore in supporting Christian political involvement is to *scale down* the massive state in Western democracies, reducing it to its biblical limits . . . The state is an inherently religious institution." (his emphasis).

This is mild compared to the positions of reconstructionists like son-in-law North who advocate public execution not just for women who undergo abortions but for those who advised them to do so. North is big on capital punishment. "When people curse their parents, it unquestionably is a capital crime. The integrity of the family must be maintained by the threat of death." Because Leviticus 24:16 says so, blasphemers are also fair game. "And he that blasphemeth the name of the Lord; he shall surely be put to death and all the congregation shall certainly stone him."

Recall that North runs the Institute for Christian Economics. "Why stoning?" he asks. Because "the implements of execution are available to everyone at virtually no cost." Not only is it free – there's nothing like a good stoning to create a warm sense of togetherness. "Executions are community projects – not with spectators who watch a professional executioner do 'his' duty, but rather with actual participants." Others who should get theirs are homosexuals, heretics, females guilty of "unchastity before marriage," and adulterers, to say nothing of murderers and rapists.[9] The great thing about reconstructionists is that they allow everyone else to feel moderate.

If the Pew survey is any guide, Americans are utterly confused in their opinions about all this. On one hand, they seem quite comfortable mixing Church and State: 69 percent of them say that "Liberals have gone too far in trying to keep religion out of schools and government." On the other, they are somewhat wary of the excessively godly: nearly half say that "Conservative Christians have gone too far in trying to impose their religious values on the country."

When it comes to law-making, 60 percent of the evangelical Christian contingent has no doubt that the "Bible should have more influence on US laws than the will of the American people." More chilling still is that, of the total American population surveyed by Pew, whether religious or not, 32 percent agree with them. If virtually a third of the country thinks the Bible is more important than democratic government and the Constitution for fashioning the laws, we should not be surprised that 67 percent of the total American population also affirm that the "United States is a Christian nation." Fully 71 percent call for "more religious influence" on American life and/or government.[10]

While it is true that opinion surveys can be mightily influenced by the way the question is posed, and that people frequently answer what they think the inquirer wants to hear, the many polls tend to bear out the same conclusions. It may be easy for outsiders to make fun of these believers but it is not wise. They should be taken seriously. To understand their agenda for the United States and the world, we need to look more closely at how and by whom their doctrines are put into practice.

WHO'S WHO ON THE RELIGIOUS RIGHT

Like the secular right, the American religious right has its funders (sometimes the same as the ones we met in the first chapter), its charismatic figures and "ideas" people, its think-tanks and mass communicators, its publications and media, its popular mass movements, and its legal defenders. There are manifold overlaps between the religious and secular right-wings and any attempt to separate them in a clinical way can only be an artificial and arbitrary exercise. Early in 2005, *Time Magazine* published its own list of the most influential individuals in this movement. Outsiders will never have heard of most of them – Billy Graham with his son and heir apparent

Franklin are doubtless the most famous. We will not try here to follow *Time's* lead in cataloguing the top twenty-five but rather look at some of the major stars in the right-wing Christian constellation that has helped to orchestrate so many electoral victories, including those of George Bush.

Let us begin with the Council for National Policy (CNP), an innocuous-sounding but secretive and effective network of highly influential people with close ties to the rest of the extreme right, including funders, think-tanks, mass organizations and communications empires. We could have just as well described the CNP in the previous chapter as it does not identify itself as specifically religious, mentioning only that its members "include many of our nation's leaders from the fields of government, business, the media, religion, and the professions."

Founded in 1981 specifically to counter the influence of the Council on Foreign Relations (which CNP members consider a "Communist Trojan Horse") the CNP is not a mass organization. It has only five or six hundred members, usually wealthy, who must pay to belong. The Council has definite "cachet" in right-wing circles and conveys social status akin to belonging to an exclusive club. It also enjoys tax-exempt status, which means that its donors can claim tax deductions for the sums they contribute to the Council.

The membership list is strictly confidential and journalists are not invited to its events. One member of the executive committee puts it bluntly, "The media should not know when or where we meet or who takes part in our programs before or after a meeting." The *New York Times*, however, gained access at least once, reporting that the CNP is made up of a "few hundred of the most powerful conservatives in the country."[11]

The Council's studiedly bland and uninformative website says

Our members are united in their belief in a free enterprise system, a strong national defense, and support for traditional Western values. They meet to share the best information available on national and world problems, know one another on a personal basis, and collaborate in achieving their shared goals.

In other words, they do a lot of networking. Sometimes they also publish the talks given by invited speakers which make up a useful compendium of the received wisdom and provide a guide to what the right wants to hear, and from whom, on subjects ranging from world politics (communism and Islam are bad) to the environment (God will fix it so don't worry).

The CNP's political program is anti-abortion, anti-gay, anti-public education, anti-tax, and anti-corporate regulation. Its great achievement is to have merged the agenda of the religious right with that of the low-tax, small-government, libertarian, and semi-secular wing of the Republican Party. At the August 2004 meeting, it bestowed on the then Senate Majority Leader (and important figure on the religious right) Bill Frist, a special award. Other featured speakers at CNP gatherings have included Donald Rumsfeld, who keynoted the first meeting they held following the invasion of Iraq (also attended by Dick Cheney). The members have also heard from the two most conservative Supreme Court Justices (Thomas and Scalia) and the former US Ambassador to the United Nations, John Bolton, as well as two former Bush Attorneys General, John Ashcroft and Alberto Gonzales.

Bush himself appeared before the CNP during his election campaign in 2000. The not-yet President is said to have promised CNP members that if elected, he would appoint only anti-abortion judges. Evangelical Christian Congressman Mike Pence knows the CNP well and calls it "the most influential gathering of conservatives in America." Its opponents call CNP members "the genuine leaders of the Republican Party."

The heads of the Christian fundamentalist right's mass organizations are in regular attendance at CNP events. These men are the generals leading the ground troops, those who will hear their message from America's pulpits on Sundays and go forth into the world to carry out their orders. Among the generals we would find, for example, the Rev. Pat Robertson, once himself a candidate for President, a noted television evangelist and former president of the Christian Coalition who told his many followers in 1998, "We've been at the back of the bus for twenty years and it's time now to use your influence on the Party at this crucial stage of our history."[12]

Now the Christian right is riding in the front of the bus, if not in chauffeured limousines. One shred of good news is that Robertson's departure from the Christian Coalition, which once boasted 400,000 members, seems to have provoked a rapid downhill slide. One report says it is no longer even paying its bills. Robertson himself remains active, however, and has proposed that the United States should have Hugo Chavez assassinated.

Contrary to the Christian Coalition, the Reverend James Dobson's organization called Focus on the Family is in rude good health and has helped to engineer the near-complete takeover of the Republican Party by religious forces in the past decade. When Dobson spoke to the Council for National Policy in 1998, he told them that 80 percent of the American people claimed the country was in a "serious moral crisis"; that these people did not identify at all with the "elites and cultural trendsetters." The Republican Party made a huge mistake, according to Dobson, in the 1996 presidential campaign when their candidate, Bob Dole, running against Bill Clinton, "did all he could to insult these good people." Dole's greatest sin was to talk only about the economy and money, with no reference to moral values.

There is a "pro-moral community out there," said Dobson, but it still lacked the votes to pass legislation in favor of school prayer, school choice and "abstinence only" sex education for teen-agers. Nor could it yet outlaw pornography, or destroy the Planned Parenthood Federation, and the National Endowment for the Arts. When Bill Clinton goes out to speak for a gay rights group, Dobson asked, "where are the Republican leaders who stand up and say this is outrageous?" After 1998, Dobson and his friends found those voices and those votes, resulting in Bush's election in 2000 and a massive majority in both houses of Congress in 2004.

Focus on the Family is a multi-million-dollar operation, said to employ as many as 1,700 people at its Colorado headquarters (this information is not available on its website). Many commentators consider it the most powerful of all Christian right organizations: It publishes seven regular magazines, dozens of books, cassettes, CDs, and supplies other products to its members. Although most of these materials have to do with marriage, life problems, and child-rearing (Dobson, originally a pediatrician, seems obsessed with obedience and control, notably the taming of "The Strong-Willed Child." A visit to the site shows that Focus has other concerns as well and has demonstrated its capacity to move civil society in its chosen direction. Focus organized a large and successful boycott of mass consumer products company Procter and Gamble to force the company to change its "pro-gay" policies (P&G had made financial contributions to some gay organizations).

Focus on the Family also organized "Justice Sunday" on January 8, 2006, simultaneously broadcast to hundreds of churches throughout America, in order to explain to churchgoers the importance of the judicial system and encourage them to support President Bush's judicial appointments of arch-conservatives to the Supreme Court and other federal courts. The judicial area is one where the Christian right has had large and measurable success (credit is also due to the secular Federalist Society which we described in the first chapter). By late 2006, George W. Bush had already had the opportunity to name not only two conservative Supreme Court justices but to make over 250 lifetime appointments to lower federal courts. Bush's appointments alone have now filled more than a quarter of all judgeships of the federal judiciary and their influence will be felt for decades.

Another Christian-right organization with designs on the judicial system is the Traditional Values Coalition, founded in 1980, which coordinates and channels the lobbying efforts of 43,000 churches and their parishioners. Its site announces "our battle plan to take back our courts from the anti-God left." The founder, Reverend Louis Sheldon, tried to put a brave face on the 2006 election results, telling the media "We know that in America the people are with us. They're just confused."

Confused or not, the electoral setback is bad news for the TVC because the House and Senate Judiciary Committees in the new legislature will be headed by Democrats, presumably well to the left of the TVC, and they may be in a position to thwart the President's nominations to the federal courts. The Coalition likes to quote its hero, Bush, who said "We need common sense judges who understand that our rights are derived from God. Those are the kind of judges I intend to put on the bench." That is precisely what he has done.

Reverend Sheldon also insisted after the 2006 mid-terms that "The issue is Iraq and the culture of corruption among a few Republican elected officials. [Still] it's very clear, we're here to stay. We're in it for the long haul. The assault on marriage, sexual predators and abortion are not going away. So, we'll go on."[13]

INVESTING IN UPHEAVAL

One of the religious right's most important financial benefactors is a member of the Council on National Policy named Howard Ahmanson, the heir to a large banking fortune and, for a time, close to R. J. Rushdoony's hard-reconstructionist Chalcedon Institute, from which he has since slightly distanced himself. He and his wife Roberta are major funders of the Institute for Religion and Democracy (IRD) which also receives money from our old friends the Bradley, Olin, Scaife, and Smith-Richardson foundations. Ahmanson doesn't say how much he hands out, but the foundations have funded the IRD with over four million dollars in the past twenty years in order to further its avowed mission, which is "to reform the social and political witness of American Churches while promoting democracy and religious freedom at home and abroad." Translated, this statement means that the IRD's speciality is to push mainstream Christian denominations further to the right and turn them into evangelical strongholds. The Protestant Episcopal Church of the United States, usually seen as the most socially up-market, WASPiest of the WASP mainstream churches, has provided the IRD with a perfect target and a test case. One must admit as well that it left itself open to such an onslaught.

The Director of Communications for the Episcopal Diocese of Washington DC, explains in a report aptly titled "Follow the Money" just how the IRD and its subsidiary groups are going about their "reform" mission thanks to the millions they receive from conservative funders.[14] The presiding Bishop of the Episcopal Church is now a woman – already anathema to the right – but the Episcopalians have further consecrated as Bishop of New Hampshire an openly gay, non-celibate man who lives with his long-term male partner. This action has allowed the IRD to drive a wedge deep into the heart of the Church, credited by the Census Bureau with 3.4 million members in 2001.

The IRD has spent almost half a million dollars on propaganda linked to Episcopalian "reform." Its goal is to force the Episcopal Church of the United States out of the worldwide Anglican Communion and replace it with the smaller and far more conservative wing of the Church with ties to the "American Anglican Council." This Council is another of Ahmanson's pet organizations, founded in 1996 to oppose gays in the Episcopal clergy and campaign for the "traditionalist" approach to biblical interpretation.

The rift is serious and goes well beyond whatever venom the IRD has been able to distil into the debate. The Archbishop of Canterbury, head of the worldwide Anglican Communion, had to become involved and he duly set up a commission that issued the "Windsor Report." This report called on the US Episcopal Church not to elect and consecrate non-celibate gay bishops, to stop blessing same-sex unions, and to issue an apology for "tearing the fabric" of the worldwide Anglican Communion.

Complicating matters is the newly elected Presiding Episcopal Bishop, Katherine Jefferts-Schori, who is definitely of the radical, pro-gay persuasion. Many accuse Jefferts-Schori of having little pastoral experience and exacerbating the rift. This ongoing drama is creating secessionist parishes, even secessionist dioceses, whose first act is to declare allegiance to the conservative American Anglican Council wing. All this delights the IRD and the Ahmansons.

The IRD also targets mainstream Presbyterians and Methodists, setting up sub-groups inside these churches to provoke similar "reform" campaigns. It justifies them, saying that the mainline churches have only themselves to blame, because they "champion leftist and secular social and political agendas along with outdated liberal theologies." The

Institute on Religion and Democracy is also opposed to anything emanating from the American National Council of Churches or from the World Council of Churches in Geneva.

MASS ORGANIZATION FOR OUR SALVATION

Sophisticated organizational, communications, and fundraising strategies are a hallmark of the Christian right just as they are of its right-wing secular brothers. Mass organizations like the National Christian Action Coalition or the Moral Majority can rely on a high-powered network composed of at least 1,600 Christian radio and 250 Christian television stations covering the entire American continent. Their media machine also includes publishing houses, magazine distribution networks, campus newspapers, and direct mail outfits that send millions of individual appeals to supporters; all of them pushing relentlessly effective demands for financial contributions. Many church leaders and pastors of the larger churches are extremely rich; they live and travel in luxurious surroundings, apparently without provoking censure from their parishioners.*

But James Dobson and Louis Sheldon are correct – there *is* a "pro-moral community out there" that follows its own moral compass. The Christian right leadership, despite its strengths, cannot always persuade that community to vote for Christian right politicians under any circumstances. Consider the saga of movie-star handsome Ralph Reed, former leader of the Christian Coalition, who face appeared on the cover of *Time Magazine* in 1995 over the caption "The Right Hand of God."

---

* Well-off friends of mine from New York once took the Concorde to Paris. Inquiring about the work of another couple on the flight, they learned that they were in charge of a large evangelical church. The pastor and his wife allowed that their parishioners were "a very giving people."

For several years, Reed acted as a senior political strategist for Bush and Cheney. He was often credited with swinging the 2000 Presidential election to Bush by dispatching 75 million "Voter Guides" to the electorate. In 2004, he brought the enormous Southern Baptist Conference, estimated at over sixteen million members, on board for the Bush–Cheney ticket. The Baptists, at his behest, sponsored and hosted a successful "Citizenship Sunday for Voter Registration."[15]

Reed seemed unstoppable – indeed as his own mother said, "I used to tell people he was going to be either President of the United States or Al Capone. Whatever he did, he was really good at it." It was thus particularly gratifying to some that Reed ended closer to Al Capone. In 2006, his own Christian constituency punished him for the good old-fashioned sin of greed. Reed was involved in sleazy business dealings with convicted lobbyist Jack Abramoff and he thereby lost the only election he ever ran, the Republican primary for Lieutenant Governor of Georgia in July 2006. His defeat could be read as a kind of premonitory warning signal for the national elections held later that year. *Time Magazine*'s headline was no longer "the right hand of God" but "the rise and fall of Ralph Reed."

Jerry Falwell, preacher and founder of the Moral Majority in the 1970s, who died in May 2007, summed up his theocratic-electoral credo: "Get them saved, get them baptized and get them registered." And indeed, these eligible Christian voters have registered in droves, they have voted, and they have largely taken over the Republican party. Their participation in national elections, although low by European standards is estimated at 56 to 58 percent, compared to the US average of 50 percent in a Presidential election year.

The former chairman of the Oregon State Republicans explains how these determined partisans can decide who will go to the National Republican Party Convention, who will write its political platform, and who will nominate its Presidential candidate. "In a State like Oregon with 600,000 registered Republicans, it is possible for 2,000 or 3,000 people to control the State party apparatus."[16] In the American political system, the States elect the President by "delivering" their electoral votes. These disciplined troops with their quasi-Leninist tactics have also helped pull the entire party to the right by attacking publicly those they call the RINOs, or Republicans in Name Only.

WHAT ABOUT THE CATHOLICS?

As noted at the outset of this chapter, Roman Catholics represent a huge slice of the US population. According to the Census Bureau and the *Statistical Abstract*, Catholics are 32 percent of all those who declared themselves Christians of one sort or another, which comes to more than 50 million people, over a sixth of the total US population. It is hard to say what portion of these Catholics can be classed as "traditionalist" or in plainer terms, politically to the right.

What we do know is that the American Catholic Church is in trouble and that this trouble has been in many ways a godsend for the most conservative wing of the Church. The ongoing, oft-suspected scandal of child-abusing priests finally broke in Boston in 2002 and since then the crisis has snowballed. Many people abused as children are now adults and are speaking out, bringing their story into the open with often startling results. Their respected association called SNAP, Survivors Network for those Abused by Priests, has 8,000 members from all over the country and acts both as a support network and an alarm-alert system.

Boston is well known in the US as a stronghold of Irish Catholicism. In 2002, several reporters for the *Boston Globe* began a path-breaking investigation of the Boston archdiocese and its cover-ups of the sexual abuse of children by some of its priests. As more and more details were revealed, pressure on Cardinal Bernard Law mounted, culminating in a letter signed by fifty-eight of his own priests calling on him to resign. Law had not just covered up for the pedophiles – he had sometimes promoted them or transferred them to other parishes, saying nothing about their histories, where they again abused children. As the Massachusetts Attorney General later said, the archdiocese engaged in "an elaborate scheme" to keep the scandal under wraps. Some victims were dissuaded from going to court by private settlements, in which case they had to promise to keep these payments secret. Cardinal Law finally presented his resignation to Pope John Paul II who accepted it and then gave him a sinecure in the Vatican.*

The *Boston Globe* won a well-deserved Pulitzer Prize for its investigations and the Boston saga launched a nationwide series of victims' "outings." The latest instalment as of this writing has taken place in Los Angeles, the largest archdiocese in the US with 4.3 million Catholics. The LA Cardinal Roger Mahoney has been more cunning than his brother from Boston. First, Mahoney used delaying tactics, exhausted all legal procedures, and refused to communicate Church documents until the United States Supreme Court at last took on the case and ruled that he had to hand over the documents which the Los Angeles District Attorney had demanded fully four years previously. Mahoney's lawyers argued "religious persecution" and "Church–State separation" to avoid having to hand over these records concerning priests. They were finally thwarted; the documents in turn opened the door to court cases brought by individual victims or groups of victims demanding damages.

---

* Cardinal Law, despite protests from many US Catholics, celebrated a mass of mourning for his benefactor when the Pope died in April 2005.

Mahoney then settled out of court with 45 victims for a tidy $60 million, an average of $1.3 million per person. The payments mean that those cases will never be tried and the priests concerned will not go to jail (whereas at least two from Boston are now serving prison terms for rape). Up to five hundred more abused people in the LA area are waiting in the wings. Can the archdiocese pursue its strategy of out-of-court settlements without going bankrupt? Apparently it can. According to Associated Press reports, it owns 1600 Los Angeles area properties valued at $4 billion. "While most of the properties are devoted to churches and schools, the archdiocese also owns oil wells, farm parcels, parking lots and commercial buildings."[17]

As in Boston and elsewhere, when complaints of abuse arose in one place, abusive Los Angeles priests were transferred to other parishes. One of them, Oliver O'Grady, was so notorious that a film called "Deliver us from Evil" has been made about him, with his full and indeed proud cooperation. The filmmaker says he shows no remorse. It is not entirely certain that the Church does either. SNAP, the victims' network, has issued a new warning concerning the *international* movement of pedophile priests. Since it has become more difficult to shift abusive priests inside the US, more and more are on the move internationally, often to Mexico or Canada. O'Grady is said to be either in Canada or in France.[18]

The Vatican now defrocks the occasional pedophile (four from Saint Louis in 2006) but the US Conference of Catholic Bishops still does not seem overly concerned with the problem. At its November 2006 meeting, marriage, contraception, Holy Communion, and homosexuality were all on the agenda, but not clerical sexual abuse. The Bishops' Conference Committee for the Protection of Children and Youth has decided that disclosing the names of known sexual predators to the public is "not appropriate" and should not become national Church policy (although some dioceses have chosen to do so).

How widespread is the problem of sexual predation inside the US Catholic Church? The man who knows more about the subject than anyone else in America and probably the world is Richard Sipe, for eighteen years a priest and a Benedictine monk. He left the priesthood and has been married for thirty-five years to a former nun; he remains deeply engaged in Church affairs. Sipe is a researcher and certified therapist; he lectures in medical schools and seminaries and has devoted his life to the study of sexual and celibate practices of Roman Catholic priests and bishops, as well as to the victims of their abuse. He has also served as an expert witness in various court cases, including the Boston cases tried before the United States District Court of Massachusetts.[19]

From his twenty-five years spent studying sex and celibacy in the American Catholic priesthood, Sipe has concluded that over the past half-century, an estimated 100,000 minors – both children and adolescents, most of them boys but thousands of girls as well – have been sexually abused by priests. At any one time, still according to Sipe, half the Roman Catholic clergy is sexually active, some with women; whereas 20 to 30 percent have a homosexual orientation and six to ten percent have been involved with minors. Most of the abusers are Catholic priests, but there are also numerous cases involving rabbis and Protestant pastors.

The official Church's reaction has been, and remains, secrecy, hypocrisy, and damage control, shunting the problem to one side or under the rug, allowing predators free rein. Their victims, whom Sipe also knows intimately and has counselled throughout his long professional career, frequently suffer permanent damage. They feel guilty, often experience sexual dysfunction even with partners they love, they lack confidence in their own judgment, cannot place trust in others, and display a host of other psychological and clinical symptoms.[20]

One cannot draw an emphatic cause-and-effect connection between the blot on the Church's honor and challenge to its credibility on one hand and the political impact of the scandals on the other; but the latter appear to have moved the Church further rightwards. According to the Pew Survey, a quarter of all Catholics (like 62 percent of evangelical Protestants) have a literalist interpretation of the Bible. The Church's most prominent conservative intellectuals have become even more prominent. The most influential Catholics in the United States today are not to be found in the upper reaches of the hierarchy which has lost part of its authority, but are rather people like Father Joseph Fessio or Father Richard John Neuhaus whose traditionalist theology many of the faithful seem to find consoling and reassuring. These men also have more clout nationally now that Benedict XVI occupies the throne of Saint Peter.

Jesuit Father Fessio is founder and director of the Ignatius Press, the foremost Catholic publishing house in America, dedicated to "the greater glory of God." It publishes both Pope John Paul II and Cardinal Ratzinger, now better known as Benedict XVI. Ratzinger was Fessio's professor and directed his thesis. Even before his elevation to the papacy, Ratzinger was considered undoubtedly the most conservative Catholic theologian of the modern era. Fessio refers, justifiably, to "my friend Pope Benedict" and is indeed Benedict's right-hand man in America. His Ignatius Press also publishes Creationist-Intelligent Design-type texts,* declaring that "Our objective is to support the teachings of the Church," by which he means the narrowest possible interpretations of those teachings.

---

* See the following chapter for a discussion of this theologically inspired "science."

Fessio also acts as provost of the quite new Ave Maria University in Naples, Florida, founded with a $250 million gift from arch-conservative Catholic layman, Thomas Monaghan, whose fortune is based on Domino's Pizzas, a huge enterprise in the US. Fessio's other project is to turn back the liturgical clock through the influence of his Oremus Institute. If Fessio has his way, the mass will be once more be said exclusively in Latin, the priest will turn his back to the people and Gregorian chant will be the only music to resound in the naves of the nation.

Father Richard John Neuhaus, once a Lutheran pastor, is the guiding spirit of the Catholic monthly *First Things*, a magazine with about 40,000 subscribers, which advocates much more involvement of religion in politics. He was already close to George W. Bush before the latter became President and is a frequent visitor to the White House, counselling the President regularly on "life issues" like stem-cell research. Bush says of Neuhaus "Father Richard helps me to articulate these religious things." Note that forty years ago American Protestants would have been enraged at the very idea of a Catholic priest having the ear of "their" President, or having anything to do with "their" government. Possible Roman Catholic influence on policy was a major campaign issue when John F. Kennedy ran for President in 1960.

Neuhaus has contributed immensely to changing that scene, and has set conservative Catholics on a course unimaginable before him. Along with President Nixon's former acolyte Charles "Chuck" Colson (who went to prison for his role in Watergate), Neuhaus was the initiator of a movement called Evangelicals and Catholics Together, or ECT. Signed by twenty prominent evangelicals and twenty equally prominent Catholics, the first ECT text was published in *First Things* in 1994 and has been followed by three further joint statements on points of doctrinal and political agreement.

At the top of their common list is abortion: ECT wants the 1973 Supreme Court *Roe v. Wade* decision reversed, even though nearly two-thirds of the American public in general is against such a move. Evangelicals and Catholics also came together to promote Mel Gibson's film *The Passion of the Christ* (required viewing in some Catholic parishes and evangelical congregations). Karl Rove, Bush's former chief strategist, loves ECT people because they contribute to what Garry Wills calls "governing from the fringes" rather than from a broad middle-of-the-road consensus which used to be the norm in American life.[21]

Meanwhile, with the support and encouragement of the ultra-conservative Vatican, which also believes in governing from the fringes, American seminaries are growing ever-more rigid, refusing to take any candidates for the priesthood who are not in agreement with *all* papal teaching. Since, as Garry Wills notes, "fewer than five percent or so of under-thirties agree with the teaching on contraception, the pool for new seminarians has shrunk drastically" and the American Church now hardly seems destined to attract creative or critical thinkers.[22] The Pope does not seem worried and acknowledges that the Church in its entirety may have to become smaller in order to remain true to itself.

CLASHING CIVILIZATIONS

Christian fundamentalists and their Muslim counterparts share at least one common characteristic: both groups believe that their own religion must either be dominant or be dominated by the baneful forces of secularism or – worse still – by another religion. Only their own is "true." For cultural and historical reasons, Christian and Muslim fanaticism express themselves in different ways but with similar results. Whereas Christian fundamentalists rarely engage in mass terrorism (although they are not above attacking or blockading abortion clinics and shooting the occasional doctor)* the results of their beliefs are as destructive to civilization, society, and unnumbered individuals as the actions of Muslim fanatics.[23] And the more the Christian right comes to dominate the political scene, the less it needs to practice low-level intimidation – the politicians can increasingly be counted upon to do it for them, and on a far grander scale.

How do fundamentalist Christians feel about Muslims? Focus on the Family sums up the attitude in an anonymous article on its site.[24] The author declares that the Church is called upon to "love Muslims by preaching Christ to them and campaigning for their religious freedom." Christ is "the response to evil in all societies" but there is no religious freedom, says the author, in any of the thirty-four Muslim countries. "Over one billion people are not allowed to hear the Gospel. This is the greatest violation of human rights in our time – yet there is little passion to see things change."

That statement is meek and mild compared to what some of the fundamentalist preachers proclaim when they address the faithful. Here is the preacher Gary Frazier at an all-day religious rally in the enormous "Village Baptist Church" in Destin, Florida, as recounted by *Toronto Star* reporter Tom Harpur:

> But [Frazier's initial, aggressive remarks] were harmless compared with the hatred against Islam that followed. Here are some direct quotes: "*Islam is an intolerant religion – and it's clear whose side we should be on in the Middle East.*" Applause greeted these words: "*Allah and Jehovah are not the same God . . . Islam is a Satanic religion . . . They're going to attack Israel for certain*
> . . . He added that the left-wing, anti-Israel media – "*for*

---

* 795 documented incidents of attacks on, or blockades of, abortion clinics occurred in 2001, according to Garry Wills in "A Country Ruled by Faith," *New York Review of Books*, November 16, 2006

example, CNN" – will never tell the world the truth about Islam. According to these three [Note SG: Ed Hindson and Tim LaHaye, about whom more in a moment, were also preaching] . . . Muslims intend ultimately "*to impose their religion on us all. A terrible, final war in the region is inevitable.*"[25]

Significant segments of the Christian right have found it easy to justify the torture of Muslims that took place in the Abu Ghraib prison at the hands of both male and female American soldiers. After all, their own President set the tone. Remember David Addington, Dick Cheney's right-hand man? He and his squads of White House and Justice Department toadying lawyers drafted the legalese to give the President the right to define and authorize torture and exonerate torturers. In August 2002, Bush's Office of Legal Counsel provided him with a memo which included the outrageous proposition that Congress lacks the power to prohibit torture undertaken at the behest of the President, acting in his capacity as Commander in Chief.*

As Columbia University law professor Michael Dorf noted, the "August 2002 memo's contentions regarding the wartime powers of the President are truly frightening." Some months after the Abu Ghraib torture scandal broke, in December 2004 the Office of Legal Counsel issued another memo softening but not repudiating the previous one. The "truly frightening" presidential powers "deserve to be repudiated expressly and unequivocally" says Professor Dorf, but so far they remain unchanged.[26]

Certain religious fundamentalist military men like General Jerry Boykin have also provided blanket anti-Muslim justification for the President. He rhetorically asked one church

---

* The then head of the Office of Legal Counsel, Jay Bybee, signed this memo and was later rewarded with a Federal judgeship, but for the *connoisseur* the document itself would seem to have Addington's fingerprints all over it.

gathering "Why is this man in the White House? The majority of Americans did not vote for him. He's in the White House because God put him there for a time such as this." And what, exactly, is this "time"? According to Boykin, America, as a Christian nation, is engaged in a battle against idolatrous Muslims. Enemies like Osama bin Laden and Saddam Hussein "will only be defeated if we come against them in the name of Jesus."

In the ensuing uproar – fortunately there are still some remaining angry secularists in the United States who complained – the Christian Coalition launched a petition supporting Boykin. James Dobson of Focus on the Family explicitly agreed with him:

> Every conservative Christian would understand the language that Gen. Boykin used to describe what is known as spiritual warfare. His words were consistent with mainstream evangelical beliefs . . ."[27]

Beyond the abominations of degrading physical torture, intentional sacrilege regarding Muslim beliefs has been frequent. Various lawsuits like one filed by Human Rights First on behalf of former detainees in Afghanistan and Iraq, cite US personnel desecrating copies of the Koran, throwing the holy book on the ground or in the toilet, stepping on it, and having a dog pick it up in its mouth, force-feeding prisoners pork and alcohol and so on.

Understandably, scholars close to the United States military are exceedingly interested in the "clash of civilizations" issue first given prominence by Professor Samuel Huntington. One officer-scholar notes that fundamentalist Islam "cannot conceive of either coexistence or political compromise. To the exponents of Holy Terror, Islam must either dominate or be dominated."[28]

Another military man, British this time, writes:

For the fundamentalist Muslim, the world is divided into two parts: areas of the globe where Islam is faithfully practiced are known as *dar al Islam* (the house of Islam), and areas which are non-Islamic are designated *dar al harb* (the house of war). Some fundamentalist Muslims would argue that a faithful Muslim's objective should be to extend the borders of *dar al Islam* until the whole of the created world is brought within the orb of Allah. [One of them] says "*our march has just begun, and Islam will end up conquering Europe and America. . . . For Islam is the only (path to) salvation. . . . It is our mission to bring salvation to the entire world.*"[29]

The point is not whether these are realistic descriptions of actual Muslim attitudes – which they may or may not be – but that the American military chooses to air these views in its peer-reviewed, scholarly journal *Parameters* and that evangelical Christians widely share these same views.

Millions of American evangelicals follow the doctrine of preachers who can hold their own against any imam. Since militant fundamentalist Muslims hold their beliefs with equivalent force, it is hard to see how the two cultural camps can be anything but enemies, particularly if they are also in control of the politics and the politicians. Each side conceives its mission as nothing less than the ultimate salvation of mankind. Each sees its intervention in this regard as part of the divine plan. Neither can allow itself to fail nor sacrifice its own God to the God of the opposite camp. It is the ideal scenario for what eighteenth-century preacher Isaac Backus, quoted at the outset of this chapter, called "mischiefs" – a word more forceful in his time than in ours for the horrors that ensue when religion and politics mix.

CURIOUSER AND CURIOUSER*

This section is devoted to total weirdness. I couldn't have invented it had I tried. Kindly fasten your seatbelt as we move from the Jesus Camp to the Hell House and from there to Armageddon itself – the final battle of the End Times between good and evil – with the Rapture Ready crowd.

Young children are weeping or rolling on the floor, apparently convulsed. With faces camouflaged, they are staging mock fights as God's army in training and praying God to put "righteous judges" in the Supreme Court. A pastor has freaked them out telling them in graphic detail about children who have died at the hands of abortionists and they promise to be the generation that will outlaw abortion. They're shouting prayers for President Bush while they lay hands on a cardboard cut-out of his likeness. They're at the "Kids on Fire" summer camp in the inaptly named town of Devil's Lake, North Dakota. The woman camp director, Pastor Becky Fischer, explains to them that "our enemies, the Muslims" send their own kids to camps from the age of five, where they learn to hate Christians and to use hand grenades. *Jesus Camp*, the film that shows all this, is not fiction but an 87-minute documentary, made by two young award-winning filmmakers from New York, Heidi Ewing and Rachel Grady.

Reverend Fischer freely admits that she is indoctrinating the children (many of whom are accompanied by their parents or other adults) but she is convinced she is doing the right thing; God's work. One mother explains, "Our children are on loan to us from God and He will judge us on how we bring them up." And to be fair, the children interviewed, some in training to become "child pastors," a growing phenomenon in

---

* "Curiouser and curiouser," cried Alice (in Wonderland). She was so much surprised that for the moment she quite forgot how to speak good English.

the United States, seem remarkably self-possessed and confident for 9- or 10-year-old kids. They too seem sure they are on God's chosen path to heaven. The film-makers are fair to their subjects; an outside observer, however, is readily persuaded that terrifying children and goading them to frenzied behavior will leave lasting scars.

Hell Houses are another feature of the evangelical landscape. The first one seems to have been invented in the late 1970s but they took off as a mass attraction in the 1990s and now number in the hundreds. They also seem to make a lot of money for their owners, because people are prepared to pay to be put through hell and scared out their wits. A lot of these customers think it's just a fun thing to do on Halloween and are not aware that the Hell House is actually a proselytizing tool to get them saved, pronto. The setting is a kind of haunted house – any house will do if you put the right equipment and sound effects in it. The visitor – the customer – proceeds through a series of horrific tableaux designed to create terror and revulsion.

Typical scenes include the murder by satanic atheists of a woman who declares her belief in God or a person being sacrificed in a devil-worshipping ritual. Then there are bloody late-term abortions with lots of screaming and gore on the floor, gays and lesbians being tortured in hell for eternity, teenage suicides brought about by the consequences of premarital sex, witches pushing students to murder their classmates – you get the idea.

The final tableau is, however, radiantly different. It is typically a portrayal of heaven. The visitor is called upon to repent his sins, accept salvation, and trust in Jesus as his Lord and Savior. A lot of the time, it seems to work. You can buy a Hell House kit from the Abundant Life Church in Arvada, Colorado, and a manual which explains how to choose a cast for the horror show, where to buy theatrical blood, and so on.

The pastor says, "We're not doing this to win a popularity contest. We're saying look, sin is hurting our nation and Jesus Christ is the answer to what you're going through." He reports about 35 percent conversions of visitors to his own Hell House, to which admission costs $7.00. He also claims that more than 500 churches in fourteen countries are now using his Hell House kits.[30]

Now for the weirdest, and doubtless the most massive phenomenon of all, the Rapture and all it entails. A bit of background: the first president of the Council for National Policy, the secretive club of right-wing leaders described earlier, was Tim LaHaye. Few non-evangelicals will have heard of him, even though *Rolling Stone* magazine has called him "the most influential American Evangelical of the last 25 years."[31] LaHaye is the co-author (with Jerry B. Jenkins) of the phenomenally successful "*Left Behind*" series of more than a dozen books published since 1995. If, like most people, you've never heard of these books either, you are missing a religious phenomenon that mirrors the success of *Harry Potter* in the secular world. With sales above 70 million volumes, a record which continues to climb, the *Left Behind* books figure in Amazon's permanent hall of fame. We shall return in a moment to the strange theology that informs the series; first we need to meet LaHaye in his political incarnation where he has been extraordinarily influential as well. His books (not counting the *Left Behind* series) have sold, get ready, 120 million copies. In the religious literature sweepstakes, LaHaye is the only competitor of the Holy Bible itself.

As a political actor, LaHaye, now eighty years old, has for decades been a hugely effective campaigner against gay rights and abortion, particularly through the American Coalition for Traditional Values that he founded and which has now grown into a network of 110,000 churches committed to getting

Christian candidates elected to office. His wife Beverly is president of Concerned Women for America, a mass membership organization of about 500,000 women who work through 1,200 local chapters across the country to influence anti-gay, anti-abortion, and pro-family legislation.

The LaHaye agenda, however, goes much further than this. His long-term goal is to abolish the First Amendment to the Constitution of the United States.* The United States should be governed, according to him, by an official religion and become a theocracy. Under such a government, religious schools would be publicly funded and the Bible, not the Constitution, would be the supreme law of the land. Genuine Christians are mandated by God to occupy all previously secular institutions.

From our previous examination of the term, the reader may recognize Tim LaHaye as a "dominionist." To be precise, he is a "pre-millennialist dominionist." He is also a "dispensationalist." Confused? Not as confused as you may be in a moment, but I shall try to make at least some sense of this doctrine. It holds that the world has always lived under a series of God's "Dispensations" or Covenants which have been in force at different historical stages; they are God's successive ways of dealing with humankind. Theologians of the dispensationalist persuasion usually class them as Patriarchal, Mosaic, and Christian; others divide them into the dispensations of innocence, government, law, grace and, finally, kingdom. Whatever the classification, the point is that God does not reveal the Truth all at once.

This addition to biblical doctrine came to America from

---

* Amendment I (1791) Religion, Speech, Press, Assembly, Petition: Congress shall make no law respecting an establishment of religion or prohibiting the free exercise thereof; or abridging the freedom of speech, or of the press, or the right of the people peaceably to assemble, and to petition the Government for a redress of grievances.

an early nineteenth-century British evangelical named John Nelson Darby, an ordained priest of the Church of Ireland who renounced the priesthood and founded the Plymouth Brethren movement. The Brethren are anti-clerical and they pay close attention to prophecy in the Bible, particularly as it concerns the Second Coming of Christ and the events they expect to precede it.

These beliefs were popularized in the post-Civil War United States by another evangelist, Dwight Moody, who produced a revised version of the Bible, a great success, but not nearly as great as the subsequent *Scofield Reference Bible*. A former failed lawyer, alcoholic, and divorcé, Cyrus Scofield, converted to Christianity, took over one of Moody's churches and spent the rest of his life in biblical study. The fruit of his theological labors was first published by no less than Oxford University Press in 1909 and the Scofield Bible went on to sell well over two million copies.

No ordinary Bible, Scofield's included a running commentary and a cross-referencing system linking various prophetic verses to each other. It was through Scofield's annotations that American fundamentalists first encountered the theology of Bishop Ussher (1581–1656) who calculated the exact date of Creation to be 4004 BC. Quiescent for a while, the doctrine returned in force with television evangelists like Jerry Falwell in the 1970s and has since become hugely popular, partly because of LaHaye's novels.

LaHaye calls the final Dispensation the End Times. Human history and society are irrevocably deteriorating and moving toward their equally inevitable conclusion. First will come the Rapture, when Christ comes to take the members of his Church who are alive at the time out of this world, "like a thief in the night." This mass disappearing act will be followed by the Tribulation, seven years of terrible suffering for those who remain on earth. Finally, the "official" Second Coming will occur and Christ will reign for a thousand years. That's the theology.*

There are, however, a few prior political requirements before any of this can come true. Jesus is not going to show up until the State of Israel has occupied the "biblical lands," otherwise known as most of the Middle East, followed by

> the rebuilding of the Third Temple on the site now occupied by the Dome of the Rock and Al-Aqsa mosques. The legions of the Antichrist will then be deployed against Israel, and their war will lead to a final showdown in the valley of Armageddon. The Jews will either burn or convert to Christianity, and the Messiah will return to earth.[32]

Now let us backtrack to the Rapture itself: In Saint Paul's teaching, "First the Christian dead will rise, then we who are still alive shall join them, caught up in clouds to meet the Lord in the air." In LaHaye's fictional version, the Rapture becomes visible to the star female character, an airline hostess, who returns to the cabin to discover that many of her passengers have disappeared, leaving their clothes neatly folded on their seats. These good airborne Christians, conveniently already in the clouds, have been "caught up" or "raptured," into heaven.

The American novelist and critic Joan Didion, reviewing LaHaye's series in the *New York Review of Books*, summarizes the Rapture's side-effects.

> Since all the true believers in the "*Left Behind*" series have vanished . . . those still on the scene are initially confused. O'Hare [the Chicago Airport] itself is littered with planes

---

* Loosely based on St. Paul's first Epistle to the Thessalonians, especially the end of Chapter IV.

that crashed on approach when their pilots disappeared. Highways are clogged with the crashes of cars with disappeared drivers. CNN runs videotape showing the disappearance of a foetus from a woman in labor and the disappearance of a bridegroom as he slips the ring on the bride's finger. Morgues and funeral homes report corpse disappearances.[33]

But what's really great about being raptured is not just driving carefully to avoid "hitting splayed and filleted corpses;" it's also the way non-Christians massively get their ghastly punishments from God. Jesus is not joking; in the series he

raised one hand and a yawning chasm opened in the earth, stretching far and wide enough to swallow all of them. They tumbled in, howling and screeching, but their wailing was soon quashed and all was silent when the earth closed itself again.

When you have been raptured, you also get to watch the Tribulation sufferings of everybody else from front-row seats on high, and the horrid spectacle of plagues, carnage, and utter desolation will be well worth it. The people who are "Left Behind," unlike their saved compatriots, were not translated, "in the twinkling of an eye" (the rapture logo is an eye) directly to heaven and these sinners are going to die excruciatingly nasty deaths, while the foresighted – those who were "rapture-ready" – watch from their perches at the right hand of God.

Later in the series we get the details of the Tribulation and the struggle against the Antichrist, a political leader, described by LaHaye as the "world's sexiest man,"* who proves how truly dreadful he is by being in favor of the United Nations

---

* Eat your heart out, George Clooney (twice winner of the title "world's sexiest man.")

and world disarmament. As we wait for Christ's definitive return, there is much mayhem and confusion on earth, but this is good news because it is fore-ordained and hastens the coming of the Lord. The thirteenth volume of La Haye's series appeared in March 2007 and looks like being the last as it is entitled *Kingdom Come: The Final Victory*. Since LaHaye turned eighty in 2006, he probably wanted to make sure of finishing.

The sticking point about the Rapture itself is that it cannot occur without the fulfillment of certain conditions, and not just those concerning Israel and the conversion of the Jews. The Signs of the End Times are varied and they are all around us, right now. You have every interest in learning to read them. The Rapture is imminent, certainly within the next forty years and you can find out how close you and your friends are either to vanishing or to horrible torment by asking Google to provide you with the Rapture Index, a kind of theological Dow Jones average of the dozens of factors that hasten or hinder it, which, in January 2008, stood at 163. Any number higher than 145 is considered a sure sign of Jesus' prompt return.

Still, among these multiple signs, events in the Middle East are especially necessary to the completion of God's plan, which is described, according to dispensationalists, in any number of biblical texts. These are dramatized by LaHaye in his series and publicized in countless hours of Christian radio and television. Joan Didion quotes one of these religious broadcasters, who is speaking about George Bush:

> It seems as if he is on an agenda from God . . . The Scriptures say God is the one who appoints leaders. If he truly knows God, that would give him a special anointing . . . At certain times, at certain hours in our country, God has had a certain man to hear His testimony.

BELIEFS HAVE FOREIGN-POLICY CONSEQUENCES

President Bush has indeed tried to remake the Middle East, so far without success unless the goal was to make matters far, far worse. He lost the 2006 mid-term elections partly on this question. The religious fundamentalists see the conquest of the Middle East for Christianity as his mission and they have been hugely disappointed with the conduct of the war in Iraq. Bush may have been mainly elected on a "straightforward business agenda" but, as Joan Didion concludes, the White House must also deal with "the coinciding fantasies of the ideologues in the Christian fundamentalist ministries and those in his own administration."

The Jewish people and Israel have a special, though ambiguous, place in right-wing ideology. Karl Rove, Bush's former White House strategic wonder boy, took advantage of this and devoted a good deal of his attention to attracting the Jewish vote that used to be almost solidly Democratic. In 2000, Bush got 17 percent of it, but increased that figure to about 30 percent in 2004. As Rove declared on NBC television, "there are no permanent majorities in American politics." He is apparently correct – the Jewish vote swung quite solidly back to the Democrats in 2006.

Rove exploited in particular a growing American phenomenon called Christian Zionism, based on the belief that in order to realize God's plan, the Jews must occupy all of Palestine, which Christian Zionists call Judea and Samaria. The State of Israel is the fulfillment of God's Covenant with Abraham (the Patriarchal Dispensation): this is why Christian Zionists are opposed to any concessions to the Palestinians, for instance trading land for peace, which sets back their religious agenda.

Now, thanks to them, fully a third of 145 Jewish settlements in "Judea," "Samaria" and, previously, Gaza have received funds directly from the Christian Friends of Israeli Communities (CFOIC). Why? Because God gave this land to the Jews 4,000 years ago.[34] The CFOIC was established in 1995 in the wake of the Oslo process and its members are deeply troubled whenever Israel seems tempted to give up land. To reinforce its resolve, they also help to finance Jewish out-migration to Israel from the US, Russia, and other countries.

As the pro-Israel pastor Jerry Falwell said, referring to the evangelical population, "There are 70 million of us" and he did not choose to hide the fact that he and other religious leaders could bring those millions to protest whenever "we sense that the government is becoming a little anti-Israel." This is logical, as the Second Coming of Christ must take place in Jerusalem (minus, needless to say, the Al-Aqsa mosque).

The CFOIC is only one of several fundamentalist groups financing such activities. The mega-ministries of Pastor John Hagee, in charge of 18,000 parishioners in San Antonio, Texas and eight television networks reaching 99 million homes, also sponsor special programs to help people emigrate to Israel to help "make it stronger." A contribution of $300 to Hagee's Exodus II program will bring Israel one more immigrant; whereas the mass banquets of his other program, Christians United for Israel, bring some 3,500 people to Washington for an evening of food and fellowship, followed the next day by intense lobbying of Congress. Many Congressional Representatives attend these CUI banquets. Why such priority attention for Israel? Hagee explains: "All other nations were created by an act of men, but Israel was created by an act of God."[35]

I cannot substantiate the following, found on the website of an outfit called Countercurrents, which I can't vouch for either, but it is frightening and plausible enough to repeat: "Figures like . . . John Hagee, who some have dubbed Pastor Strangelove, believe a nuclear attack by the US against Iran would set off a battle of Armageddon in the Middle East; he and his allies are literally pushing the Bush administration to attack for that reason."[36]

That makes them the allies of the neo-cons who also want to bomb Iran, but one should note that the main interest of Israel to the Rapture crowd is its role as a trigger for Jesus Christ's return. The American Jewish leader, Abraham Foxman of the Anti-Defamation League, has grasped this. As he said in late 2005, "If Israel is not useful to rapture-ready Evangelicals, it might as well not exist." Israel indeed figures in Rapture theology as a kind of landing pad for the Lord. Foxman also cited various evangelical groups, like Focus on the Family, overtly out to "Christianize America." Other Jewish leaders have criticized Foxman, however, for breaking with these Christians whom they see as allies.[37]

One man who oversees the cooperation between Christian Fundamentalists and Jews in Israel is Rabbi Yechiel Eckstein, who left Foxman's Anti-Defamation League to found the International Fellowship of Christians and Jews. To pay for the emigration of Soviet Jews to Israel, he made a television commercial based on Isaiah 49:22 "I shall beckon to the Gentiles." The Gentiles got the message. They came through with huge sums of money and Rabbi Eckstein and his organization were launched.

Eckstein now hands out millions of dollars yearly to charities of his choosing inside Israel, where his International Fellowship is the second largest charitable foundation in the country and an unofficial advisor to the government. Abraham Foxman refers to such activities as "pandering to Christians" but it is doubtful that either the Jews or the Christians concerned are listening.[38]

Perhaps they should be listening, especially the Jews. The Christian evangelical pre-millennial dispensationalists "know" that only 144,000 Jews will ultimately be saved and survive the final battle with the Antichrist at Armageddon.* The rest will be condemned to hell – which means that in these evangelical eyes, seven and a half million Jews in America alone are destined for eternal suffering. The fundamentalists seem not to be shedding many tears over their supposed fate.

Why should anyone care – particularly anyone outside the United States – about these beyond-belief beliefs of millions of Americans? People should care for two paramount reasons – aside from the obvious one that theocracy and democracy are incompatible. First, whichever political party is in power, this theology will continue to have considerable influence over United States policy toward Israel, the Middle East, and many other issues. Second, it has a direct and deleterious impact on United States ecological policy, or the lack of same.

The attitude of the Christian right, especially the part of it to which we've devoted the most attention, toward the environment is frightening in the extreme. Bill Moyers, a well known producer and journalist with the Public Broadcasting System, has written a long and chilling essay, called accurately enough "Welcome to Doomsday."[39]

This right-wing theology is not merely crazy; it is actively destructive, as great a threat to the environment as it is to a sane foreign policy. Millions of believers are convinced that environmental disasters are actually good news since they foretell Christ's return. Don't count on their numerous Congressional representatives to pass flood control measures for New Orleans, forbid cutting down forests or disallow drilling for oil in Alaska.

* I have also seen the figure 155,000, Jews saved but 144,000 corresponds better to 12,000 each from the twelve tribes of Israel. In either case, it's not many.

In Rapture or Dispensationalist theology, the ecological crisis cannot even be recognized for what it is. Just as a war with Islam in the Middle East is not to be feared but welcomed, so the collapse of ecological systems and their consequences, like Hurricane Katrina, are sure signs that the Apocalypse is on its way. Moyers cites author Barbara Rossing who points out in her book *The Rapture Exposed*, that the basic Rapture credo is final: "The world cannot be saved." Believers are thus relieved of all responsibility for "the environment, violence, and everything else except their personal salvation. The earth suffers the same fate as the unsaved. All are destroyed." A more mean-spirited, ungenerous, and finally un-Christian religion would be hard to imagine.

Meanwhile, the Lord will provide in his own good time. Global warming is in any case a myth. It is heresy to claim that resources are limited; God has enough for everyone. His generosity also confers the right to unlimited exploitation of the earth because He originally gave Dominion over it to man.

SOME CONCLUSIONS: ALL IS NOT LOST

Reading this chapter is likely to be as depressing as writing it. The combination of crazed theology, mass delusion, and ordinary selfishness can make democracy seem impossible and solutions to today's challenges unattainable. The "long march through the institutions" seems to be reaching its final miles. Let us nonetheless try to discern some hopeful signs, not least because there are some.

As we have noted, not all religious people, not all evangelicals, hold the same dominionist or reconstructionist perspectives. Some evangelicals are beginning to turn green. One of their prominent coalitions, the National Association of Evangelicals (of which the disgraced pastor Ted Haggard was head) has adopted an *Evangelical Call to Civic Responsibility*, affirming that "God-given dominion is a sacred responsibility to steward the earth and not a license to abuse the creation of which we are a part." A "dispensation" is often translated as a way of governing or administering affairs, but for many evangelicals the word also implies "stewardship," and it is one of God's ways of making us accountable.

Support for Bush's war and for his Middle East policy in general has plummeted. Weapons of mass destruction were sheer inventions, even though people believed in them, and Iraq is an unholy mess. Bush's credibility and his approval ratings have hit bottom, whether or not he qualifies as born-again. A recent tell-all book by David Kuo, who spent a couple of years in the White House on the faith-based initiatives desk, exposes how people – supposedly Christians – at the top of the administration were laughing at him behind his back for the sincerity of his Christian beliefs. People can recognize hypocrisy when they see it.

Perhaps material and cultural change in the United States will come above all for the simple reason that the people are not being served. One can understand that women in the heartland may welcome religious conviction on the part of their husbands because it keeps them away from traditional male pursuits like drinking, whoring, and gambling. American evangelicals are mostly not rich; many are quite poor. Because they are also often uneducated, they may, for a while, put "moral" policies – on abortion, homosexuals, and so on – in first place, but presumably not forever.

American infrastructure is crumbling. Public transport is virtually non-existent. Public schools are disintegrating and sometimes dangerous; this is also why so many on the Christian right have opted for homeschooling. Decent health care, like quality education, is outrageously expensive or unavailable to ordinary low-income families, even though they have jobs. The return of the Lord is all very well and religion may provide some solace to people who feel helpless in difficult times, but ordinary Americans must, even as they await the Rapture, live in the here and now.

The political task for those who live inside or outside the United States is to aid the return of reason and to isolate the politicians who bow to theology and the pressures of the religious right rather than to democracy and the law.

4

EXTINGUISHING THE ENLIGHTENMENT: THE ASSAULT ON KNOWLEDGE

By firm immutable immortal laws / Impressed on Nature by the GREAT FIRST CAUSE / Say, Muse! How rose from elemental strife / Organic forms, and kindled into life . . ., Hence without parent by spontaneous birth / Rise the first specks of animated earth / From Nature's womb the plant or insect swims / And buds or breathes, with microscopic limbs . . .

> Erasmus Darwin (Grandfather of Charles Darwin, 1731–1802), *The Temple of Nature*

If an intelligent designer used his skill, cunning and craft to make all these things, the fact that most of them go extinct is an embarrassment. Why have they all gone extinct if he is so intelligent?

> Kenneth Miller, Professor of Biology, Brown University in Providence, Rhode Island

At some point in the past twenty years the expression "dumbing down" entered the standard English vocabulary, particularly that of its American variant, and is now a dues-paying, fully accredited member of the language, although my computer stubbornly insists on underlining "dumbing" in red. I have searched unsuccessfully for the origins of the phrase (I even wrote to the *New York Times* language expert William Safire, who didn't answer) but the usage had surely become common before 1996 when arch-neo-con Phyllis Schlafly used it in a vituperative attack on educational standards in the US. In many ways the term merely encapsulates complaints heard since the time of Plato. The concept "involves a claim about the simplification of culture, education, and thought, a decline in creativity and innovation, a degradation of artistic, cultural, and intellectual standards, or the undermining of the very idea of a standard, and the trivialization of cultural, artistic, and academic creations."[1]

Although I agree that it is unmistakably taking place, I have no pretensions here to examine fully this decline in the United States, nor the institutions that promote it (the schools, the media, and so on). Such critiques have been expertly and repeatedly undertaken over several decades by scholars of culture more qualified than I. My aim here is rather to describe some of the ways that American right-wing shock troops are waging war against science, education, and the fragile progress of the human spirit over the past several centuries. Their goal is to "dumb down" any part of the acquired wisdom of humanity that does not fit their dogma.

SCIENCE AND RELIGION: WORLDS APART

The religious right is deeply preoccupied with the significance of life on earth and the ultimate truth about human beings. So is science. There the resemblance between scientific inquiry and religious activity ends. The two worldviews are incompatible. If you asked a scientist to describe the place of the earth in the cosmos and the place of human beings in the great scheme of things, she might say something like "Here we are, marooned on a tiny, imperfect sphere whizzing at nearly 30 kilometers a second around an insignificant star we call the sun. Our planet is an infinitesimal speck in one galaxy among hundreds of billions of galaxies in an out-of-the-way corner of a universe we can't even see the end of – and which for all we know may be only one among billions of other universes."

Let us try to make an everyday comparison. If the universe – the one of which we have some limited knowledge – were the size of our puny planet, then the place of the earth in it might be likened to a single cell of a bacterium on the handle of a tool in the bottom drawer of a garage workbench in a nondescript suburb of Kansas City or Swindon. Such a view certainly does not exclude religion, which like science (and sometimes more than science) tries to confront ultimate questions. Where did this or any other universe come from to begin with? What is Time? Light? Gravity? How and where did life begin and where do we come from? Why is the universe orderly? Why are natural phenomena predictable? How is it that our minds can discover natural laws at all and sometimes invent the mathematical formulas that only later turn out to have applications in nature? Science does not negate religion but it places us, as well as our surroundings, in a perspective approaching objectivity.

No one likes to feel unimportant, whether locally or cosmically. Religious authorities have fought an unremitting war against any downgrading of Man's standing or the assigning of low relative importance to the earth he inhabits compared to the universe. It took the Roman Catholic Church centuries to admit the truth of the Copernican revolution, to accept that the earth orbits the sun, not vice-versa. Galileo's famous *"Eppur si muove"* muttered in distress as he surrendered to the Inquisition still resounds wherever rational people gather.* A good Christian still, Galileo said, "The Bible shows the way to go to heaven, not the way the heavens go."[2] They burnt his book anyway and kept him under house arrest for the rest of his life. Not until the time of Pope John-Paul II ("Truth cannot contradict truth") was Galileo rehabilitated.

So the doctrine of "Creationism" in the United States held by innumerable individuals who believe literally in the Genesis story of creation – six days, Adam and Eve, the serpent, the apple, the lot – is nothing new. It is a holdover from ages past, the sort of poetic mythmaking religion has been broadcasting, defending and, when it could, imposing as literal truth for centuries. Since the first concern of religiously oriented people is generally to understand what God has in mind for them personally, they are understandably fascinated by a story that pretends to explain why they are here, on this particular earth, in the first place.

For the Christian, the Bible recounts – in more or less metaphorical terms depending on the intellectual sophistication of the reader – how God relates to his Creation, the world and to Man who stands at the summit of the natural order. The Creation story, in which the serpent tempts Eve to disobey God and eat the fruit of the Tree of Knowledge, explains how sin enters the world. Man, a term that "embraces woman" (as one involuntarily witty French dictionary puts it), is sinful; because this "original" sin is an evil stain from which no one can escape, passed down through the generations. In the fullness of biblical time, God decides man should have a chance for redemption and sends his "only begotten Son" to shed his blood in which the sins of the world shall be washed away and

---

* "And yet it does move" (the earth is in orbit around a stationary sun).

the slate of sin wiped clean – but only if you believe in Jesus Christ, the son of God.

The sequence is important: without Eve's transgression of God's law, no original sin; without sin and humanity's resulting guilt, no need for a Redeemer; without such a need, no Jesus Christ as the answer to human spiritual destitution. The Old and the New Testaments are inseparable, the Prophets prepare the way and one divinely-scripted event leads to another. For many Christian believers, therefore, the Old Testament has to be literally true – otherwise, who knows? – the New Testament and with it Christ's life, death on the cross and resurrection might be called into doubt or even become irrelevant to the human condition.

According to the biblical view, the various physical features of the earth and living things in God's creation also bear witness to his will; divine providence has always provided and will continue to provide for our material wants; he also has a plan for every individual human being. As the old revivalist hymn goes, "He's got the whole world in his hand." God has humankind's ultimate salvation at heart and the Bible is the Baedeker to guide the species' feet on the straight and narrow path. Follow it and you can live forever; stray and you're done for.

If you know how to read the sacred texts, every living thing, every event on earth past or present conveys God's will. God's initial intentions are consigned in the Bible but he continues throughout human history to make them clear. His word is the same thing as his action; this is why Saint John's Gospel begins with the famous affirmation "In the beginning was the Word." In God's grammar, all verbs are in the "performative" tense, he need only "speak the word," as in the biblical verse "And God said, 'let there be light' and there was light." Most importantly from suffering humanity's point of view, his decisions can be swayed by prayer. For the believer, events occur, things happen to us for reasons we cannot always fathom but we can sometimes alter the outcome by humbly beseeching God.

This is a crude summary. One can repeat the main point in an even briefer statement: religious belief and scientific method based on the examination of natural causes and experimentally confirmed hypotheses, as well as the possibility of proving these hypotheses false, have nothing in common except, sometimes, for a sense of beauty and wonder.

Nor is it any wonder that science and religion are destined to square off and fight an endless match. Anyone keeping score would have to admit that throughout most of the recorded history of civilization on our minor planet, religion has won. To be more precise, *monotheistic* religion has won in *Western or Judeo-Christian* civilization, the one with which we are mostly concerned here.* The Greeks, highly eclectic worshipers, with the right god or goddess for every occasion, made remarkable scientific headway before an Empire of skilled, successful, and equally polytheistic engineers replaced them as world leaders, at least in the West. When monotheism took over from that Empire, however, the jig was up. Scientific inquiry and freedom to speculate quickly became frozen in place. Aristotle was the only pagan authority admitted in the West as a kind of honorary theologian, and the thaw of the orthodox ice sheet did not even begin until roughly four centuries ago – a fraction of our particular civilization's existence.

Monotheistic humans somehow never seem content with just believing in, praising, worshiping, beseeching and sometimes making sacrifices to their God: they are obsessed with proving his existence, deciphering his will, and making other

---

* Yes, polytheistic Hindus, monotheistic Moslems and doubtless people of all other persuasions can be quite nasty to their neighbors as well, but I am trying to stick to the subject.

people conform to his alleged laws whether they want to or not. Left to itself, monotheism seems historically destined to become an excuse for unnumbered wars, witch-hunts, bloody crusades, and murders. Believers are forever appealing to God's earth-centered concerns; to the commands he is supposed to have uttered in remote eras or the traces he is supposed to have left behind like so many significant artefacts. These are often literary artefacts like Bible stories. Believers, being human, need desperately to justify their own prejudices and desires by getting their Creator's approval; they also need him in order to condemn disturbing, "deviant" practices, particularly where sexuality is concerned. The Creator, conveniently, never talks back.

In monotheistic religions, he is known, however, to have made especially strict rules about who can enjoy pleasurable carnal activities with whom, at what age, under what legal regime and with what reproductive consequences, if any. To help humans stick to his plan, he works though self-appointed spokespersons (in the case of Christianity, priests and pastors) who have a more direct line to the deity than other people and whose job it is to state and restate what is licit and illicit.

It is probably the case as well that most humans are programmed to prefer certainty to doubt, clear instructions to personal solution-seeking, and revelation to reliance on the slow progress of reason. Other peoples' beliefs and their "abnormal" (read: different) behavior create anxiety. Democracy is also distressing because it gives power to ordinary mortals rather than to an omniscient and omnipotent God or at least to his authorized representatives on earth who enjoy divine rights.

Faced with that kind of competition, not just from God himself but from such momentously important matters as sex and reproduction, self-preservation, and a sure-fire antidote to dread, it is astonishing science has progressed so far and so fast. Too far and too fast, at least for the Almighty's storm troopers in the United States. Even scientists – one is tempted to say especially scientists – do not always understand what these people are up to, nor why. Too often they consider religious fanatics beneath contempt and not worthy of serious notice. The religious demolition enterprise is, however, only beginning and it is being driven forward with finesse and cunning. And not just by those Americans and others too hastily call "Creationists" or "Jesus Freaks" but by a highly educated and articulate cadre of well-dressed, presentable people. The religious program is progressing so fast, in fact, that the apparent triumph of science, even in the West, is under threat and may be far more fragile than we might assume.

THE GULLIBILITY GAP

Calling all anthropologists: We need you, not in South America but in South Dakota; not in Oceania but in Oklahoma. We need serious scientific work on the tribal culture of the inhabitants of the country which remains, for the moment at least, the most powerful on earth, and I don't mean the culture of Native Americans. Despite membership in all manner of rich-country organizations and international institutions; despite boasting many of the best universities in the world; despite the presence on its soil of 400,000 European scientists (most of whom have no intention of returning to Europe); neither the letter nor the spirit of science touches the majority of the people of the United States.

It may be hard to credit, but hark to the results of the "primetime poll" taken in February 2004 by the reputable organization ABC News. With a margin of error of three percentage points one way or the other, the poll showed that fully 61 percent of Americans believe that the account of creation in the book of Genesis is "literally true, meaning it happened that way word for word" (text of the pollsters' question). Sixty percent believe the story of a global flood and Noah's ark; even more – 64 percent – agree that Moses parted the waters of the Red Sea to save the fleeing Jews from Pharaoh's chariots in hot pursuit.

Among Protestants, three-quarters believe – or at least told the pollsters they did – in the Creation story and a huge 79 percent took the Red Sea account as fact. Those calling themselves evangelical Protestants were 90 percent on board for the Genesis account of God's Creation of the world in six days (with a day off on Sunday), word for word. Only three in ten of those questioned said No, these stories are "meant as a lesson, but are not to be taken literally." The rest – between six and ten percent depending on which story was mentioned (Moses getting top marks for credibility) – either didn't answer or didn't know.

US Catholics showed themselves slightly less credulous with one-half believing in literal six-day Creation and in Moses' parting of the Red Sea. Perhaps most surprising of all, among those who said they had "no religion," a quarter still believed in the six-day Creation and a third subscribed to the Red Sea legend. The oftener the people questioned went to Church, the more literal-minded they were with regard to the Bible.*³

Another poll by the Harris organization found that 93 percent of American Christians believe in miracles (and 95 percent in heaven). Recall that at least three-quarters of the US population classes itself as "Christian," then do the simple

---

* The only encouraging feature of this ABC News Poll is that, on the other question asked, only 8 percent of the respondents (and 12 percent of the evangelicals) said that the Jews, including those alive today, are "collectively responsible for the death of Jesus." That's still too many, but despite some literalist interpretations of the New Testament and the widely attended Mel Gibson film "The Passion of the Christ," on many screens in the United States at the time the poll was taken, most people showed good judgment.

calculation 93 percent of 75 percent and the conclusion is that seven out of ten Americans consider miracles a realistic possibility. With figures like these in front of you, you may be less surprised that so many in the US were prepared to believe in "weapons of mass destruction" or in the direct implication of Saddam Hussein and Iraq in the terrorist attacks of September 11. Their relative loss of confidence in George W. Bush is a positive sign but one must assume that the gullibility factor and blind trust in whatever fictions may be affirmed by personages (or texts) considered authoritative are still present.

PRAISE THE LORD (AND ADAM SMITH)

Religion is also winning the race against science and rationality in the world at large where the big news is the spectacular spread of pentecostalism (from its origins and base made in USA, where else?), a generic name for revivalist religions of collective enthusiasm and ecstasy. According to a report by *The Economist* which credits the movement with at least half a billion followers worldwide already, it is "not only burning through the 'cities of the dispossessed' . . . [but] also consuming the business and professional elites of the developing world."[4]

The Economist, not atypically, sees this wildfire religious movement as a sign of our own version of modernity and sheds an Adam Smithian light on the stunning success of revivalist religion. Rather than a monopoly – such as the one the Catholic Church long enjoyed – the revivalists are model small capitalist entrepreneurs.

First off, there's plenty of healthy competition between churches to attract followers. Huge incentives exist to outperform the other purveyors of salvation, because if you don't give your spiritual customers what they want, they can and will turn away and go elsewhere. The barriers to entry in the field are low because you need virtually no capital; only charisma, to start a church. Unlike strictly hierarchical religions such as Catholicism, which insist on long and rigorous training for the priesthood, no qualifications are required to praise the Lord loud and clear and dispense salvation to all and sundry. The pentecostalists make full use of the talents of women worshipers as well as men, so there is also lots of innovation.*

Pentecostalism, in a new twist on Calvinism (which holds that worldly success displays God's favor) encourages self-confidence and success in business. The bookshops attached to the mega-churches are full of Christian literature as one would expect, but also feature plenty of tomes on management. Such Churches can also provide a handsome pay-off and you needn't wait for the afterlife to collect it. If you are among the most effective pastors of these growing flocks, the religious lottery may afford you huge material rewards. The local fame of some of these charismatic wonder-boys and, increasingly, girls, may also lead them into politics. In short, pentecostalism is a capitalist dream come true.

Europe (along with China and probably some other parts of Asia) stands out as an island of rationality in a world where religion is gaining the high ground. The same ABC poll showing the predominance of literal belief in the word of the Bible, identified the believers as more likely to be "Protestants (particularly evangelicals), Southerners, blacks, lower-income and less-educated Americans," which would be a quite good summary of the rise of religion world-wide where most people are also non-white, poor, and unschooled. If we hope to continue to celebrate reason and a rational attitude toward life in the world at large, we are certainly not taking the right road by

---

* A French friend recounts an experience in a poor neighborhood of Recife, Brazil, where his brother is a Catholic priest: On the central square are no fewer than three pentecostalist churches, all equipped with powerful sound systems, all simultaneously blaring their competing services into the square. The din is tremendous and it's impossible to understand anything but no doubt the capitalist ideal of free and unhindered competition is well served.

leaving the global South to its present fate, in poverty and ignorance. We should also take care that standards of living and education are not eroded in Europe itself, where the same causes could be counted upon to produce the same effects.

YOU CALL THIS SCIENCE?

Let us now return to the Creationists in the United States. Nearly everyone has heard of them. Yes, there really is a museum in Arkansas whose exhibits "prove" that dinosaurs and people co-existed on earth. It attracts busloads of visitors to the Ozark mountain town of Eureka Springs, which boasts a thriving tourist trade centered on an extensive Christian theme park.

The museum will present you with Adam and Eve in the same Garden-of-Eden tableau as a tyrannosaurus rex. The T-rex does the decent thing and abstains from eating them, but this is normal because we are still in the time of peaceful coexistence before sin enters the world, so death is not yet known. So why aren't there any dinosaurs around right now? Because they were wiped out by the flood, you dummy. If you stay on for an evening in Eureka Springs, you can go to the Great Passion Play – over seven million other people have – with hundreds of extras and Roman legions galore

The commercial success of the Eureka Springs museum has not been lost on other religious entrepreneurs in, for example, Cincinnati and Dallas, where similar Creationist museums were as of early 2007 under construction. If you send a donation to the one in Cincinnati, you can receive in exchange a leather-bound, limited edition volume of Bishop Usshers' *The Annals of the World* (first published in Latin in 1650, the English posthumous edition dates from 1658). The reader will recall that Ussher calculated creation to have taken place in 4004 BC. The museum promises to "counter evolutionary natural history museums that turn countless minds against Christ and Scripture."

And yes, there really are school districts where creationism is taught in parallel to, or in place of, scientific accounts of the earth's formation and the subsequent evolution of life. By 2005, according to one expert witness, anti-evolutionary ideas were being taught in 82 school districts in 30 US states.[5] The bigots imposing these doctrines do not necessarily belong to the fundamentalist variety, known within the evangelical fold as "young-earth creationists." The evangelicals of the genus Eureka Springs are arguably the least dangerous of the anti-Science, pro-God brigades. It's too easy to refute their rants and too hard not to laugh. None of which implies such people are utterly harmless, if only because, as we have just seen, there are so many of them and they are culturally conditioned to believe anything.

Far more threatening are the proponents of so-called Intelligent Design. I should not even talk about them here because part of their strategy consists in planting the seeds of controversy and encouraging insidious doubts in peoples' minds. They never miss the opportunity to point out that their ideas are being discussed, as I will do here, and are thereby in a sense being taken seriously.

DEVIOUS BY DESIGN

Let us nonetheless discuss them and begin at the beginning, which is to say with the creation of the world. Did anyone do it? If so, who? Whereas the "young-earth" creationists have no doubts on this point and loudly proclaim God's six-day handiwork, the Intelligent Design, or ID, people never make a claim for God, nor does his name come into their arguments, even though their ultimate intentions may be clear.

Their best-known think-tank is called the Discovery

Institute, founded in 1996. With its offshoot the Center for the Renewal of Science and Culture (CRSC) Discovery is spearheading the fight against "scientific materialism." People at this Institute and its subsidiary, both located in a suburb of Seattle (close to Microsoft), practice what they call the "wedge strategy." Their aims became known through a document of that name leaked from the CRSC in 1999 in which they set out the plan "to replace materialistic explanations with the theistic understanding that nature and human beings are created by God."

Just as you would split a log by hammering a sharp wedge into it, so they hope to use "thin-edge" tactics to split the trunk of the scientific tree at its weakest point. One of the most visible among Discovery Institute staff, William Dembski, says that science undermines faith and "this is going to stop." Although he is a devout evangelical, he never speaks in public about God, stressing only "cultural engagement" and affirming that "science has something to hide."[6]

These new religious warriors, like their brothers in the secular right-wing institutions, have no financial problems. Their money comes from some of the usual suspects among right-wing foundations (see Chapter I) and from private donors like the reconstructionist Howard Ahmanson, who knows a thing or two about wedge strategy. He practices it, as we saw in the preceding chapter, to split open the mainstream churches and drag them into the arch-conservative fold.

The IDers are far from stupid; they are in fact exceptionally bright and well educated: William Dembski has a Ph.D. in mathematics from the University of Chicago and took another doctorate in philosophy from the University of Illinois before doing a couple of other scientific post-doc degrees and finding time for a Masters in divinity from Princeton. The Discovery Institute does not mention that Dembski was ejected from a teaching position at Baylor

University (even though it is a Baptist-dominated school) largely due to protests from the faculty. Nor does it point to his teaching activities and directorship at the Center for Science and Theology at the Southern Baptist Theological Seminary (and later at the Southwestern Baptist Seminary).

Dembski's co-editor for the Discovery collective volume *Darwinism, Design and Public Education*, Stephen Meyer, has a Ph.D. in the History of the Philosophy of Science from Cambridge. Their jointly edited book is published by the respectable Michigan State University Press. Other fancy degrees among Discovery's fellows are Phillip Johnson's JD – he taught law at Berkeley for 25 years – and the multiple attainments of Donald Kennedy, including a Ph.D. in biology from Harvard and membership in the American Academy of Sciences. Michael Behe, another leading figure whose stock in trade and rallying cry is the "irreducible complexity" of life, has a Ph.D. in biochemistry from the University of Pennsylvania and teaches biology at Lehigh University, a secular institution. In other words, don't get into an argument with Discovery on the basis of academic credentials.

Unless you are very, very sure of yourself, don't try to skewer them in debate on general principles either. A talent for manipulating language and for extraordinarily good PR is a hallmark of the religious right and their practiced rhetoric is likely to be slicker than yours. They employ, in fact, several experts with Ph.D.s in rhetoric, speech, and communications studies on their team. The Intelligent Designers' objectives are always couched in language making them sound quite reasonable; they want, for example: "a more scientifically inclusive and controversy-based approach to teaching biological evolution."

The Institute's website underlines their concern for the "future of democratic institutions, religion and public life and reform of the law." They believe in "God-given reason" (the Founding Fathers might have said as much), the "permanence of human nature", and "free market economics domestically and internationally." Just your typical upstanding, reasonable, civic-minded – though perhaps a tad conservative – Americans, and far better trained intellectually than most, right? Look again.

Their ultimate aim is to discredit the scientific method itself so that God comes into his own as a causative factor in natural phenomena. Unless they are challenged and defeated on that terrain, they can weasel their way out of just about any other charge. I am not a scientist but I shall try to explain what the fight is about where Darwinism is concerned. The contest is between the overwhelming number of scientists and educated people on one side and these sophisticated creationists on the other. The first group sees evolution as the long process of random variations in populations living in diverse environments, combined with natural selection; the second claims that this process cannot have taken place randomly and required the intervention of an Intelligence intent upon a particular outcome, that is, us.

ANCESTRAL ANTI-EVOLUTION: THE SCOPES TRIAL

The Discovery Institute belongs to the latest flowering of a long anti-scientific American tradition. Uniquely among the peoples of developed countries, Americans have been arguing about evolution virtually since the conclusions of the *Origin of Species*, published by Charles Darwin in 1859, reached the shores of the United States.*

---

* Full title: *On the Origin of Species by Means of Natural Selection, or the Preservation of Favoured Races in the Struggle for Life*, John Murray, Albemarle Street, London, 1859. Many revised editions followed in quick succession in which Darwin made useful additions and refuted the arguments of his detractors.

The most famous historical episode in this ongoing debate took place in Tennessee in the summer of 1925: the Scopes trial (popularly known as the "Monkey Trial"). John Scopes, a high school biology teacher, backed by the American Civil Liberties Union, was tried for teaching evolution in contravention of a Tennessee law.

The lawyers for the prosecution and the defense were among the most celebrated men in the country. For the prosecution, William Jennings Bryan, who had been the unsuccessful Democratic candidate for President three times (1896, 1904, 1908) and was considered by many the best orator in the nation. For the defense, Clarence Darrow, was the country's top criminal lawyer who travelled from Chicago to defend Scopes without fee.

Bryan was a uniquely American mixture, quintessentially of his time and place, rooted in nineteenth-century populist politics and in southern Illinois. He was an important figure in the Progressive movement and a champion of working people. He campaigned against the big, predatory corporations, especially the banks and the railroads and he fought for women's suffrage. He was a prominent activist in every social justice campaign of his time, but he was also a prohibitionist (in favor of outlawing alcohol) and a Christian fundamentalist.

The trial attracted huge attention. It was the first ever to be broadcast nationwide on the radio and a hundred journalists came to the small Tennessee town of Dayton to cover it. A high point was the joust between Bryan and Darrow conducted on the courthouse lawn so that the huge crowds outside could be accommodated. Darrow called Bryan himself as a witness in order to cross-examine him on the Genesis account of Creation and the age of the earth. Here is the eyewitness account of famous journalist and sharp wit H. L. Mencken, writing in the *Baltimore Evening Sun*:

The youthful Attorney General Stewart, desperately trying to bring the performance within legal bounds asked, "What is the meaning of this harangue?" "To show up fundamentalism" shouted Mr Darrow . . . in one of the few moments of anger he showed, "to prevent bigots and ignoramuses from controlling the educational system of the United States." Mr Bryan sprang to his feet, his face purple, and shook his fist in the face of Mr Darrow while he cried "To protect the word of God from the greatest atheist and agnostic in the United States."*

When he couldn't answer a question, Bryan fell back on the authority of the Bible. The judge would not allow expert scientific witnesses to testify in favor of the biology teacher and after eleven days, Scopes was found guilty and fined 100 dollars. The trial has since inspired books, plays, and movies, but its chief lesson for us today is that the same battle lines are still drawn in the United States. The difference is that the anti-evolutionists have learned from experience, the ground has shifted and the attack on Darwin is both more sophisticated and more convincing to the uninitiated than it once was.

HAS DARWIN STOOD THE TEST OF TIME?

The Discovery Institute is now without contest the leader of these anti-science, far more savvy opponents. Active in denying human-induced climate change or ozone depletion and a major contributor to the effort that led to the federal ban on most stem cell research (which the Democrats have promised to reverse); they still reserve most of their energy for their principal *bête noire* Charles Darwin. While they employ cos-

---

* Five days after the trial ended, on July 21, 1925, Bryan, still in Dayton, Tennessee, died in his sleep.

mologists, astronomers, and meteorologists, their biologists are on the front lines.

The Darwinian explanation of evolution and natural selection is one of the most solidly established scientific theories ever put forward; over nearly a century and a half, the master's fundamental insights have been refined and supplemented (notably through genetics) but never refuted. One can almost feel admiration for the IDers, trying to discredit a theory backed by such overwhelming evidence when they might have chosen a softer target. Why they decided to lay siege to this scientific monument remains mysterious – others might have been more easily overthrown or at least fissured. They must believe that God reveals himself in the details of biology more readily than elsewhere. What is the science they must argue against?

Now, as then, Darwin's theory of evolution rests on three basic claims:

- There is variation in some characteristics among individuals in a given population;
- That variation is heritable; that is, genes can be passed from parent to offspring;
- There are different survival and reproductive rates among individuals carrying the different variations of a characteristic depending on the environment inhabited by the carriers.[7]

Darwin says nothing at all about the *direction* that selection of characteristics may take and the notion of "progress" toward any particular goal is foreign to him, although he does clearly say in his later work, *The Descent of Man* (1870), that man is descended from "lower" forms of life. Man as a species, however, follows exactly the same rules as those noted above, with new traits like the capacity to reason and use language contributing to human reproductive success. The name of the evolutionary game, whatever the species, is to have more, hardier, better-adapted offspring than others in the same population, but this is not a teleological process (i.e. driven toward some preordained goal) any more than it is a theological one.

Most species are not "successful," or at least not for long as science measures "long." Ninety-nine percent of all species that have ever lived have in fact become extinct. Although our own species may seem to us immutable, we lack perspective. Like any other mammals, we are necessarily still evolving, but nature inexorably eliminates the typical mammalian species within about ten million years and if we allow nature to take its course, our turn will also come. These observations might inspire a definition of *homo sapiens* as "the only species capable of self-annihilation within a much briefer period," but that is another story.

How do the Intelligent Design people hope to undermine a theory that has demonstrated its robustness time and again? The problem is that, although they certainly do not convince trained scientists, the ID people use both secular and Christian institutions as megaphones and target the public through the popular media. Their founder and Chairperson, Bruce Chapman, according to the 1999 leaked "wedge" document, possesses a remarkable address book, bulging with accommodating media contacts.

I-Designers often argue from analogy, which, as any scientist will readily affirm, means nothing at all in terms of proof although it may be taken as such by the untrained observer. If A is "like" B in some respects, this does not mean that A is identical to or behaves like B. Take Discovery's Michael Behe who likes to begin his talks with the mousetrap. If the mousetrap lacks any one of its component parts, it won't function; it is "irreducibly complex," and it has been designed by an intelligence for a purpose, which is to catch mice. Even very simple components of lower organisms like the bacterial flagellum, which Behe has studied in depth, display, "like" the mousetrap, irreducible complexity.

The coming together of their component parts through evolution is, according to Behe and his ID colleagues, so unlikely that it is mathematically impossible. It would have required more time than the entire history of the universe for these components to evolve together; and since this is impossible, the only alternative is that they must have been designed so that they would fit together.

But Darwin doesn't say this. Unfortunately for Behe's argument, not only have less complex mousetraps actually been invented and less complex organisms fulfilling exactly the same functions actually been discovered – the doctrine of irreducible complexity makes no sense scientifically.

As Darwin wrote in 1870, "When one part is modified, other parts change through the principle of correlation." In more modern language, from evolutionary biologist H. Allen Orr's review of Behe's book, *Darwin's Black Box: The Biochemical Challenge to Evolution*,[8]

> Behe's colossal mistake is that, in rejecting these [evolutionary] possibilities, he concludes that no Darwinian solution remains. But one does. It is this: An irreducibly complex system can be built gradually by adding parts that, while initially just advantageous, become – because of later changes – essential. The logic is very simple. Some part (A) initially does some job (and not very well, perhaps). Another part (B) later gets added because it helps A. This new part isn't essential, it merely improves things. But later on, A (or something else) may change in such a way that B now becomes indispensable. This process continues as further parts get folded into the system. And at the end of the day, many parts may all be required.[9]

Although it may be perfectly true that complex structures will not work without all of their component parts and the odds of these having arisen spontaneously *all together* so that the organism could function are so small as to be impossible, this is not at all Darwin's argument. The IDer's "colossal mistake" is to fall into the trap logicians and scientists call the "retrospective fallacy:" they begin from an outcome observed at present. Then they demand in advance that particular outcome; as opposed to a different, equally functional one, thereby tremendously stacking the odds.

I quoted Kenneth Miller, a professor of biology at Brown University (and a practicing Catholic) at the top of this chapter to the effect that if the Designer is so intelligent, why have nearly all the creatures he designed gone extinct? What an embarrassment! Miller also provides a telling comparison in refutation of the ID arguments. The odds, he explains, of a poker player drawing a pre-ordained hand of, say, two black tens, two red queens and the ace of spades may indeed be incredibly small, but all you need for evolution is to draw "a pair" – natural selection will, over time, do the rest and here the odds improve immeasurably. Selection can furthermore take any one of a great many paths and does not occur in the same way for all organisms. For example, the proteins occurring in different species may vary by 90 percent yet still have the same function.

Nor can the IDers be allowed to get away with the kind of logical fallacy that starts from the obvious to reach the unacceptable: "Some complex physical or biological phenomena are not yet explained by science (obvious); *therefore* this or that so-far-unexplained phenomenon must be considered evidence that a supernatural power decided to bring about the said phenomenon (unacceptable)." The language may be more erudite, but this is on a par with explaining that rain falls because of the tribe's prayers to the rain-god. Down that road lies the disintegration and the eventual demise of science.

The legal scholar Ronald Dworkin has put it cogently:

> Indeed, divine intervention would then be available even as a rival to a fully adequate conventional explanation. Why should we prefer a climatologist's account of global warming, which suggests that the process will continue unless and until people reduce the level of their carbon pollution of the atmosphere, to the rival account that a god is warming the planet for his own purposes and will cool it again when he wishes?[10]

Since this is exactly what many religious people do believe about global warming, it is fair to conclude that the religiously-led assault against science and knowledge threatens not just the Enlightenment, but life on earth itself.

Not all religious people try to use the crutch of God to strike down Darwin. Although the know-nothing President George W. Bush has famously said "The jury is still out on evolution" and, along with the former Senate Majority Leader Bill Frist (himself an MD) wanted "both sides taught" in the public schools; this was not the view of Pope John Paul II who said "Evolution is no longer a mere hypothesis." Making this papal view more explicit still, the Director of the Vatican Observatory, astronomer and priest Father George V. Coyne, has said that Intelligent Design "belittles God;" that "science and religion are totally separate pursuits;" that it is wrong to believe that the Bible can or should be used as a "source of scientific knowledge."

Coyne has also publicly rebuked Cardinal Christoph Schoenborn of Vienna for his widely publicized anti-Darwinist, pro-design views. Schoenborn wrote in the *New York Times* – not generally the first place to announce new developments in Catholic teaching – that evolution cannot be reduced to "chance and necessity;" there is rather an "internal finality" and a Divine plan. Father Coyne explains that this is most definitely not Church teaching and the Cardinal is "in error on at least five fundamental issues."[11] Let us hope Coyne's view will prevail: Schoenborn is known to be close to Pope Benedict XVI and one wonders if his sortie in the *Times* was meant as a harbinger of Catholic doctrinal backtracking to come on evolution.

EVOLVING INTELLIGENT DESIGN

Ironically, Intelligent Design itself, whatever its view of Darwin, is like any other organism, institution, or doctrine: it is constantly evolving as its environment changes. The I-Designers are a slippery lot. Like evolution itself, they employ both chance and necessity to best effect. They never claim to see design *everywhere*, so when they are confronted with irrefutable proof that this or that organism or component of an organism shows no sign of design but can be explained by natural selection; they simply shift their ground.

Unlike genuine science, Intelligent Design never makes testable predictions – in other words, its claims are not "falsifiable" – the acid test for a scientific hypothesis. You have to be able at least to imagine evidence that would refute the hypothesis, but no conceivable evidence can knock down the claims of Intelligent Design enthusiasts. They can avoid ever being tested, first because they are deliberately vague about when and how the "designer" is supposed to have intervened. Second, they never say "Every structure in nature has been designed" but rather "Science ought to be able to find evidence for design in nature" – two totally different propositions.

The *New Scientist* calls the latest ruse of the Intelligent Designers "the God Lab." Since the Discovery Institute and the Center for the Renewal of Science and Culture can deliver only so much in terms of credibility, the same coterie of well-funded people has opened a new, secretive research facility in the same Seattle suburb called the Biologic Institute. When the *New Scientist* journalist came to call, the only person willing to open the door and his mouth was dismissed immediately thereafter. But not before he let the cat out of the bag.[12]

This hapless informant, a certain George Weber, recited the usual lesson to the *NS* reporter. Some features of living organisms are too complex to have evolved without intervention and the new Institute was there to detect it – whereupon the director of Biologic, Dr Douglas Axe, gave him the axe. Weber, he said, was "found to have seriously misunderstood the purpose of Biologic and to have misrepresented it." Anyone familiar with the literature emanating from the Discovery Institute or from its fellows like Behe and Dembski would say, rather, that Weber had understood this purpose perfectly. Biologic intends to do lab science to search for the Designer's handiwork, and Axe, who has a doctorate in molecular biology and has done post-doc work in a lab in Cambridge, England, is to lead this work.

FROM DAYTON, TENNESSEE TO DOVER, PENNSYLVANIA: DARWIN ON TRIAL

Clearly one reason for the establishment of the Biologic Institute was the stinging setback dealt to ID people in a landmark legal battle decided in December 2005. From the Scopes trial onward, such matters have been settled through the courts in the United States and in this one, Federal Judge John E. Jones III handed down a long negative opinion in the case of *Kitzmiller* et al. v. *Dover Area School District*. A group of parents whose children go to school in Dover, Pennsylvania took the School Board to court because the latter insisted that biology teachers must read a statement affirming that

Darwinism is nothing but a theory and as such is not proved; while proposing another textbook in which ID is the central concept. The parents won.

Judge Jones, despite being a Bush appointee and a self-declared Republican, refused to allow the statement or the teaching of the ID doctrine in public schools because it was nothing but creationism in fancy dress, and thus stands in violation of the First Amendment. Judge Jones wrote:

> The overwhelming evidence at trial established that ID is a religious view, a mere re-labelling of creationism, and not a scientific theory.[13]

The trial lasted three months and legal costs came to a shade over a million dollars, a huge sum for the district school board which, as the guilty party, was expected to pay. Subsequently, four states, apparently fearing similar lawsuits, took ID off the school curriculum, in a singular victory for reason. Another such victory occurred even before the trial ended. In the November 2005 local elections, voters threw out all the members of the Dover school board who had voted for the ID statement.

Such victories are often aided by the action of organizations like the venerable American Civil Liberties Union, founded 1920. It was already present at the Scopes trial and now handles over 6000 court cases a year thanks to the support of its half million members. A more specialized organization is Americans United for the Separation of Church and State, which has 75,000 members and has been litigating and educating for sixty years. Its objective is to defend the First Amendment and to "keep America from establishing a state church and from becoming a church state." There are still plenty of Americans prepared to defend the Constitution against all comers, secular and religious.

However, it is still early days to rejoice. Locally, many high-school biology teachers admit that they are simply skipping over the subject of evolution in order to avoid clashes with fundamentalist parents. Some choose euphemisms, preferring to speak to their students about "change over time" rather than pronouncing the dread "e-word" (as it is now known in some circles). Since the Dover trial, the indefatigable Discovery Institute fellows have been on the road, using their accommodating media contacts in attempts to prove Judge Jones was wrong. One of the arguments Jones used in his 139-page opinion was that ID "has not generated peer-reviewed publications." Now, Douglas Axe, the director of Biologic, has published two peer-reviewed papers in a reputable molecular biology journal that William Dembski cites as evidence for the ID case.

Unless scholarly journal editors are especially vigilant, more of these carefully worded papers may sneak through the peer review process. The I-Designers are after scientific respectability and legitimacy and to that end they are refining their strategy at every step. As another *New Scientist* journalist reported on the current situation:

> Sometime in the past few years, those who question the findings of mainstream science ceased to be laughable Luddites and, to a significant number of people, became an accepted voice in public debate about science. And when that voice's opinion is not only accepted but also suits voters' prejudices, Dembski's work is done.[14]

ID people are making headway because they are working in a fertile and receptive terrain. In the United States, evolution and Darwinism are still live issues – indeed personal insults to some. Alone among citizens of the wealthier, presumably better-educated countries, Americans are, for example, loathe to accept the scientifically established fact that they, like all other humans, share 98 percent of their genes with chimpanzees – two-thirds of Americans, in fact, angrily reject the notion that they might share even half.

FIGHTERS FOR THE ENLIGHTENMENT: TO THE BARRICADES!

The best-selling author and biologist Richard Dawkins (*The God Delusion*) is seriously alarmed at the onward march of religion and its attempts to trample on science. So are a number of Nobel laureates and other prominent scientists who gathered at the Salk Institute in La Jolla, California in November 2006 for the first "Beyond Belief" conference.* In cooperation with the Science Network, a nascent television project, the participants acknowledged that religion was winning over reason in the popular mind and asked themselves what they could do about it. If, they said, we are to avoid the "twilight for the Enlightenment project and the beginning of a new age of unreason" then we had better go about creating a "new rational narrative as poetic and powerful as those that have traditionally sustained societies."[15]

The question they seem not yet to have faced is whether the "poetic and powerful" can come together with the "rational," or more simply, whether individuals, even those as determined and talented as these scientists, can create new mythic structures *ex nihilo*. "Myth" in this sense does not imply truth or falsehood, but rather encapsulates the stated goal of the Beyond Belief believers – the creation of a "poetic and powerful narrative," compelling enough to capture and inhabit the

---

* The second Beyond Belief Conference took place in early November 2007 focusing specifically on the Enlightenment. It will become available as a video-stream but as of this writing (mid-November 2007) no reports were available.

popular imagination. Science indisputably has a beautiful and awe-inspiring tale to tell – and too often hides its light under a bushel, if a biblical allusion is acceptable in this context. This, however, is unlikely to be enough to influence mass opinion. Cultural hegemony, as we saw in earlier chapters, depends on a lot more than a few isolated scientists, however brilliant they may be.

Although the Beyond Believers have defined the first important M, Mission, they will need to get four other down-to-earth "M"s under control. That is, they will need Money, Management, Media, and Marketing if they hope to create a successful final M, for Myth. Furthermore, should they try to fulfill all these functions themselves, they will find no time for their labs, teaching, running the New York City Hayden Planetarium and various other vital day-jobs. Recall Focus on the Family which employs 1,700 people or the Heritage Foundation, which supplies "an average of 6.5 media interviews every working day."

That, multiplied by about a hundred and two, is what the new Enlightenment Fighters must do. They need to build the Enlightenment version of the Discovery Institute (and of the Heritage Foundation and all the other rightwing ideology factories for that matter), create a rationalistic replacement for the Center for the Renewal of Science and Culture and generally line up the cannon against the rest of the anti-scientific armada. This long-haul, hard-slog work has not even begun.

To begin at all, they must try to find the most basic of the 'M's – Money – without which the others are likely to remain dim and distant hopes. They need, in fact, about half a dozen Templeton Foundations squarely on the side of science. The Templeton Foundation is a deeply ambiguous honey pot full of huge amounts of cash that has been funding prizes and research projects for two decades. No rationalist would argue with its banner headline: "Supporting science, Investing in the big questions" nor with its motto: "How little we know, how eager to learn." The foundation also announces up front that it does not support the Intelligent Design movement, is not associated with the Christian Right and is not a religious organization. So far so good.

But when it comes to its "Core Themes," the Templeton focus seems more than a little blurred where science is concerned. To allow the reader to judge, here is the list of all 31 of these themes:

Creativity, Curiosity, Emergence, Entrepreneurship, Evolution, Forgiveness, Freedom & Free Will, Future-Mindedness, Generosity, Gratitude, Honesty, Humility, Human Flourishing, Infinity, Mind & Intelligence, New Concepts of God, Prayer & Meditation, Progress, Purpose, Reliability, Science and Religion, Self-Control, Spiritual Capital, Spiritual Development, Spiritual Transformation, Spirituality & Health, Thrift, Ultimate Reality, Unconditional Love, Wisdom, Worship.

Whereas scientists are undoubtedly curious about evolution, mind & intelligence and possibly infinity; economists interested in thrift and entrepreneurship and anthropologists and moral philosophers involved in many of the rest of these categories; the cards do seem quite heavily stacked in favor of the sacred.

This assessment is confirmed when one checks out the prizes. The Templeton Foundation rests on the fortune of a legendary stock-market speculator, John Templeton, now in his 90s and as far as I know still enjoying life in the Bahamas. His lucrative stock-picking has allowed the foundation, still a family affair, to give the largest individual cash award in the world and this prize of £800,000 pounds ($1.6 million; €1.2 million) is the one for which it is best known to the public. The Templeton

Prize dwarfs the amount a Nobel laureate can expect to pocket. The winners have tended to be either cosmologists or theologians; all are conscientiously trying to smooth out the sheets so that science and religion can lie down together in the same bed. Richard Dawkins refers to the Templeton Prize as "a very large sum of money given . . . usually to a scientist who is prepared to say something nice about religion."

But Templeton also gives out many smaller prizes – to religious journalists or films with spiritual themes for instance. When I looked at its "Freedom Prizes" the penny dropped, the veil was rent, the scales fell from my eyes, or whatever metaphor you prefer to designate the moment of truth revealed; in the present case the fact that Templeton is way, way to the right and nowhere else.

These "Freedom Prizes" are selected and administered by the Atlas Foundation (a transparent reference to Ayn Rand's ultra-neo-liberal novel *Atlas Shrugged*) and the prizes are awarded to members of a huge network of neo-liberal, Hayekian-type think-tanks around the world. Twenty-six of these think-tanks won a Freedom Prize in 2006 "for excellence in promoting liberty." More to the point is that there are now 481 of these think-tanks to choose from if you take the word of Atlas's site. The "liberty" involved is Hayek's economic freedom, and freedom from government regulation, taxes, public services, and so on.

Atlas also specializes in helping people of like mind to set up their own think-tanks from Albania to Zambia, and putting the true believers in touch with each other to form broad networks. Their handy catalog identifies 81 such institutions in Latin America (including 24 in Argentina alone), 41 in the Asia-Pacific region, 22 in the Mid-East or Africa, 149 in Eastern and Western Europe – I counted over 50 in Eastern Europe for which no separate total is available. The champion, as one would expect, is the US with 158 but Canada has 21 and the UK 18.

The existence of these 481 centers of neo-liberal or libertarian thought may well exaggerate their actual impact – for example, in the 11 centers in France, I could not identify a single well-known French intellectual, except for one economics professor at the most right-wing section of the university, a past president of Hayek's Mont Pèlerin society. Still, the speed with which they have moved, for example into Eastern Europe or some of the more IMF-infested countries of Latin America like Argentina is truly impressive. These people are organized, they run high-performance networks and they are results-oriented.

The Templeton–Atlas alliance is one more indicator of the need for progressives to counter the opposition by learning from them. One person who has understood this is a man who helped to finance the Beyond Belief conference, San Diego businessman and investor Robert Zeps, identified in the *New York Times* piece about that conference as "anti-Templeton." I tracked him down and asked him what he understood by that phrase and if he thought of himself as a pioneer. Robert Zeps was kind enough to reply to my inquiry:

> I am NOT anti-Templeton in terms of funding scientists to say mean things about religion. I (simply believe) that all study should be free of any particular agenda other than learning. One of the problems I see is that rich people . . . tend not to bother about these issues, happy to fund cancer research etc. but with no motive to fight the conservatives. Most take the position that the religious right are just nuts who are loud but frankly undeserving of a response. So in some ways I do find myself a pioneer and hope that many of my wealthy friends will follow my lead and throw some money the way of The Science Network for example. I am going to put some considerable effort into this! I believe that Bill Gates and Steve Jobs and pretty much all of the tech age

wealth is firmly on the side of science and they need to step up and say so in a way that is felt by the anti-science lobby.[16]

One wishes him, so to speak, godspeed; meanwhile, the assault on the Enlightenment is in full swing. Defensive action will take more than money, although money is an obvious first step. The "regressives" are streets ahead of the progressives when it comes to the four Ms: because progressives still don't understand the need to support ideas – in this case, the greatest ideas humankind has ever come up with concerning the nature of the universe, the structure of physical reality, and the gorgeous proliferation of life,

Stemming the assault on science in the United States may demand a different approach as well. Although perhaps inevitable in the present American context of aggressive evangelicals, militant atheism à la Dawkins to counter them may not necessarily be the best way to proceed. At least to me, it seems that the focus should not be on pitting believers against atheists – and not just because there are so many more of the former. Centuries of debate – whether between learned professors or donkey-drivers – have established that arguments about the existence and intentions of God never have been, and never will be, resolved.

On the other hand, both believers and atheists can vigorously defend, and win, the argument concerning the need for separation of Church and State and for keeping all religious belief systems out of the public sphere. This is what the French finally managed in 1905 after the long-dominant Catholic Church was obliged to leave the affairs of the Republic to secular, elected representatives. In France, the same rules apply to other religions as well.

Thomas Jefferson got it right in my view when he called for the "wall of separation." Many scientists are religious believers; this does not prevent them from doing fine research because they leave their beliefs at the door before entering the lab. Why must atheism be a prerequisite, as Dawkins insists it must, for the progress of humankind?

It is quite possible that neuroscience, evolutionary biology, and anthropology will present us with firm evidence that those of our ancestors who believed in protective supernatural beings thereby gained a survival advantage over those who didn't – such a finding would be perfectly plausible. As a species, we may now be hard-wired to believe in powers superior to our own that can help us to make our way through life.

Education of the whole society seems the only antidote to mass credulity and this is another good reason for excluding prayer from public schools, one of the neo-cons' favorite hobby-horses. People must receive the tools necessary for critical thought and that includes critical thought about the Deity, if any, and all his or her works. In the United States, obscurantist religion in particular perfectly fits the Marxist qualifier "opium of the people," but any frontal attack would immediately run up against the First Amendment: "Congress shall make no law respecting an establishment of religion or prohibiting the free exercise thereof. . ." The Communists used coercive action to rid the deluded masses of their illusions – thereby making the cure worse than the disease. Goethe said "The only thing history teaches us is that nobody ever learns anything from history," but that much at least, we ought to have learned.

Collective monotheistic religious beliefs (and rivalries) may have become dysfunctional and destructive – I personally think they have – but individual belief or disbelief in God is still an intensely private matter and protected – as it should be – in democratic societies. Judging from everything we can observe, religion consoles millions and helps them to live in less distress than would otherwise be the case. Instead of accepting such consolation, should they revolt? Maybe, but convincing them to do so and offering them an alternative is a quite different political battle from fighting against religion itself. So long as believers do not try to impose their beliefs on everyone else, as the Discovery evangelical Christians relentlessly try to do, Jefferson's "wall of separation" ought to be enough for anyone. Right now, however, it needs emergency repairs and perhaps even some barbed wire festooned across the top.

Finally, how is one to treat the argument concerning "tolerance" – your belief is as good as mine, and other relativist notions of that kind? Here I stand firmly on the side of the absolutist camp. Freedom of religion, inscribed in the Constitution, is a hard-won right for which far too many were massacred individually and collectively ("Kill them all: God will recognize his own)" and martyred in the most barbaric ways. If only to honor the memory of these countless victims, freedom of worship deserves protection, so long as it does not impinge on other people's rights, including the right to live in peace and not be witch-hunted by fanatics.

The same goes for freedom of individual speech. If I want to stand on the corner and proclaim that the moon is made of green cheese, I should be allowed to do so, but a science teacher has not only the right but the duty to give students enough knowledge and methodological skills to understand that my belief, however passionately held, is always ignorant, superstitious, and wrong. The Dover, Pennsylvania parents were right to be "intolerant" of Intelligent Design, first because it is demonstrably false and second because it impinges on the inalienable right of children to be taught the most accurate knowledge available to their time. How else are they to learn to cope with the future?

Furthermore, belief, not in a bearded-man-in-the-sky but in a universal intelligence embodying all matter, energy, consciousness, and time is at least as plausible as Dawkins's arch materialism and leaves all the room necessary for superior science.

THE HOMESCHOOLING MOVEMENT*

In the previous chapter we looked briefly at the theocratic teachings of R. J. Rushdoony and the Chalcedon Institute, intent upon throttling the Constitution and instating the Bible, specifically the Old Testament and Mosaic law, as the supreme authority of the land. Rushdoony was a pioneer of the large and growing movement to remove American children from public schools and train them at home, using special textbooks guaranteed to uphold fundamentalist prejudices. This is another clear and present danger to the Republic. It is a crime against human intelligence and reason, not a phenomenon to be "tolerated" even though it is now protected by innumerable court decisions. The degraded condition of many public schools in the United States may evoke a measure of sympathy for homeschooling parents (a few of whom are progressives) but the answer to that problem is not to cram children full of anti-scientific and irrational propaganda but to invest in the public schools, pay teachers more, and so on.

Let me begin this part with a digression, which may turn out not to be one. When I was in public elementary school in the United States, we had a daily ritual. Every morning, before beginning our lessons, we stood next to our desks, placed our right hands on our hearts, gazed up at the Stars and Stripes proudly displayed above the teacher's desk and recited the Pledge of Allegiance. "I pledge allegiance to the flag of the United States of America and to the Republic for which it

---

* People in the homeschooling movement always spell it as a single word, without a hyphen.

stands, one nation, indivisible, with liberty and justice for all."
Great words, good words for kids to remember all their lives,
which, as my own evidence shows, we do.

Sometime in the early 1950s, a Catholic organization called
the Knights of Columbus lobbied hard to wedge God into the
pledge and in 1954, it was duly changed to hail "one nation
under God, indivisible . . ." President Eisenhower approved
the change, saying, "In this way we are reaffirming the tran-
scendence of religious faith in America's heritage and future;
in this way we shall constantly strengthen those spiritual
weapons which forever will be our country's most powerful
resource in peace and war."*

Eisenhower thus imprinted on millions of tiny minds the
idea that patriotism is wedded to religion and vice versa;
whereas my own tiny mind was given to contemplate daily
some of the greatest ideals republican government ever developed, all in about 25 words. President Eisenhower muddied
the waters and ignored the First Amendment, but nobody
seems to have minded much, perhaps because no child can
be obliged to recite the pledge, even though he/she will
inevitably hear it recited every day. The Supreme Court established this principle, even for the earlier version, in 1943. A
kid of eight or nine would feel very strange and lonely not
reciting it along with his classmates, but (s)he doesn't have
to. Not satisfied, the religious "pro-life" (code for "anti-
abortion") forces now want to push through another change,
so that the pledge ends, "with liberty and justice for all, *born
and unborn.*" Mercifully, they have so far failed.

Why have I introduced the Pledge of Allegiance here?
Because it was one of those common customs like singing the

---

* Francis Bellamy, a Christian Socialist, wrote the initial version to celebrate the 400th anniversary of the discovery of America on Columbus Day
in October 1892. His granddaughter said at the time of the change that he
would not have approved the insertion of "under God."

national anthem at baseball games or marching and having a picnic and fireworks on the 4th of July, that reinforce the notion not just of patriotism but of a shared destiny, of citizens together extolling the civic virtues that make them what they are. Once God gets into it, that sense is diminished, or so it seems to me, because he is necessarily going to exclude some people.

The homeschooling movement will exclude millions more from the community of citizenship. That is, in fact, the point: they should learn to obey the Bible alone. Children put through this particular educational mill will identify themselves above all as evangelical, God-fearing Christians; not as American citizens, republicans, and democrats, with a small "r" and a small "d."

TEACHING OR PREACHING?

The Southern Baptists are not worried about such matters. With sixteen million members, theirs is the largest Protestant denomination in the United States and much of their leadership now equates registering children in public schools with "child abuse." Here is the forthright message from one of them: "If you like sexually transmitted diseases, shootings and high teen pregnancy rates, by all means, send your children to public schools."*

To root out these evils, and in light of the "spiritual, moral, and academic decay in the government schools," Southern Baptists intend to move toward Christian teaching via the

---

* The Southern Baptist Convention, its formal name, is a perfect example of the rightward shift in American religion and politics. In the late 1970s it underwent a "conservative resurgence" or a "fundamentalist takeover," depending on your point of view. The more liberal wings hived off into a confusing array of much smaller organizations and churches. An earlier split had occurred in 1845 when the majority took a position in favor of slavery. "Southern" in this context, however, has nothing to do with geography: "Southern" Baptists are to be found throughout the United States.

"Exit Strategy" (from public schools), orchestrated by an ancillary organization which borrows from the Old Testament to call itself the Exodus Mandate. These Baptists are onto something: they have noticed that the more secular the education young people receive, the more likely they are to stop going to Church, particularly when they reach high school and college age. Says another leading proponent of the movement,

> Christian parents are obligated to provide their children with a Christ-centered education. Anyone who thinks that a few hours of youth group and church will have more influence on a child's faith and worldview than forty to fifty hours a week of public school classes, activities, and homework is simply not being honest with himself.[17]

Numerous estimates indicate that homeschooling in the United States already involves at least two and a half million pupils from kindergarten to 12th grade. The movement has also become big business: sales of curricular requirements, textbooks, computer programs etc. for those students already surpass $1 billion a year. If Southern Baptist parents follow the call of their pastors and theologians, they can easily double or triple those figures.

Members of the Baptist hierarchy claim that they concluded only reluctantly and with sorrow that they must call for homeschooling throughout America. They say they could no longer wait because

> [public schools] are not even neutral on many crucial issues which are important to people of faith. Unfortunately, public education has been hijacked by people who reject biblical teachings on man's origin, the proper role of sex and the acceptability of homosexuality. These are non-compromising issues for Christians."[18]

As usual, sex looms large on the Christian agenda and California Christians in particular have expressed alarm that it will soon be illegal to "discriminate" against homosexuals in the curriculum; that sexual deviance, as Christians define it, must be "tolerated." What they term the onslaught of the "organized homosexual lobby" augments an already long list of evils catalogued by Bruce Shortt in his short book *The Harsh Truth about Public Schools*. This book is published by the Chalcedon Foundation, as we know the mouthpiece of one of the religious right's most far-out millennialist-dominionist-hard reconstructionist institutions. Shortt's book is promoted on many other sites like WorldNetDaily. So what is the "harsh truth?" It is the

> inescapably anti-Christian thrust of any governmental school system and the inevitable results: moral relativism (no fixed standards), academic dumbing down, far-left programs, near absence of discipline, and the persistent but pitiable rationalizations offered by government education professionals.

Another ancillary organization called "Homeschooling Family to Family" is dedicated to encouraging each family already homeschooling its children to convince another family to do the same and to give them all the moral support they need along the way. These proselytizers understand that many parents are worried about not doing their Christian duty but hesitate to make the leap of faith to homeschooling because they are afraid they will not be up to the job and that their children will suffer. Homeschooling Family to Family builds their self-confidence, points the way to the broad network of support groups, helps bring homeschooled children together in a variety of extra-curricular and sports activities so that they are "socialized" with each other. In short, it leads the new and inexperienced parents to the stage where they can in turn become a support family. In other contexts, this strategy might

be called "viral marketing." Whatever it's called, it is destined
to increase the number of children stuffed with the evangelical
curriculum not just on Sundays but every weekday as well.

Europeans reading this may be by now in an advanced state
of incredulity. Doesn't the government intervene? Can you
just pull your child out of a state-run or state-approved school
and teach them any rubbish you like? The answers are (1) no,
the government does not intervene and (2) yes, you can teach
nonsense – though it wasn't always that way. Education is the
province of the individual states and nearly all of them used to
have laws, particularly concerning teacher qualifications and
certification.

That they no longer do is largely thanks to the tenacity of
another evangelical organization, the Home School Legal
Defense Association (HSLDA), which now has more than
80,000 member families contributing financially to its work.
Two dogged, specialized lawyers, attorneys Mike Smith and
Michael Farris, founded HSLDA in the early 1980s and began
systematically chipping away at legal teaching requirements.
Within a mere ten years, after a string of victorious court challenges, they got rid of state laws fixing standards for teacher
certification and made homeschooling legal in all fifty states.

This is why the number of children in the system has shot
up from about 300,000 in 1990 to the estimated 2.5 million
today. In some states like Virginia, parents are not even
required to have a high-school diploma to teach their own
children: it is enough that they claim a "religious exemption."
There is no state regulation, much less federal government
regulation, of the homeschool curriculum. Nor is there any
oversight of textbooks, several of which take the "young-
earth" creationist position with the Bible account of Genesis
baldly presented as "science." The Dover, Pennsylvania trial
was an added spur to many families who resented the court's
refusal to allow the teaching of Intelligent Design in public

schools. Now parents can legally teach, and refuse to teach, whatever they please.[19]

As for the curriculum, evolution is taboo, of course, but the inventiveness of some of the "science" texts beats the best of science fiction. A quick magical mystery tour includes such incontrovertible facts as these:

- Creation of the earth took place about 6,000 years ago – sorry about the repetition, the reader already knows this;
- Carbon and other radiometric dating methods, which purport to show rocks older than 6,000 years, are unreliable;
- Being homosexual reduces life expectancy at age twenty by at least eight to twenty years and substantially increases the risk of contracting breast cancer;
- Climate change will not occur because God supplies "checks and balances" so there "is no danger of a global warming disaster;"
- The Grand Canyon was carved out by the Flood;
- If you have heard that the starlight we see now was emitted billions of years ago, this is an illusion. The speed of light used to be much faster than it is now.

We are not yet in a position to announce that the moon is made of green cheese, but please be patient, our scientists are working on the problem.

WHAT HAPPENS THEN?

So here we have all these really well-home-educated, properly indoctrinated young people eager to pursue their education at university level. Where can they go next? There are plenty of Christian colleges like the Bob Jones University or Jerry Falwell's Liberty University or the reconstructionist Regent

University, but some students will want a more elite education. Surely, however, homeschooled graduates cannot be admitted to a legitimate secular college or university? Yes, they can be and they are. Except for the very top institutions, most of the college admissions offices rely on standardized, computer-corrected exams stressing factual knowledge which are not designed to highlight or judge whether the student understands basic scientific concepts.

If these students entering secular establishments of higher learning take a first-year biology, geology, or astronomy course to satisfy the science requirement, they are in for a nasty shock. To shield their tender sensibilities, yet provide in full measure for their future, at least one institution caters to the needs of the brightest homeschool graduates. Patrick Henry College, a small school (about 250 students) set in beautiful rural Virginia within striking distance of Washington, DC, was founded in the year 2000 to cater to homeschooled evangelicals. It is succeeding beyond expectations. So far, every one of its graduates who has applied to law school, including the most prestigious, has been admitted – a 100 percent record many older and more prestigious educational institutions would envy. PHC students are sought-after in conservative Washington DC circles, where many have found internships or entry-level jobs in Congress, in key federal agencies including the FBI, and even in the White House.*[20]

Such coups are not uniquely due to evangelically minded

* Patrick Henry, one of the most famous orators in American history, pleaded with his fellow Virginians to join the revolution already underway in Massachusetts. Most schoolchildren used to be able to recite the end of his great speech, delivered on March 23, 1775: "Is life so dear, or peace so sweet, as to be purchased at the price of chains and slavery? Forbid it, Almighty God! I know not what course others may take; but as for me, give me liberty or give me death!" The slogan of the college that bears his name is "For Christ and for liberty," but the liberty proclaimed is rather more Hayekian than Revolutionary. Read or listen to Patrick Henry's inspiring rhetorical and political triumph at www.history.org/media/audio.cfm.

bureaucrats or politicians making room for the new right-wing blood: Patrick Henry graduates are undeniably good at their jobs. The College prepares them to be effective politicians, debaters, and lawyers with a curriculum heavy on logic, rhetoric, writing, and speech and communications skills (just like the Discovery Institute). Many of them major in government and PHC conscientiously prepares them for "careers of influence" as its former president put it. This former president is none other than Michael Farris – one of the crusading lawyers for the Home School Legal Defense Association who beat back the state laws preventing homeschooling in all fifty states.

Patrick Henry College has twice won the US "moot court" championship, in which students prepare legal briefs and defend them in a mock court. Aristocratic Balliol College of mighty Oxford, England, had better look to its laurels and hang its head – the Patrick Henry debating team has twice won debating competitions against Balliol, once in the US, once in Britain.

Michael Farris called his institution the first member of the "Evangelical Ivy League;" the students call their alma mater "Harvard for Homeschoolers." The rules are stringent, the dress code strict, the politics Bush-Cheynian, the morals pure and all incoming students must sign a faith statement including the proposition concerning Satan and hell, the place where "all who die outside of Christ shall be confined in conscious torment for eternity." More and more of the Patrick Henry College contingent will head straight for law-school or directly for Washington. One of their star debaters could well become the future lawyer who argues successfully in the Supreme Court to reverse *Roe* v. *Wade*.[21]

A CAUTIONARY NOTE IN CONCLUSION

The assault against the Enlightenment comes from below – from young-earth creationists and from uneducated parents bringing up children who will be less educated still. It comes from above – from sophisticated advocates with Ph.D.s allied with complacent media helping them to spread anti-scientific propaganda. Between these two millstones, above and below, rational thought and democratic practice may well be ground exceedingly fine. Do not believe that it is possible to engage in "dialogue" with these people, whether they come from the bottom or the top of the cultural heap. They do not want to discuss anything. They want to convert you and have their way, period. If you refuse conversion, they will apply coercion as soon as they take power and while waiting, they will employ various ruses.

Take it from Joe Bageant, a gifted writer who knows them of old. He was born among them, his brother is a fundamentalist preacher, he returns to his family – good, kind people who love him even though they can't talk to each other. Bageant knows whereof he speaks and we should open our ears when he tells us what world these people inhabit:

> Religious fundamentalists experience archaic states of liminal consciousness of a type long atrophied or lost to most of us. [They experience] vestigial ecstatic states such as adoration and ecstatic rapture, . . . that are little accessed by modern humans; states that lie outside reason and logic and are indeed antithetical to them.

When Bageant goes back to see his fundamentalist family and friends, he doesn't go to church with them because he knows it's too dangerous. He is still prone to ecstatic states and realizes that he too can succumb to the weeping, speaking-in-tongues persona that still lurks beneath his own progressive political surface. "It is some primitive social submersion thing and you are not as strong as you might think." A kind of group psychosis takes hold, the believer experiences blessed feelings of emotional release, "beautiful anxious joy and well-being and, yes, love."

If you stay with and participate in the cult, you can absorb this wonder drug whenever you like. Otherwise it wears off. Most people who have experienced its powerful effects stay with it and I for one, the author, do not intend to throw the first stone at them. They have lousy jobs or no job, they are working longer hours for less; a single visit to the doctor for their child costs a day's wages, they are chronically overdrawn on their credit cards and at the mercy of bill collectors. Now the subprime mortgage crisis is turfing them out of their homes. Religion is far more gratifying than the grim realities of working-class or even middle-class life in the United States and provides a sense of belonging no other institution can touch.

Next to the intense pleasure of membership in the warmth of the fold, cold reason offers few attractions. Those inside the cult can huddle together and stop feeling threatened, for a time, by those outside who do not share their vision. If push comes to shove, cult members do not care about the hard-won democratic structures of the country because they no longer benefit from them. America, whether ruled by the Republicans or the Democrats has little to offer them except hard work when they can find it and total insecurity when they can't. A theocracy would suit them very well, thank you, and non-believers have no rights. Fundamentalist Muslims are living in similar conditions and are on exactly the same trip.

We are not talking about rational argument or nor even about "may-the-best-doctrine-win" religious competition. The stakes are higher, because they imply definitively stamping out the worldview and the human progress that came with the Enlightenment, in exchange for the fundamentalist doctrine of biblical law that does indeed provide a sense of security. In the United States, there are about three times more working-class people whose education stopped, at best, with high school than there are college-educated, middle-class Americans.

All fanatical persuasions and practices follow the same rules. Years ago in Paris I saw the play *Rhinoceros* by Eugene Ionesco. In it, the playwright maps the transition, under increasing pressure, of many characters from ordinary humans to rhinoceros. Quite normal citizens undergo the metamorphosis, no matter how much they may resist, right up to the last one. Ionesco was proposing a parable about fascism or communism but religious fundamentalism is the same.

As Joe Bageant says to the rest of us well-educated, intelligent, tolerant, middle-class, democratic, dialogue-promoting types, "Wake up. You have worse enemies than you know."*

* The quotes are from Joe Bageant, "Hung over in the end times," November 11, 2004, but I fervently encourage a visit to his site at www.joe-bageant.com for an uninhibited taste of contemporary America, particularly religious America, rendered in fearless and funny prose. His book *Deer Hunting with Jesus: Dispatches from America's Class War* was scheduled for publication by Crown in 2007.

5

LOBBIES, CORRIDORS, AND SEATS OF POWER

We can have democracy in this country or great wealth concentrated in the hands of a few, but we cannot have both.

Justice Louis Brandeis, Supreme Court Justice
from 1916 to 1939

The first "lobby" was exactly that: the lobby of the House of Commons where representatives of special interest groups waited to pounce upon Members and defend their cause. American chauvinists may say that the original lobby of influence was that of the Willard Hotel in Washington, where President Ulysses S. Grant drank brandy and smoked cigars with cronies while waiting for White House refurbishment after a fire. The truth is that the Brits got there first, linguistically at least, because in the United States the practice of lobbying itself is as old as the Republic. In the 1880s, US railroad lobbyists brazenly handed out checks to legislators on the very floor of the House and the Senate. Since the nineteenth century, the techniques have become rather more sophisticated, slick, and expensive.

In the first chapter of this book, we saw how intellectuals, foundations, and think-tanks changed the American cultural landscape, but we mostly left out the contributions of big business to the great ideological shift. In Chapter 2, we looked in a limited way at the impact of lobbies like AIPAC (the "Israel lobby,") which have their own staff to press their cause. Other interest groups employ staffs but also seek out the services of specialized firms to get their line across. According to the watchdog group LobbyWatch, between 1998 and 2004, the top ten clients of the US lobbying industry handed out nearly a billion dollars to public relations companies to help them get their way with the government. These sums are in addition to their own paid staffs, some of which are quite large.

It is worth recalling here that lobbying in the US is a perfectly normal activity, protected by the Bill of Rights and seen as an expression of "free speech." If you want to know how much this or that lobby spends, there is no need to look for the information under stones and in dark corners – it's in the Congressional Quarterly and on the site of the Federal Election Commission. Groups like LobbyWatch are valuable because they compile and make sense of the data but they don't need to steal it or rely on leaks as they would have to do in Europe.

It is instructive to note that the top ten lobbies include both the American Medical Association and the American Hospital Association, doubtless diligently campaigning so that ordinary Americans will never, ever receive government-sponsored, cheaper or – heaven forbid – free national health care. Also present on the big spenders list are transnational corporation umbrella organizations, and a couple of Military Industrial Complex charter members.*[1]

The rest of the top one hundred clients list of lobby-power reads like a catalog of the usual suspects – the oil, automotive, communications, software, banking, insurance, military, electronics, and pharmaceutical industries. The only vaguely citizen-related lobby expenditures listed come from the Farm Bureau (representing the largest farmers and agribusinesses), the AFL-CIO (trade unions,)† the Association of Trial Lawyers and three associations of older people including the high-powered American Association of Retired People. The reader may remember that three surveys of the Congress classed the latter at the top of the list of the most effective lobbies in Washington, along with the gun lobby, the National Rifle Association and AIPAC. The general rule, however, is a scene dominated by big business or big business umbrella groups.

The high-flying corporate umbrella group Business Roundtable is number eight on the LobbyWatch list. It proclaims itself an association for the Chief Executive Officers of major US corporations. Their companies collectively rake in $4.5 trillion in annual revenues and, in 2005, handed out $112 billion in dividends to their shareholders. These companies also gave $7 billion to charity (that is, six percent of the amount paid to shareholders) which, judging from their sales, they could well afford. The Business Roundtable spent over

---

* The top ten line-up in order is the Chamber of Commerce, Altria Group (food and tobacco, several cigarette brands), General Electric (no.7 Pentagon supplier), American Medical Association, Northrop Grumman (no. 4 Pentagon supplier), Edison Electric Institute (nuclear industry umbrella), Verizon Communications, Business Roundtable, American Hospital Association, Pharmaceutical Research and Manufacturers.
† The American Federation of Labor and Congress of Industrial Organizations merged in 1955 to form the unified AFL-CIO which has about thirteen million members.

$5 million lobbying in just the last six months of 2006 according to the *Congressional Quarterly's* "Political Money Line" section.

The most venerable lobby of all, defending the interests of its members for nearly a century, is at the top of the big spenders' list. The US Chamber of Commerce spent $205 million on outside lobbying services between 1998 and 2004. That sum was niggardly compared to what it spent in the electoral year of 2006 for lobbying activities and political campaign contributions. That year the C of C and its affiliate, the US C of C Institute for Legal Reform, spent fully $72 million, an average of $6 million a month in addition to the cost of in-house staff. It listed fifty-six professional paid lobbyists working to influence the executive and legislative branches of government.

Whereas the Business Roundtable is strictly for the *crème de la crème* of corporate management, the Chamber of Commerce claims to represent three million businesses of all shapes and sizes, including self-employed individuals. Its "core mission is to fight for business and free enterprise before Congress, the White House, regulatory agencies, the courts. . . ." To carry out this mission, it maintains a permanent staff of over three hundred "top policy experts, lobbyists, lawyers and communicators."

THE CHAMBER OF COMMERCE AND THE CULTURE WARS: THE POWELL PRESCRIPTION

These preliminaries show that it is high time we gave business its due: just like the neo-cons and the foundations, the corporate sector had its own parallel cultural right-wing agenda, even though it had to be pushed to adopt it. A hugely influential document called the *"Powell Memorandum"* played in the world of free enterprise a role akin to that of a "Capitalist Manifesto."[2]

In August 1971, Lewis F. Powell, a distinguished corporate lawyer who also served on eleven company boards, responded to a request from his friend Eugene Sydnor, Director of the US Chamber of Commerce. Perhaps not coincidentally, President Nixon shortly afterwards named Powell to the United States Supreme Court where he served from 1972 until 1987.* His memo to Sydnor, eventually leaked, was titled *"Confidential Memorandum: Attack of American Free Enterprise System."* Never before in American history, according to Powell, had the free enterprise, i.e. capitalist system, been exposed to such threats. The attackers were numerous and determined, they had a broad base in American society and they were "gaining momentum and converts." As he saw it, leftists of all stripes were winning the ideological fight in the universities, the media, the intellectual and literary journals, in science, the arts – even in the courts and the churches. Business seemed unable to defend itself, much less retaliate – to the contrary, as he put it, the free enterprise system "tolerates, if not participates in, its own destruction."

Powell was right. Partly due to the anti-Vietnam War movement, partly because of the student revolts and the civil rights and feminist movements, the New Left in 1971 was rapidly gaining strength. The radical campus movement was in full swing: Powell cited one poll of student opinion showing that "Almost half the students favored socialization of basic US industries." More broadly appealing to public opinion and therefore especially scary to people like Powell was Ralph Nader whose attacks on business abuses had made him the "idol of millions of Americans."

Other subversives and saboteurs he identified were busy denouncing everything from corporate collusion in poisoning

---

* Once on the Supreme Court, Powell was moderate on racial and social issues, but he also extended the legal rights of business.

the environment and the food supply to tax breaks for corporations and the rich; some anti-business activists were even resorting to physical attacks against corporations and banks. Although he did not express the situation in such terms, Powell recognized that there was a Gramscian left in the US well on its way to establishing cultural hegemony at the cost of free enterprise.

Most alarming of all in Powell's eyes, at the very time more and more people wanted to interfere with business and get it under control, corporate leadership was apathetic, responding to attacks on its integrity and its right to manage its own affairs with "appeasement, ineptitude and ignoring the problem." If business could not, or would not, fight back, he predicted that its very survival was at stake.

On this basis, seventy years after Lenin, Powell laid out a capitalist "*What is to be done.*"*

Here is a summary of his memo to Sydnor of the C of C. First, business has to recognize the problem and accept it as a top priority for the attention of corporate leadership. Just running one's business profitably is no longer enough: business leaders must protect and preserve the system itself from destruction. Corporations should name a high-ranking corporate officer like an executive vice-president responsible for the counter-attack, overseeing the public relations department but doing far more than just PR. Once individual corporations have named their ideological executives, they need to coordinate. Powell's Leninist plan recognizes that

> independent and uncoordinated activity by individual corporations will not be sufficient. Strength lies in organization, in careful long-range planning and implementation, in consistency of action over an indefinite period of years, in the scale

* He writes "What specifically should be done?" and it is not sure he is conscious of the Leninist allusion although he mentions Marx and Marxism at various points in his memo.

of financing available only through joint effort, and in the political power available only through united actions and national organizations.

In this sustained warfare, the Chamber of Commerce is called upon to become the Pentagon, the war-room of free enterprise. It holds a strategic position, it is trusted by its many members and it has troops in hundreds of local Chambers who will be ready to serve and play a supportive role. The fight must begin on the college campuses of the nation, which Powell sees as the most dynamic source of the attack on the system. Social science and political science faculties are the worst, spearheading the anti-corporate movement with influential and charismatic teachers, producing effective writers, including authors of textbooks, and lecturers who spread poisonous revolutionary doctrines among the young and teach them to distrust and despise free enterprise.

To counter all this, the C of C must assemble a cadre of "highly qualified scholars in the social sciences who do believe in the system;" create a staff of professional speakers and a speakers' bureau (which will call not just on scholars but on top corporate executives). It must establish panels of "independent" experts to evaluate and criticize textbooks, because if "the authors, publishers and users of the textbooks know that they will be subjected . . . to review and critique by eminent scholars who believe in the American system," they will be more careful in what they write and "a more rational balance can be expected."

Business should demand "equal time" on campus with the communists and leftists, but what if no groups in the universities want to invite the C of C speakers? This could happen "unless the Chamber aggressively insisted on the right to be heard" and publicly denounced university administrations which did not allow the expression of "diverse views." Here the essential ingredients are "attractive, articulate and well-informed speakers" and especially "to exert whatever degree of pressure – publicly and privately – may be necessary" to make sure they get plenty of exposure. In the longer term, business must also exert pressure for better balance of teachers on the various faculties. The universities are the first priority, but the C of C should also develop programs adapted for high schools, graduate schools of business, and law schools.

These educational efforts will have an impact in the longer term, but the media – especially television – are feeding millions of people the "most insidious type of criticism of the enterprise system" every day. The criticism may result from "hostility or economic ignorance" but whatever the motives, it must be fought because it is eroding confidence in the system. Although TV is the principal target, radio and the press also deserve attention. The C of C methods must be the same as those used in the universities – a blend of experts, pressure, and ideological production, the recruiting of "staffs of eminent scholars, writers, and speakers who will do the thinking, the analysis, the writing and the speaking," with the back-up of competent communications support staffs. Powell understands too that the C of C's cadre of scholars will have to publish in reputable journals and "incentives might be devised to induce more 'publishing' by independent scholars who do believe in the system." Like money?

Powell wants to see ideological action on the move throughout the culture – in the popular and more intellectual publications, on the newsstands, in the paperback books you can buy at the airport; he wants paid advertisements and points out that if "American business devoted only ten percent of its annual advertising budget to this overall purpose, it would be a statesman-like expenditure."

Given the totally transformed scene we confront in the twenty-first century, it may be hard to believe that the campuses and television were once hotbeds of radicalism or

that serious men like Powell could argue in 1971 that "few elements of American society today have as little influence in
government as the American businessman." This "forgotten
man," he says, is ignored in Washington, whereas politicians
"stampede to support almost any legislation related to 'con-
sumerism' or to the 'environment'" – because that is what they
think the public wants. That public must be educated, but so
must the politicians themselves. The answer is to build up the
political power of business and grab the spotlight rather than
shrinking away from it.

> [S]uch power must be assiduously cultivated and when nec-
> essary, used aggressively and with determination, without
> embarrassment and without the reluctance which has been so
> characteristic of American business. As unwelcome as it may
> be to the Chamber, it should consider assuming a broader
> and more vigorous role in the political arena.

Powell sees other opportunities for promoting the cause of
free enterprise. To deal with the judicial system whose decisions are increasingly limiting the freedom of business, the C
of C must also have a cadre of highly competent lawyers and
counter the claims of the American Civil Liberties Union and
the labor unions in court. It can also have an impact among
the 20 million ordinary American shareholders who have a
financial interest in strengthening business. But wherever the
cultural offensive is waged, it must be done with a "more
aggressive attitude."

All this is going to cost a great deal of money and require
the participation of top management. The cadre of speakers,
scholars, lawyers, and the C of C's own personnel must earn
competitive salaries and the Chamber itself must grow bigger,
more professional, and restructure its management. But the
inputs of money and time will be worth it: cultural offensive

is the only answer because, as Powell concludes, "business and the enterprise system are in deep trouble, and the hour is late." We need only breathe the air of the present, twenty-first-century climate to recognize the spectacular success of the Powell prescription. The C of C not only became the far larger and more professional (and aggressive) organization he wanted but business dug deep into its pockets. It helped to build up the think-tanks like Heritage and the American Enterprise Institute as well as a variety of its own ideological lobbying organizations and movements. These efforts bore fruit in the 1980s when it cooperated fully with the Reagan administration's "[keep your] hands-off business" approach. With George W. Bush, corporate dominance has reached undreamed of heights and it is unlikely a future Democratic presidency could challenge this presence in significant ways.[3]

Thirty-five years after Powell administered his shock-treatment, among its listed accomplishments in 2006, the Chamber "successfully blocked efforts to raise the minimum wage . . . that would have increased [it] to $7.25 an hours over two years." Fortunately, the newly elected Congress with a Democratic majority voted in early 2007 to raise the wage to that level. The Chamber of Commerce expressed disappointment that the minimum wage, which had been stagnating for years at $5.15 (Euros 3.50 or £2.50 at November 2007 exchange rates) did not stay there. Despite this long-delayed increase, the subject of the minimum wage deserves a bit of elaboration because it shows where the US stands on labor issues. We shall return to the C of C and other lobbies presently.

LIVING ON A SHOESTRING – SO WHERE ARE THE SHOES?

One of the laws passed under Franklin Roosevelt's New Deal established for the first time in 1938 a federal minimum wage.

"Federal" means that no individual state can pay under that rate. Over half of the American states also have minimum wage laws and when that is the case, workers are entitled to receive the higher wage set by the state. In 2007, before Congress voted the recent increase, the minimum had been stuck at $5.15 an hour for a decade. In constant dollars, this was less that the $6.28 a worker was making in 1950 and a huge drop from the minimum wage buying power in 1968, which was $9.28. A wage of $5.15 an hour is impossible to live on decently, which is one reason so many Americans are "maxed out" on their credit cards. Without family solidarity or access to food banks and other charity, the slightest mishap, like a car-repair or a child's high fever becomes a tragedy.

At $5.15 per hour, you could earn the miserable, below-poverty level yearly salary of $10,712, but in that case, you would have to work forty hours a week fifty-two weeks a year. This gets you the equivalent in continental Europe or Ireland of €7,284; in the UK £5,248 a year; that is, €607 or £437 per month. In 2009, when the new wage increase takes full effect, the minimum wage worker can look forward to an annual income of $15,080 a year, but again only if he/she works forty hours a week fifty-two weeks a year. Now the comparison with Europe and the UK becomes €10,254 and £7,389 a year; or €854 and £615 a month. Better, but not exactly seventh heaven and still way below 1968 US purchasing power levels. Note that the ironically named "Fair Labor Standards Act" does not require paid holidays or sick leave. The rule of thumb for American workers and employers is simple: "no pay for time not worked." Just avoid being sick or going on holiday. Overtime is paid time-and-a-half above forty hours a week.

How bad is the real situation for working people? It is both better and worse than these raw figures suggest. Although the minimum wage, even at $7.25, is no bed of roses, the latest available US Department of Labor statistics show that *average* hourly earnings were in 2005 a shade over $17 an hour or €11.56 / £8.33. In the manufacturing sector, which is shedding jobs as trees shed leaves in the fall, hourly wages of specialized workers can be quite high, well into the $20s. The *median* US wage (as many workers above it as below it) in 2005 was $46,326 a year and the median weekly wage $638. However, compared to the year 2000, this median yearly wage was down by $1,273. During those five Bush years of "compassionate conservatism," from 2000–5, four million people were added to the official poverty rolls for a total of 37 million people or 12.6 percent of the population. Official poverty line definitions underestimate the number of people living in extremely adverse conditions.

The Department of Labor counts the number of people actually paid at or below the minimum wage as only 2.5 percent of the waged labor force. This is a stark improvement from a quarter century ago; in 1980, 15 percent of wage-earners were classed in that category (although the wage was then higher in terms of purchasing power). Discrimination is still obvious, however: women make up fully two-thirds of all workers paid at or below minimum wage level.

Despite the obvious hardships for the nearly two million people at the bottom of the heap, the real problems for most workers lie elsewhere. Sixty percent of all working Americans earn hourly wages, not monthly salaries and this proportion of the total labor force has scarcely varied since the 1970s. Sorry about all the numbers, but we need them to understand the plight of millions of American job-holders.

Although it is true that unemployment in the US is, strictly speaking, under five percent, this figure does not take into account the huge prison population of over two million and it particularly excludes vast numbers of involuntary part-time workers. In 2005, more than 75 million workers earned hourly rates, some of them decent rates, but 21 percent of them, 15.8 million, worked less than 34 hours a week whereas most of them would have preferred working fulltime. Six million other hourly wage-earners also worked from 45 to 60-plus hours a week – the Bureau of Labor Statistics stops counting at sixty. You would stop counting too if you were working five twelve-hour days a week (or six ten-hour ones). Although the Bureau does not say so, these are on the whole people holding down two part-time jobs rather than people earning significant overtime pay.

Poorly paid workers are overwhelmingly concentrated in the "service occupations" which now make up about four-fifths of the total US economy. The worst off, mostly women, are employed in "food preparation and serving related occupations" and in retail sales.[4] As well-paying manufacturing jobs are steadily lost to China and other low-wage countries, people whose jobs disappear are forced to find new employment in low-pay service jobs where they may even earn *less* than the minimum wage. The rock bottom wage for occupations like restaurant waiter or waitress is legally – get ready – $2.13 an hour. Food-servers are expected to survive on tips. Foreigners dining out in the United States do not understand such barbaric customs and often leave disappointingly small change behind whereas 20 percent of the bill would be more appropriate. Waitresses fight not to have to serve foreigners, especially Brits . . .*

I know this because I have read Barbara Ehrenreich's remarkable book *Nickel and Dimed* in which she chronicles the life of a woman, herself, caught in such occupations. In her case, it was voluntary. She moved from Florida to Maine to Minnesota, working as a waitress, a hotel maid, a cleaning woman, a nursing home aide and a Wal-Mart sales clerk. She learned that even the lowliest occupations require exhausting mental and physical effort and that one job is not enough. If you insist on living

---

* To understand why tipping, especially in the US, is indeed a barbaric custom, see Daniele Archibugi's economic, sociological, and ethical analysis: "Tips and Democracy," *Dissent*, vol. 51, no. 2, Spring 2004, pp. 59–64 and his website at www.danielearchibugi.org.

indoors rather than in your car or on the street, you need at least two. If you are from out of town and have no family to fall back on, you are never going to save enough money to pay three months' advance rent on a room or a flat and you will have to live in motels. Even the down-market ones are expensive.

Ehrenreich, a professional writer, did this work as a social experiment – she had the education and social status to make her getaway once she had gathered her material and she possessed the skills to tell the story. Above all, she knew the situation was temporary and that she could escape at any time, for example if she fell ill. Most people stuck in these jobs are just plain stuck and their situation is not going to improve. As Holly Sklar points out, food preparers and servers must often depend on food banks to feed their families; health-care aides can't afford health insurance and childcare workers can't save enough for the education of their own children.[5]

The US economy siphons ever-greater wealth from working people to those already best-off rather than satisfying the need for food, shelter, clothing, transport, health, education, and so on of every person in the population, regardless of birth, race, or station in life. To most Americans, this seems the natural order of things and it is astonishing to observe that they remain on the whole good-humored and optimistic. Although I can no longer track down the reference, I distinctly recall a poll showing that with regard to their own wealth and status, 19 percent of Americans questioned believed that they themselves were in the top one percent of all income earners. A further 20 percent said, No, they were not yet in the top one percent but they would be one day.

THE TOP-HEAVY WEALTH PYRAMID

In reality, they have few grounds for optimism. American wealth is hugely skewed and is growing more so by the day.

The point of the pyramid in the USA is made of solid gold; the base of base metal. Again sorry for all the figures, but you can perhaps forgive them since some are quite attention-grabbing.

In 1980, the ratio of the earnings of a corporate Chief Executive Officer to the earnings of the average worker was 42 to 1. By 2002, the CEO was earning more than 400 times the pay of the average worker. We can show this contrast in another way. In 1968, the highest paid CEO in the United States made as much money as 127 average workers and 239 minimum wage workers. In 2005, the highest paid CEO received as much as 7,443 average workers and 23,282 minimum-wage workers.[6] Other comparisons show how much more society values CEOs than, say, public schoolteachers. Here the ratio was one CEO=63 average schoolteachers in 1990 but 264 teachers in 2001.[7]

The top one percent of the US population has captured a third of the total national wealth and the next 19 percent a further 51 percent, meaning that the top 20 percent of Americans hold 84 percent of total net worth (assets minus debts). This leaves just 16 percent for the remaining 80 percent of the population.* When only financial wealth is considered (no houses or other fixed assets counted), the top one percent has 40 percent of it, and the top 20 percent a staggering 91 percent. Between 1973 and 2005, real incomes for the top five percent went up by over half.[8]

This is nothing compared to the top 0.001%. I tend to get lost in these tiny percentages and lurch between the US and European notation systems: what I mean here is one person in 10,000, or about 30,000 Americans altogether, who are truly the Happy Few. From the late 1960s to the late 1990s, they increased their share of total American income from 0.5 percent to 2.5 percent. Expressed differently, these super-rich

* Worldwide, wealth is skewed in about the same proportions.

had as much income as 15 percent of the (poor) population of the United States, probably the only country in the world where 30,000=45,000,000.[9]

That gives the story for income. Let us now hark back to the story of net worth, which is total wealth, comprising all assets including those that cannot readily be converted to cash (like real estate, private jets, or yachts), minus debts. According to Federal Reserve figures, in the decade from 1995 to 2004, the net worth the bottom quarter of the US population increased by eight percent, while the worth of the top ten percent shot up by 77 percent (reflecting large increases in house prices among other factors).

In terms of net worth, one can refine even further the figure of 30,000=45 million people, a comparison which counts only their income. The higher you go on the ladder of success, the greater the concentration of wealth. Every year, the business magazine *Forbes* provides its list of billionaires, eagerly awaited by the rich and famous. In early 2007, the top 400 Americans had total wealth of $1.25 trillion or, if you prefer $1,250 billion. How much is that? It is ten percent of total US Gross Domestic Product, which the Organization for Economic Cooperation and Development (OECD) placed in 2005 at $12,428 billion.[10]

Despite globalization, which everywhere is sucking wealth upwards and concentrating it in the bejewelled hands of people in other parts of the world, the 2007 world crop of Forbes billionaires list is still 40 percent American. You already know that Bill Gates is the richest man on earth with $56 billion according to the Forbes 2007 list. But what about the Walton family of Wal-Mart fame; one of the places Barbara Ehrenreich worked for a pittance? Wal-Mart's orientation is unabashedly right-religious; it is in their monster stores that the books of the *Left Behind* series about Armageddon and the Rapture first began flying off the shelves. The Lord has certainly provided for the founding family: Six members of this clan dwarf Gates' stature with a total haul for the family of over $83 billion in 2007. Meanwhile, during the golden Bush years from 2000 to 2005, the number of "severely poor" Americans increased by 26 percent (to 16 million). Wages, the main source of income for most people, fell by 6.5 percent between 2001 and 2004.

PLENTY OF CHILDREN LEFT BEHIND

The chasm in American wealth distribution is unlikely to be bridged any time soon. The poor are stuck at the bottom partly because education, potentially the great equalizer, is failing them and the school system is geared to keeping them where they are.

According to the American comic actor W. C. Fields, "No man who hates children can be entirely bad." Well, George Bush has tried to convince the nation that he loves children. His concern is enshrined in the law called No Child Left Behind (NCLB), passed in 2002. The US has a Department of Education (4,500 employees and a $71 billion budget) but there is no such thing as a national curriculum or national examinations as is usual in Europe.

The system for funding public education in the US is extremely complex and depends on all three levels of government: federal, state, and local.[11]* The federal government gives grants to states, supposedly on criteria of need and probably also based on their political leanings and how much influence their political representatives have in Washington. Total

---

* "Public education" in this context and in what follows means free public schools in kindergarten and grades one through 12 or "K-12" in US statistics. Colleges (universities) may be public or private and their quality and prestige vary enormously but none of them is free. Students without full scholarships always pay some tuition. The full cost of a year at one of the top universities in 2006–7 was about $45,000.

spending on education from all sources – federal, state, and local – for the year 2004–5 in all 50 states came to $419 billion (for about 48 million schoolchildren) of which the federal government provided only nine percent. The importance of Federal grants to the 50 states varies; in 2005, for example, they counted for 17 percent of the total education budget in South Dakota but only three percent in New Jersey. The rest of the schools' money comes from a mix of state and local taxes.

The states are divided into myriad school districts – more than 15,000 for the entire United States – whose school boards have a large measure of autonomy.* Recall the court case concerning the teaching of Intelligent Design brought by parents against the school district of Dover, Pennsylvania. No one at the state level of Pennsylvania, much less the federal government, was dictating to the Dover school board what it could and couldn't teach. School boards also enjoy varying measures of financial autonomy; because of differences in funds raised through local property taxes, some are far more opulent than others.

The proportion contributed to the public education budget by state and local sources also varies enormously from one state to another. In 2004–5, the two extremes of state contributions were Vermont whose government provided 87 percent of total funds; and Nevada, where the state contributed only 27 percent. The national average for contributions by state governments the same year was 47 percent of total education budgets. Funding drawn from local government contributions reverses these proportions – 65 percent in Nevada and six percent in Vermont – with all kinds of mixes in between. The national average for local funding was 43 percent of total

---

* 15,000 reflects profound reform and concentration of school districts – sixty years ago there were over 120,000.

education budgets. These percentages tell us nothing, however, about the total size of the budget, nor how much it can buy.

For that information, we need to know how much money is actually spent per district per child in the public schools. The top funders are New Jersey and New York, spending $13,370 and $12,879 on average for each pupil. At the bottom are Arizona and Utah ($5,474 and $5,032) and the national average is $8,661. Thus some states are spending on each child 150 percent of the national average, others only 60 percent of it. Once again, however, averages and "funds per pupil" do not tell the whole story. Local funding in this multi-ingredient financial soup is crucial because each school district is dependent to some degree on local taxes levied on private property.

Consequently, the amount spent per child can vary enormously from school to school, even within the same state. The children of wealthy suburban property owners can expect good libraries, well-equipped science labs and plenty of computers in their schools, not to mention gyms and sports facilities. Inner-city kids must often be content with obsolete text-books, grimy, run-down buildings, and limited facilities. Guess which group will get college preparation courses, foreign language training, science, art, music . . . In short, the system is rigged.

Neo-conservatives think children are getting too much. When a Senior Fellow of the neo-con Manhattan Institute learned that New York had increased school spending by a further five percent and was second only to New Jersey in per-pupil outlays at close to $12,900, he angrily denounced the "spending frenzy for state schools . . . [the figure] really highlights how indefensible it is to be increasing spending this much." This gentleman was not heard to complain that some school districts on posh Long Island spend $16,200 per student, but it is well known that art, music, history, games, and so on are "frills" when offered to poor children but necessities for rich ones.[12]

Aside from its small contribution to the overall state education budgets, the federal government sets standards and mandates compliance by the states with federal programs. Among its special projects are the "Teachers Incentive Fund" to reward teachers who accept jobs in particularly disadvantaged school districts; research support to determine the most effective teaching methods; grants to college students who major in math, science, engineering, "critical foreign languages" and the like.

No Child Left Behind (NCLB) is the federal government's most ambitious educational initiative by far. This law, passed in 2002, increased at a stroke the national government's involvement in education, which was previously limited mostly to providing special help to children "at risk" (physically or mentally impaired or otherwise severely disadvantaged). No Child Left Behind, as seen by federal government spokespersons, claims to "help schools improve by focusing on accountability for results, freedom for states and communities, proven education methods, and choices for parents." The law stipulates that the states must cooperate in assessing their pupils, regularly testing the English language skills (mainly reading) of at least 95 percent of all children enrolled. In 2007, standardized math tests were being phased in as well. The overall goal is "grade level proficiency for all by 2014."

"Grade level proficiency" simply means that every kid in, say, fourth grade should be able to read as well as the average kid in fourth grade as fixed by a government benchmark. Each school must collate the test scores of its pupils in order to pass the Acceptable Yearly Progress test. NCLB introduces competition between schools by giving parents the freedom to transfer their children to schools boasting better progress performance records. The government also helps the schools by sharing its research on educational methods through the "What Works Clearing House."

When one browses the Department of Education site and checks out the "Blue Ribbon Schools Program," it is clear that some schools are, to their credit, making a genuine effort and improving their results. More children are indeed achieving "grade-level" results from year to year; this includes, for instance, an inner city school in Houston, Texas where the kids are 97 percent black (the other three percent are Hispanic). The Secretary of Education says that, nation wide, reading scores for nine year olds have increased more in the past five years than in the previous twenty-eight years; that gaps between black/Hispanic and white children are gradually closing.[13]

So much the better, but the NCLB law has no pretensions to equalizing total funding for American schools and no commitment to really giving each American child an equal chance, no matter how rich or poor their parents are, what color they are, or where they live. Seen from the perspective of the teachers and the state education authorities, the NCLB is nowhere near the rousing success story the federal government trumpets. The powerful National Education Association (NEA, whose excellent and thorough research I've used above) has 2.7 million members – teachers and other education personnel – and it is harshly critical of NCLB. So is the Center on Education Policy, an "independent advocate for improved public schools that monitors school reform policies to determine their effect."

Both these organizations have done broad surveys and what they hear from the grass roots is not encouraging. First off, the NCLB law is 1,100 pages long and, five years after its passage, schools supervisors are still trying to sort out exactly what is required of them. The law mandates extra burdens for schools; local districts have to pay for "more bureaucracy, standardized testing, transportation, private tutoring, and other costly demands," but the government does not reimburse them for these extra costs. To the contrary: federal grants to schools have been reduced and frozen and are at least $9.5 billion less than had been promised for implementing the law. Two-thirds of all districts reported equal or lower funding for the 2006–7 school year compared to 2005–6.

All over the country, schools are expected to do more with less. The NCLB law specifies that schools not making "Adequate Yearly Progress" for two years in a row must provide private tutoring for the students falling behind. This is fine in theory, but the providers of these services include profit-making companies and non-profit groups, often many different ones serving the same population, and schools are supposed to monitor these tutors at their own expense. Thirty-eight states reported they were not able to oversee "whether those providers are effectively raising test scores" for the pupils concerned. Not only must the schools pay for the tutoring but they also have to find funds for extra staff in order to comply with the law's monitoring requirements.

Meanwhile, education professionals report, the NCLB "eliminates programs proven to help students succeed, such as comprehensive school reform, drop-out prevention, parental assistance centers and history, arts and foreign language education." Because the federal government grades schools solely according to their results on standardized reading (and now math) tests; because schools are punished with further extra costs (and less money) if they are not up to scratch, thousands of them are coping with the financial crunch by cutting back on other subjects. Teachers of English as a second language are dismissed, even in districts with majority immigrant populations. Since 2002 when the law was passed, "71 percent of the nation's 15,000 school districts have reduced time spent on subjects like art, social studies, and history." So much for leveling the playing field and even modest training in critical thinking.

The future looks bleak. In accordance with the NCLB law, a school that has not reached the Adequate Yearly Progress target for five years running must be "restructured" – again at the expense of the state, not the federal government. No one quite knows what this provision will entail. In California, eight percent of public schools are already marked for "restructuring," but evidence of poor performance in many other states will soon kick in. The states already know that they will again face a shortfall of millions if not billions of dollars.[14]

All this sounds like a long-term strategy to downgrade one of the few remaining public services in the United States. Allow the quality to decline sufficiently and parents will be prepared to make any sacrifice for their children's education. Those who can afford it will send their children to private schools, often run by one or another religion. Neo-liberals will chant the "free to choose" mantra and push for a nationwide school-voucher system. What is there to choose between a dilapidated, perhaps dangerous school and a clean, orderly, well-equipped one where the atmosphere is conducive to learning? Of course, it will cost something, but that's life, isn't it? People get what they deserve; so do their children.

If the parents can make the sacrifice, it will be their offspring's ticket to the future, because when a child has been left behind by the public school system, (s)he will have no opportunity to obtain a higher education. A college degree is costly, most students need to borrow to obtain it, but about a million are now getting one every year because it has become indispensable for a decent career – even to get a foot on the first rung of the ladder. The US used to be a place where, in a single generation, poor or immigrant children could leap the hurdles separating lower from middle class. One salary was enough for a family to live in dignity and education provided the road "onwards and upwards." That era is long gone. Today, America more and more resembles a feudal society in which privilege is hereditary and most people remain trapped in the class into which they were born.

Census bureau figures confirm that a college degree is a requirement for a successful life today. In 2005, only 28 percent of Americans over twenty-five had graduated from a four-year college or gone on for a higher academic qualification (a masters or doctoral degree) or a professional degree in a field like law or medicine. Nearly half the country (46 percent) in 2005 had only a high-school diploma. An additional 15 percent of school drop-outs lacked even that; the rest had "some college." What can these different categories expect from life? Median earnings (as many people above the figure as below it) of high-school graduates in 2005 were $26,500 but only $17,400 to $20,300 without a high school diploma. A four-year college degree in contrast was worth a median $43,100 on the job market and a masters degree $52,000 – earnings double those of someone with only a high-school diploma. Over a lifetime, the financial difference in educational attainment can often be measured in millions.[15]

These class distinctions are self-perpetuating and reinforced daily in the "land of equal opportunity." Even a top university like the California Institute of Technology, credited with a scrupulously fair admissions policy for choosing among many applicants (for example not giving preference to children of its alumni) contributes to this process despite its high ideals.

(CalTech's) admissions officers, by their own account, find it painfully necessary to reject candidates who have passion and talent but who, having attended inferior high schools, lack the advanced placement courses and test scores proving strong science preparation.

The *New York Times* published the "honest talk" a former college president said he had always wanted to deliver to his first year students – but never dared give.

> More than half of the freshmen at selective colleges, public and private, come from the highest earning quarter of households. Tell me the ZIP code and I'll tell you what kind of college a high school graduate most likely attends.

Race and gender inequality still present some serious problems in American society, but in the social stratum inhabited by the kind of people who attend the good, selective US universities these are no longer dominant issues. The obstacle to advancement is not race or gender but poverty, which is to say the problem is class.[16]

POST-BUSH IMPROVEMENTS?

The National Education Association with its 2.7 million members and chapters in all fifty states is in a sense a "lobby" but unfortunately not a very successful one. A successful lobby gets legislation passed that favors the interests of its constituents and obtains federal money for the purposes it specifies. Is the shift to a Democrat-dominated Congress going to make a difference on the Washington scene?

Perhaps so, marginally. Whatever their party, however, any Congressional representatives can be counted on to vote mostly for the transnational corporate agenda. As the *Washington Post* reported in March 2005, "Fortune 500 companies . . . are emerging as the earliest beneficiaries of a government controlled by President Bush and the largest GOP House and Senate majority in half a century."[17]

The new Congress is not likely to reverse this process significantly for one paramount reason: the system of political campaign financing. Dozens of members of Congress are themselves millionaires, probably at least a quarter of the total, which is lucky for them, given the cost of political campaigns. The 2004 presidential election pitted two extremely wealthy men, George Bush and John Kerry, against each other. Congress may "represent" Americans in the electoral sense, but certainly not sociologically.

The financing system institutionalizes corruption while calling it by another name and the corporate constituency is easily the largest contributor to electoral campaigns. Every time legislation is passed to "reform" the system, clever lawyers find loopholes you could drive a campaign bus through. Corporate donors hedge their bets and fund both parties although the Republicans have had a definite edge, generally collecting 55 percent of the total. In 2005–6, "industry groups" gave $311 million to political candidates – "organized labor" (which we shall look at in a moment), accounted for 19 percent of these funds – not quite $60 million – while over $250 million came from business.* Tax cuts for the wealthy, a Bush specialty, may also cause grateful donors to open their hearts and their wallets for the party that takes such pity on rich people.

Corporate interests are thereby diligently served. The stagnation of the minimum wage at $5.15 an hour for a decade was a lavish gift to employers. The "Bankruptcy Abuse

---

* The top industry contributions to political candidates in 2005–6 (amounts in $ millions) came from: Finance/Insurance (52), Health Care (41), Energy/Natural Resources (22), Business & Retail Services (22), Communications/Technology (21), Transportation (21), Real Estate/Construction (20), Agriculture (18), Law (14). The total was up by $45 million compared to the 2003–4 electoral cycle.

Prevention" law of 2005 represents, according to lawyers, "a big win for commercial landlords;" while the National Rifle Association is as ever riding high. Firearms remain the only unregulated "consumer good" sold to the American public and the gun industry will be further shielded by the ban on class-action lawsuits through the "Protection of Lawful Commerce of Arms" bill. This bill, passed by the previous Republican Congress, was co-sponsored by fifty-two Democrats.

Once in a while, a corporate demand goes unmet. For example, Congress has not outlawed class action lawsuits by employees against companies, despite loud complaints from retailers like Wal-Mart. Several courts have found the company, now the world's largest employer, guilty of various abuses and Wal-Mart owes compensation to many of its workers or former workers.

What is the latest news about that perennial favorite, the military-industrial complex? In 2006, a courageous Congress stood up to George Bush, who had requested a defense budget of $513.3 billion. Putting its collective foot down, Congress awarded him only $512.9 billion. This included $50 billion in "Emergency Costs for the Global War on Terror" (the GWOT is always capitalized on Capitol Hill) and $86 billion for weapons procurement, a nice contribution to corporate balance sheets.[18]

What, then, of the "good guys" who can be expected to try and help ordinary Americans? This is where trade unions come in: they too are a lobby and they are fighting corporate interests in order to advance working people's rights. Most of their political campaign money ($59.5 million in 2005–6) predictably goes to Democratic candidates. Although the Chamber of Commerce lost the fight on the minimum wage bill when the Democrats regained power, it still hoped to beat back another union effort called the Employee Free Choice Act. The C of C called it the No Choice Act.

The present procedure for organizing a trade union on a work-site, at least in theory, is the following. When the workers of a given employer want to form a union, 30 percent of them can petition the National Labor Relations Board (another Roosevelt New Deal invention). The NLRB will then duly send out an official to set up and observe the vote to determine whether the majority of the workers in question wants to form a union or not. The vote is by secret ballot, guaranteed by the NLRB. The unions have good reasons for wanting to change this procedure, but if you were to read only the Congressional testimony of Mr CC of the C of C (Charles Cohen, expert witness for the Chamber of Commerce), you would think the union hierarchy, notably the AFL-CIO, was out to destroy democracy-as-we-know-it. Cohen, a specialized labor lawyer, cites many Supreme Court decisions and claims that

> The threat . . . is the Employee Free Choice Act –more accurately [. . .] described as the Employee No Choice Act, [which] would, in nearly all cases, eliminate government supervised secret ballot elections and instead turn the National Labor Relations Board into a card-counting agency. The motivating force . . . is the steady decline in union membership among the private sector workforce in the United States. Unions today represent only about 7.4% of the private sector workforce, about half of the rate twenty years ago.[19]

If, however, you listen also to the unions and particularly to their members who have been sacked for trying to form a union, the picture changes. The AFL-CIO can show that one in five workers who try to organize their workplace lose their jobs. Somehow, American employers just do not love unions. Even when the workers get as far as collecting enough signatures and petitioning the National Labor Relations Board;

even when the Board comes in and organizes a secret ballot; even when the workers win the vote; still over a third of employers procrastinate and never agree to sign a union contract. So nothing changes.

Employers use other tactics as well. Still according to AFL-CIO, half of all companies threaten to close the plant if it is unionized (but only one percent actually do so). They manipulate pre-election information; employers do not allow union representatives from outside to visit the workplace, whereas private, paid anti-union consultants are free to spread whatever propaganda they choose among the workers. Over 90 percent of employers require that their workforce attend closed-door meetings organized specifically against unionization where they will only hear the boss's side of the story. Meanwhile, still according to union sources, 60 million non-unionized workers say they want to have a union in their workplace and 77 percent of the American public supports them.[20]

This is why the unions propose the Employee Free Choice Act. If half the workers sign cards saying they want a union, they can have one. As the relevant Congressional sub-Committee chairperson, George Miller, puts it,

> The Employee Free Choice Act is very simple. It says that if a majority of workers in a workplace sign authorization cards in support of a union, then they get a union. That's it. Workers are still free to choose a National Labor Relations Board election if they wish.

The act would also establish stronger penalties for violations of employee rights when workers seek to form a union and during first-contract negotiations. Independent mediation and arbitration for first-contract disputes would also be available.

The bill passed the House easily in March 2007. In the

Senate, however, a two-thirds majority (so 60 votes) was needed to halt debate and bring the bill to the floor for a vote. Here it lost, by 51 to 48. The AFL-CIO has not given up, however, and points to increasing support, including that of sixteen state governors and all the major Democratic party candidates for President. They will try again later but that means a wait until 2009 at the least and the lobbyists for the other side are not going to give up easily.

One of these lobbyists, a particularly rabid enemy of labor, figures on the distinguished list of "The Thirteen Scariest People in America" compiled by a group of independent journalists on an alternative website.[21] This coveted award goes to Richard Berman, a Washington PR man whose specialty is inventing innocent, public-spirited sounding entities whose vocation is to spread anti-union, anti-worker propaganda.

They have names like the Employment Policies Institute, the Center for Consumer Freedom, or the Center for Union Facts. Mr Berman is Executive Director of all these innocuously named front groups, which, because they are supposed to be "non-profit" think-tanks, receive tax-exempt status. Once the fronts are established, Berman solicits charitable "donations" from his corporate clients who can also claim tax-exemption on them; he then uses the money to campaign for corporate interests. It's a neat, if totally dishonest system, ethically speaking, but so far, it seems to be legal. The "think-tanks" produce "reports" that Berman then peddles to the press, carefully omitting any mention of Berman's connections to industry clients and rarely informing readers that the source of the report is a Berman front group. His targets have included – for the tobacco industry – mandatory non-smoking areas in restaurants, and studies showing that smoking causes lung cancer and heart disease. For the purveyors of junk food, whether manufacturers or restaurant chains, he attacks efforts to cut junk food consumption.

Berman brags that his lobbying firm is different from others because "We always have a knife in our teeth" and because he only goes after the "big issues" that are most important to shareholder value – like keeping wages and benefits low for workers and taxes low for employers. Every time a scientific study appears showing the harmful effects and public health crises due to cigarettes, alcohol, sugar, or fat-laced foods, Berman removes the knife from his teeth and plunges it into the heart of the messenger. His blanket tactic is to make war against what he calls the "Nanny Culture – the growing fraternity of food cops, health care enforcers, anti-meat activists and meddling bureaucrats who know 'what's best for you.'" Since Mr Berman is said to rake in about $10 million a year, the Nanny-killing strategy must be working.[22]

CORPORATE BUYERS, CLIMATE LIARS

The neo-liberal United States, especially under Bush, has walked on two legs: lies and denial. The dire consequences of both will drag on for decades. The contest for "Most Dangerous Lie" is doubtless between Iraq and climate change. It's a tough call, but I vote for climate change because it is the issue on which the top management of corporate and political America, basically a few hundred people, have long called the shots for the entire planet. These men (plus a few women) are the ones responsible for the *Financial Times* headline proclaiming "World faces more disease, starvation and mass migration."[23]

Although the human suffering caused by the invasion of Iraq already reaches well beyond the borders of that miserable country; although the encouragement and ammunition this war has given to terrorist organizations will have untold bloody consequences for thousands; climate change will cause afflictions on a scale as yet unimagined and perhaps unimaginable. The horrors to come, far sooner than previously supposed, sound like a biblical catalog of plagues. As the scientist Martin Parry, co-chair of the UN's Intergovernmental Panel on Climate Change, speaking of the impact, explains "It's exactly what you don't want."

There will be much more water in already humid areas and far more severe drought where it is already dry. The scientists predict an extra 250 million victims of hunger, far more widespread malaria, dengue fever, yellow fever, and Nile fever; heavier rainstorms, more frequent hurricanes, floods putting millions at risk, wildfires, severe crop failures, the death of coral reefs. They foresee accelerated species extinction plus another fifty million climate refugees on the move, not by 2100 as reported earlier, but tomorrow, by 2010. And as always, the poor will suffer most. In Europe, the foretaste was the wildfire attacking Olympia in Greece, site of the first Olympic games in 776 BC. In the United States, fires attacked even the rich and famous, in Malibu, California. No one is sheltered.

The United Nations Intergovernmental Panel on Climate Change, IPCC, probably represents the broadest scientific consensus in human history. Set up by the UN in 1988, its reports have become increasingly alarmed and alarming. Should we believe these reports? Inherently, yes, because they are extraordinarily conservative, "even timid," as George Monbiot says, charting the process that leads to their publication.[24]

Monbiot, a journalist and writer with a scientific background, has followed the subject of climate change closely for years and knows many of the people involved; his book *Heat* is a best-seller, he has made a film about climate change for Britain's Channel Four; in short he is a credible witness. How do IPCC reports reach the public?

First the hundreds of scientists confront the evidence and

achieve, or not, agreement about it. No consensus, no publication. When they are finally ready to publish, the politicians swoop down and "seek to excise anything which threatens their interests." The United States is always in the front ranks brandishing the scissors; China, Russia, and Saudi Arabia are its chief accomplices and I shall not insult the reader by explaining why. The scientists then fight back, trying to preserve the integrity of their work but they always have to concede some points. This time, according to one of the scientists involved in the 2007 report, most references to positive feedbacks (self-reinforcing processes accelerating climate change) had to be junked at the demand of governments.

This, says Monbiot, is "the opposite of the story endlessly repeated in the right-wing press: that the IPCC, in collusion with governments, is conspiring to exaggerate the science." In this conservative fantasy, the world's most constrained, least adventuresome scientific body becomes part of a mass green conspiracy out to prove deliberate scientific falsehoods and to destroy economic prosperity. The line the right wing takes may remind the reader of the Discovery Institute's methods: people who claim that climate change is coming or is already upon us are trying to "stifle debate" and have "something to hide." Those who disbelieve and speak out against the majority are courageous victims who are "being censored."

Let's be serious. Where is the real skulduggery in this story? Who are the victims? Let us call a star witness to testify before the court of opinion. Exxon Mobil, please take the stand. It is true, is it not, that in terms of sales, you are the world's top transnational corporation. In 2006, your profits hit an all-time record for all corporations of 40 billion dollars. Have you not used this vast wealth to deceive and mislead public opinion about climate change?

Exxon would be laughing its head off. True, its sales are higher than those of any other transnational corporation in the world; true, it salted away record profits of $40 billion in 2006, but all the opinions it wanted to buy and all the propaganda it wanted to spread came incredibly cheap. You would think that the hacks, the "experts" prepared to cross the borders of honorable professional conduct would at least have become seriously rich, but the craven scientists and activists on Exxon's payroll have apparently been willing to work for a pittance. We learn this from an excellent report prepared by the Union of Concerned Scientists (UCS) in Cambridge, Massachusetts. Between 1998 and 2005, Exxon funnelled a paltry $16 million to a "network of 43 advocacy organizations that seek to confuse the public on global warming science." For this tiny investment, tiny at least on the Exxonian scale, they have helped to retard climate action for years.*

The UCS report *Smoke, Mirrors, and Hot Air* is subtitled "How Exxon Mobil uses Big Tobacco's Tactics to 'Manufacture Uncertainty' on Climate Change." Here the reader may wish to recall the pioneering work, noted above, of Richard Berman on behalf of the tobacco industry recycled here for another noble cause. The methods are tried, if not true. Here's what you need to do:

- Raise doubts about even the most indisputable scientific evidence; play the "uncertainty" card to the utmost;
- Set up and fund a number of front organizations with public-spirited names to create the impression that those who deny climate change are a broad consensus of reputable scientists, rather than the small but close-knit fraternity they actually are, specialized in misrepresenting scientific findings;
- Use the same "experts" to discredit the genuinely broad

* Exxon declared $14.5 million in lobbying expenditures for 2006 according to the *Congressional Quarterly*.

scientific consensus that declares, on the basis of the best
available evidence, that climate change is occurring;

– Project your own "experts" to the press, continue to tout
their publications even when their bona fide scientific
colleagues have denounced and refuted these publications;

– Portray opposition to action on climate change as a positive quest for "sound science" rather than as business
self-interest;

– Avoid all mention of the corporate connections of your
front groups and paid spokespersons;

– Use your privileged access to the government to block
action and shape both executive and legislative attitudes;
suggest key personnel who can fill strategic government
jobs; provide "spin" to government communications on
climate change.

The whole of the Union of Concerned Scientists report is
worth reading but I especially enjoyed the annexes listing the
people and organizations benefiting from Exxon's largesse.
We find some of our old friends from Chapter I like the
Heritage Foundation, the American Enterprise Institute or
the Federalist Society, with other special climate denial Exxon
favorites like the Competitive Enterprise Institute and the
George C. Marshall Institute. One can also note that some of
Exxon's "experts" act as spokespersons for nine or ten of their
front organizations, creating a fake impression of diversity.

Memos from various corporate entities that UCS obtained
via the Freedom of Information Act show how thorough,
effective, and cynical these people can be and how they plan
their work. The annexes also include some juicy contributions from the oil industry umbrella group, the American
Petroleum Institute; others show the connections between
people who once upon a time worked for Big Tobacco and

now serve Big Oil, placing their dubious skills at the service of the global warming denial industry.[25]

For nearly two decades, this industry has staved off reality and prevented Americans from looking it in the face, beginning in the late 1980s. Although various scholars had already published evidence of the increases of greenhouse gases in the atmosphere, the first official notice taken of the phenomenon was at an international conference called by the Canadian government in 1988. The consensus document issued by that conference spoke of the effects of global warming that would be "second only to global nuclear war." To avoid such drastic consequences, humanity had to act fast to reduce greenhouse gas emissions.[26]

The Toronto conference warning triggered the reaction of the United Nations. In record time, it established the Intergovernmental Panel on Climate Change, IPCC; this organization now includes about 2,500 scientists from over eighty countries. They have divided themselves into three working groups: Group One makes and refines the scientific diagnosis of global warming and climate change; Group Two charts the expected impacts; Group Three is responsible for recommending the necessary strategic responses. The latest report of Working Group Two on impacts, issued in early April 2007, is the one cited above, and once more, the corporate lies machine has gone into high gear. The difference between 1990 and 2007 is that today, Bush and Exxon should be feeling a little more lonely.

Their side is finally losing the argument, but not before doing enormous damage. As soon as the IPCC's first synthesis report came out in 1990, the denial lobby was ready for it. When the United Nations set up the IPCC, a flock of transnational corporations, mostly from the petroleum and automotive industries, simultaneously put together the Global Climate Coalition, with the usual high-sounding aims and the real goal of preventing any action whatever to slow or halt greenhouse gas production. The GCC called instead for "more research" and "voluntary measures" (always the standard recommendations of the corporate lobbying industry).

This worked quite well for about a decade but then began to unravel. In 1997, British Petroleum's CEO John Browne announced that his company would withdraw; BP was joined the next year by Shell, which also saw itself henceforward as an "energy" company as opposed to an "oil" company. The GCC ship had slowly begun to founder and other prominent desertions – like Ford and Daimler – followed, until finally the Coalition was pronounced dead in early 2001. Its spokesman told the press, "We have achieved what we wanted to accomplish with the Kyoto Protocol," which the US has never signed.

A personal note : I published my own first contribution on the subject as a chapter in *Global Warming: The Greenpeace Report*, edited by Jeremy Leggett, which appeared in 1990, right after the first IPCC synthesis report. Most of the chapters were by climate and environmental scientists; mine dealt with the economic system that hastened and sustained climate change. This book rings as true now as it did seventeen years ago and looking at the contributions, I cannot find a single one that subsequent research has called into question much less disproved. We knew all the facts we needed to know almost two decades ago and we knew the risks were severe enough to start changing our collective behavior and our governments' policies without delay.[27]

You can read Jeremy Leggett's introduction to the *Greenpeace Report* for some vintage quotes from the denial industry. As soon as the IPCC synthesis came out, the *Wall Street Journal* countered with its typical accusations of "scientific faddism" and "unreliability." Above all, the newspaper instructed, do nothing. "We hope the President hangs tough on this one," said the *WSJ*. He did. The President at the time was also named Bush and his offspring is still doing nothing.

Well, no, not exactly nothing. In fact, the White House, in cooperation with Exxon and the Petroleum Institute, has done rather a lot. The Bush White House has specialized in naming former lobbyists to top jobs in government agencies they previously sought to deregulate or destroy. Thus a timber industry lobbyist took charge of the forest service, one from the mining industry was named to oversee public lands and, until 2005 when he was forced to resign, Philip Cooney was chief of staff of the White House Council on Environmental Quality, an institution that shapes much of the country's policy on the environment. Mr Cooney had spent the previous fifteen years at the American Petroleum Institute in charge of its "climate team."

Greenpeace documented the Exxon–White House link in 2003, publicizing an e-mail obtained through the Freedom of Information Act.* In this cosy and conspiratorial-sounding memo, Mr Myron Ebell writes to Mr Cooney. Mr Ebell is an employee of the Competitive Enterprise Institute which, according to the Union of Concerned Scientists' report, received between 1998 and 2005 $2 million from Exxon, making it the best-funded of all Exxon's front organizations. It is Cooney who has initiated the exchange – Ebell begins his memo with "Thanks for calling and asking for our help."

What help could Mr Cooney need and Mr Ebell provide? Cooney's problem was this: Somehow, the United States government's Environmental Protection Agency had got the bizarre idea that its mission was to protect the environment. This misapprehension had caused the EPA to prepare a study for the United Nations on climate change, the US *Climate*

---

* You have to wonder when they will get rid of the Freedom of Information Act . . .

Action Report of 2002; a report specifically recognizing that human activity was the cause of climate change. The EPA report, drawn up by scientists from US government, industry, and universities further forecast major impacts of global warming on America itself and called for action to minimize their economic consequences. Although it did not go so far as to call for a reduction of greenhouse gas emissions, the EPA report announced that since it was too late to stop the predicted impacts through a reduction program, one should at least prepare to deal with the consequences.

All this was a stark departure from previous US statements and the media seized upon it. It got huge play. At last, the United States had officially recognized that the climate was changing, that something had to be done. Cooney's emergency cry for help to Ebell was prompted by the media storm. Ebell gave this advice: "Drive a wedge between the President and those in the Administration who think that they are serving the President's interests by publishing this rubbish." He outlined a plan to make the head of the Environmental Protection Agency the scapegoat and force her to resign.[28]

The EPA probably thought it was safe in publishing because the report had been approved by all the relevant governmental agencies, but it reckoned without Exxon. Two days after Cooney got the e-mail from Ebell, Bush repudiated the scientists' report, saying it had been "put out by the bureaucracy." In May 2003, after several more incidents of high level interference, Ms Christine Todd Whitman, the embattled head of the EPA, resigned.

Cooney, however, continued as Editor-in-Chief of environmental publications. Although his academic degrees are in economics and law, he made hundreds of changes to various scientific documents, excising and softening them and adding weasel words like "potentially" or "might" where scientists saw certainty and direct human responsibility for climate change. In March 2005, a veteran official of the government's climate-change research program called Rick Piltz had had enough. He resigned and subsequently took his story, plus documents he had "liberated" to the *New York Times*, providing it with the perfect "Fox Guards Henhouse" revelations: Man spends fifteen years at American Petroleum Institute in charge of climate; Man becomes White House official, Man systematically doctors scientific studies to favor oil industry's interests . . .

The White House Press Secretary did his best to convince the media that the "interagency review process" justified political actors meddling with scientific documents. The media didn't buy it and Cooney resigned next day. A few days later he was hired by? You are allowed only one guess.*

There is a sequel. Nearly two years later, in March 2007, the Congressional Committee on Oversight and Government Reform held hearings and called Philip Cooney as a witness. In his prepared testimony, Cooney assured the Committee of his "high standard of integrity" and informed members that "each day that I served over four years, I worked very hard to advance the Administration's stated goals and policies." An impartial observer might note that this was precisely the problem. Cooney tried to hide behind the Administration's "Policy Book" and a report from the National Academy of Sciences dating from 2001 which, to give him his due and the benefit of the doubt , was couched in particularly fuzzy language. He claimed he often used direct quotes from the NAS study in his own "review comments."

Cooney definitely had a point, however, when he explained to the Congressional Committee that, within a month of his resignation, his action was implicitly confirmed by "all three branches of government." In June 2005, the Senate indeed

* Exxon.

defeated legislation for a "mandatory, national cap and trade system for greenhouse gases." The US Court of Appeals did uphold the decision of the Environmental Protection Agency *not* to regulate CO2 under the Clean Air Act. Finally, the jamboree G-8 meeting of the heads of State and Government at Gleneagles accepted Bush's refusal to take a stand and issued a particularly weak and waffling statement on global warming.

Oil rather than blood often seems to course through the veins of President Bush and Vice-President Cheney. But it is not just the obstruction of the executive branch that has criminally delayed action on global warming in the United States. The Congress, the Courts, and federal agency personnel are part of the web. The problem is not so much that the spokespersons for industry leave their Washington lobby offices to become high-level bureaucrats. The problem is that they never really leave. They continue to do the same work in government that they did in K Street, Washington's PR thoroughfare.

ISOLATED INCIDENTS? LOOK AGAIN

Cooney and the others we have met along the way are members of a proliferating fraternity. Government manipulation, distortion, and censorship of scientific information have become routine and we have once more the documentary evidence to prove it thanks to the work of the Union of Concerned Scientists and the Government Accountability Project. These two organizations surveyed hundreds of government scientists working on climate questions in several federal agencies and departments, including Agriculture, Energy, and Defense; NASA, the National Oceanic and Atmospheric Administration (NOAA); the Environmental Protection Agency and several others. The UCS-GAP researchers note that about 2,000 government scientists spend at least part of their time on climate-related issues; they sent their questionnaires to 1,500 of them and 308 responded. They also studied thousands of pages of government documents obtained through the Freedom of Information Act or from insiders and they carried out forty in-depth interviews.[29]

The results are discouraging and disquieting. Nearly half the respondents (46 percent) had "perceived or personally experienced pressure" to eliminate words like "climate change" or "global warming" from their communications. Forty-three percent had perceived or personally experienced changes and edits by their superiors and reviewers that altered the meaning of scientific findings; while over a third reported that statements by officials at their agencies misrepresented the scientists' findings.

Asked to quantify the number of incidents of political interference of all kinds over the past five years, 150 scientists listed a total of 435 incidents. The more frequently a climate scientist's work touched on politically sensitive or controversial issues, the more the scientist reported interference. From this evidence, one can conclude that Philip Cooney may be a spectacular example, but in the Washington climate science world, his conduct was fairly routine.

Scientists at NASA in particular complained of having funds withdrawn from their research in earth science and shifted to Mars or the moon; one at the US Geological Survey said, "US satellite programs are in severe jeopardy. [Because of funding cuts] the loss of continuity in observational satellite data will impair progress in climate science." Morale is sinking. Another scientist at the Environmental Protection Agency said, "I am close to retirement and feel that I will no longer be able to use my abilities to produce scientific information of use to the American public. The last years of my career are being squandered for political reasons." The scientists feel they are victims of "incredible bureaucratization"

intent on "crippling our scientific productivity." The USC
survey also asked respondents to choose the most appropriate
word in the following statement: "Today's environment for
federal government climate science is (better, worse, same)
compared with five years ago." Sixty-seven percent said it was
worse.

All this political filtering and interference remind one of
the worst regimes in recent history; of Hitler's contempt
for "Jewish physics" and the Soviet Union's promotion of
Lyssenko's erroneous biological theories; their purges of scientists whose work displeased the rulers and did not conform
to official truth. How is the present American administration
any different? True, it does not put offending scientific workers in camps or liquidate them. It accepts, however, that it will
not get the accurate science it needs to make policy decisions.
With their professional integrity in question, scientists who
consider themselves public servants will look elsewhere and
the government will be unable to attract scientific talent.

As summed up by a scientist at the Department of
Agriculture who responded to the UCS survey, "The results
of science should not be diluted or adjusted to justify policy.
This particular Administration has gone beyond reasonable
boundaries . . . To be in denial on climate change is a crime
against the Nation." Crime is the correct word. When scientific integrity and the free flow of information on vital issues
is not valued, indeed rejected, the welfare of present and
future generations is under direct attack. In government-
dictated science as in war, truth is the first casualty and it is
the people who suffer.*

---

* The US House of Representatives Committee on Oversight and
Government Reform has published a full and damning report based on
27,000 pages of documentation (December 2007). Entitled "Political
Interference with Climate Change Science under the Bush Administration,"
it more than confirms this criminal tampering.

CONCLUSION: WHY UNDERTAKE THIS BOOK?

The direction American thought and culture takes affects everyone in the world and no one who has come this far will be surprised to learn that I find this direction grievously mistaken. Religious and secular conservative pressures have changed the nature of the country and its values. Why pretend to be neutral on the subject? Neutrality in social commentary and in the so-called social sciences is impossible anyway and authors should make their biases known. I hope to have done so, while remaining fair-minded.

I worry that much of America and many Americans – though very far from all, thank God – have become mean-spirited and fearful; that American perceptions have shifted; that they are no longer the ones I grew up with and never will be again. I owe America and Americans and my own family and background a tremendous debt. Please let me indulge in a short personal narrative here. I was born and raised in the US, of solid American "stock" (as the somewhat zoological expression goes). My paternal grandmother Stanley's ancestors arrived in the Massachusetts Bay Colony from England in 1632. They were religious dissidents who initiated the family genius for selling potentially valuable property cheap and moving on (a good portion of Harvard Square in Cambridge, Massachusetts for starters).

My mother's side included an officer in the Revolutionary War who spent the terrible winter of 1777–8 at Valley Forge with General Washington's ragtag, frozen, battle-weary, hungry, disease-ridden army. He died in 1812 in North Carolina, having freed his slaves. When I learned about Col. Vance, he made me happy for a week

The Vances too moved on and my mother's branch home-steaded in Southern Illinois on the rich land of the corn belt. In 1822, Samuel Vance and his team of oxen plowed part of the Chicago–Vincennes road, now Illinois Route 1. He donated twenty-six acres to the town of Paris, Illinois to build the new county seat, still at the center of Edgar County. One of his grandsons went "back East," at least as far as Ohio, to attend medical school and one of his children was my mother. The last of my forebears to reach American shores, my pater-nal great-grandfather Alfred Akers, arrived just at the end of the Civil War. An apprentice tin-smith from Kings Lynn, Norfolk, he had a bad fight with his boss's son, took the first boat to New York, then a barge to the end of the Erie Canal and ended up in Akron, Ohio, where he established a success-ful roofing and construction company. The outcome of all this traveling was, eventually, me.

I'm proud of these people and these origins and I've tried to be true to them in writing this book. I hope that this history, plus an adult life spent in France (where my studies and subsequent marriage brought me and where I later became a citizen) provide a vantage point combining proximity and distance – emotionally, intellectually, geo-graphically – for observing changing American attitudes and politics during the latter half of the twentieth century and beyond.

The dominant self-image of Americans is still a combination of the melting pot and, usually (although less often than before), enlightenment values with a dash of the hardy frontier spirit thrown in. Most Americans feel as though they belong to God's chosen people. Patriotic displays are not seen as "corny," "kitsch," or embarrassing but as bearing witness to ideals which should be shared by all right-thinking people. The United States is perhaps the only nation in the world where a prohibition on flag-burning could be seriously proposed as a Constitutional amendment without provoking general hilarity.

American perceptions of their own history – at least those instilled in me – might be summed up as follows. The American Revolutionary War was a heroic moment, inaugurating an entirely new phase in human affairs and a victory won against tremendous odds. The Constitution and the Bill of Rights are unique documents, and continue to protect hard-won freedoms. The Civil War was a harrowing moment for the country, but in spite of everything, Americans managed to abolish slavery, however great the problems of racism and poverty may remain. The American stance in the First and Second World Wars was exemplary.

Nor, in this traditional view, could one improve upon American standards of personal behavior. You should be strong and count on yourself; you should not blame others for your failings but work hard to correct them; just as you should work hard, period. If you did, then you could accomplish anything. That went for women as well as men, at least in my family. Along with self-reliance came a duty to others, to those who needed help and were less fortunate. Especially if you were privileged, as I was, you were expected to give back generously to the community, with time and resources and with gratitude for what you had received.

Religion generally reinforced these secular values. In the America of the mid-twentieth century, nearly everyone went to church, as the majority still do. My family's was the Protestant Episcopal Church, and as I have already written elsewhere, I owe it a great debt as well. I shall never write as well as I would like, but the prose style of the services, the Saint James Bible and the Book of Common Prayer correspond to a period of splendor in the English language and I am grateful to have had it so often in my ear.

The schools did not stress (an understatement) the history of American interventionism and the negative side of its national actions; neither did they concentrate on racism, maltreatment of immigrants, union-busting and the early manifestations of corporate control or capitalist greed. We heard in school about the robber barons, about strikes brutally repressed or the Ku Klux Klan but looked on them not as structural features of our country but as painful aberrations that a good dose of democracy would correct.

When President Eisenhower said farewell and told the country to beware of the "Military–Industrial Complex" whose increasing power risked creating, in its own interest, a permanent war economy, we took him seriously. The Vietnam War later caused many Americans to stop and reflect on their country's role abroad. The nineteen sixties and seventies were tumultuous, witnessing face-offs between new attitudes and traditional ones and they resulted in the development of a new and far more radical political consciousness in significant segments of the US population.

These attitudes and beliefs combined to create what successive Presidents, from the 1930s onwards, called the New Deal or the Great Society or by some other name, but the idea was the same. America could only be great as a nation when it shared. Presidents can only lead when the people follow and they follow because they all have a stake in the country. The "land of opportunity" was not supposed to be an empty phrase but an accurate description of the United States and its capacity to include everyone. Naïve, surely; impossibly virtuous, probably; silent about a great many horrible episodes at home and abroad, undoubtedly – but still close enough.

Today, even the world of the seventies, much less the fifties, seems barely recognizable. The question I ask myself, and have constantly asked myself as I have been writing this book, is this: Will it be possible to return to a more generous, though surely less innocent, American culture and politics; or are the changes wrought by fifty years of manufacturing and imposing neo-liberal or neo-conservative secular and religious ideology and values permanent?

Today, winners take all, losers nothing. The riches of some are obscene; so is the poverty of others. The corporate and financial leadership has, deep down, nothing but contempt for the weak. Rather than fellow-creatures deserving our help, the poor deserve what they get – which is very little indeed. The government is content to watch from the sidelines as the achievements of the civil rights movement are beaten back. These attitudes, as Hurricane Katrina dramatically displayed to the world, will prevail unless and until public opinion demands change. It shows, for now, few signs of revolt, particularly among the poor themselves.

As economic inequalities advance, the result is the destruction of social cohesion and solidarity. In the disaster of New Orleans, foreign governments were quicker to offer help than Washington. Indeed, why bother with poor, mostly black people who were unable to escape? They too got what they deserved.

Psychologists at Princeton University recently used magnetic resonance imaging to measure the responses of students' brains to photographs of people from various social groups. The prefrontal cortex normally lights up in response to "socially significant stimuli" but the researchers were

> shocked to discover that photos of people belonging to "extreme" out-groups, such as drug addicts, stimulated no activity in this region at all, suggesting that the viewers considered them to be less than human. "It is just what you see with homeless people or beggars in the street," says (a psychologist), "people treat them like piles of garbage."*

Although no one should doubt that many classic, good, kind Americans remain, the vast majority has no idea whatsoever what their government and corporations are doing at home, much less in the world at large. No one encourages them to grasp the political, economic, and strategic objectives of the elite; they do not see, except in extreme cases like Iraq, how their country's actions take their toll on other nations and other peoples.

The media fulfill their function of what media critic Herbert Schiller called "Dumbing down, American style."[1] Most people get their news exclusively from television where the dividing line between information and entertainment grows ever more tenuous, giving rise to the hideous neologism "infotainment." Five or six transnational corporations hold a virtual monopoly over broadcasting, they are not interested in providing Americans with analysis. What they do not control, the religious broadcasting systems do. Americans almost never receive any cultural input that does not come from America itself – that is, from corporate or corporate-

---

* There is hope, however. It was enough to ask any question about the person in the photograph, such as "What food do you think this beggar might prefer?" to light up the brain zone. See Mark Buchanan, "Are We Born Prejudiced?," *New Scientist*, March 17, 2007

religious sources. For example, foreign films represent a mere one percent of American movie attendance, restricted to upper-class cognoscenti in large cities. The "quality papers" like the *New York Times* or the *Washington Post* are also geographically and numerically limited in circulation.

As for the Enlightenment, as we have seen, "creationism" is now legally taught in many states to "balance" Darwinism and evolution; even though it sometimes takes the sham-scientific form of "intelligent design." The leadership's disdain for science is hurting people and the planet. No stem cell research means no cures for presently incurable diseases; rejection of climate science in the country responsible for a quarter of all CO2 emissions means a hotter, potentially devastated planet. Evidence-based, scientific solutions to problems systematically take a back seat to corporate interests, like those of the oil industry, and to know-nothing religious denial.

Some public schools are doing better than ten years ago and are improving their teaching, particularly of reading, writing, and math; but many are still crumbling, and they rarely equip students to think critically. Education is also infested with religious cranks and in the universities, the neo-con thought police threaten professors with dismissal and condemn them to a spineless "neutrality."

Religion seems to have less and less to do with loving one's neighbor and doing unto others as you would have others do unto you; more and more to do with rejoicing that your neighbor will be burnt to a crisp when Christ returns, serving the sinner right. In Rome, wits say that the letters on Vatican City automobile licence plates, marked SCV (for Stato della Città del Vaticano) actually stand for "Se Christo Vedesse" – "If Christ were to see . . ." One could say the same about much of the religious doctrine and practice drummed into the American faithful today.

Measures of social control are generally effective; they include keeping more than two million underclass, troublesome, mostly minority men behind bars; hundreds of thousands of them for non-violent drug offences. The US rate of imprisonment per 100,000 people (773) is the highest in the world.

In sum, the ideology-inequality factory is turning out goods most people buy without even knowing it. The price is too high and we are all paying it, including those of us who do not live in the United States.

Some revisionists are now rueful that Abraham Lincoln, instead of waging the Civil War, didn't just let the South secede. This is not entirely a joke. Without "Dixie," they point out that life would have been easier for everyone, and Democratic Party strategists today would not have to write books with titles like *How Democrats Can Win without the South*[2] or hunt for a presidential candidate who can please the Bible Belt.

An economic historian from the University of California, Roger Ransom, has taken the secessionist proposition seriously and constructed a counterfactual, "what if?" scenario. His book called *The Confederate States of America: What Might Have Been*[3] changes some military details resulting in a Civil War stalemate rather than a Northern victory. Lincoln, under pressure from France and Britain as well as his own electorate, signs a peace treaty with the Confederacy and the South becomes an independent country. Over the following decade, world demand for cotton declines and the slaves are set free because they are no longer profitable. They live on as second-class citizens in a kind of American-style apartheid system, while the North tries to prevent them from crossing the international border.

Well, Lincoln didn't lose, the South didn't become an independent country and progressives must still try to live with, or fight against, Southern and increasingly Western conservatism which infects other parts of the country as well. So the progressives can continue to lose.

But they could also win. It is worth remembering old, comforting words like "This too will pass" or "nothing lasts forever." From 2005 to 2007, since I started work on this book, neo-liberals and neo-cons in the United States have taken several severe hits. As we have seen, a Pennsylvania district court condemned a local school board that wanted to teach creationism. The lobbying scandal around Jack Abramoff caught many Republican Congressional representatives in its sticky net. The prominent neo-con I. Lewis "Scooter" Libby, Dick Cheney's former chief of staff, was tried and convicted of perjury and sent to prison in disgrace. Paul Wolfowitz got chucked out of the World Bank, Karl Rove has left the White House. Iraq is an unholy mess and Bush's popularity is at an all time low. People jokingly argue about whether Bush is *the* worst President in American history or only one of the worst. Best of all, the Republican majority in both the House and the Senate has been thrown out.

Economist Paul Krugman feels sure that Americans are fed up with growing inequalities. Distractions like September 11 can last only so long and you can't prevent poor people from voting forever. He thinks that the Democrats, "who spent most of the Clinton years trying to reassure rich people and corporations" are going to have to change radically.[4]

More comfort is at hand when we recall Lincoln's famous wisdom: "You can fool some of the people all of the time and all of the people some of the time, but . . ." You know the rest – even though George Bush and his team are still trying to fool all of the people all of the time. Why should they succeed or, more pessimistically, how can we make sure they fail? Even the billions spent on the production and dissemination of neo-liberal ideology; even the additional billions of the right-wing religious networks may not be enough to fool all of the people – or at least a significant electoral majority – all of the time. As noted at the outset, Americans have changed their minds about President Bush who, in 2005, was "honest" and "good;" but in 2007 "incompetent" and "arrogant."

Despite the Democrats' genius for snatching defeat from the jaws of victory, the next President will probably come from their ranks – not because they are so brilliant but because Bush is so loathed. If you look at the local newspapers in the United States, at the pictures of the young soldiers who have lost their lives or their limbs in Iraq, you will see that they come from the heartland, from small towns you never heard of. The children of the rich do not join the military. Those who do see it as an opportunity to learn a trade and take a social step forwards. Their families are those trusting, patriotic, often evangelical Christians that traditionally vote Republican. These families are bolting. If the Democrats win in 2008, as now seems likely, within two or three years, Iraq will be *their* war, and they have no idea how to exit – at least none they have told the American people about. Remembering the upheavals that accompanied the long delayed exit from Vietnam, I refuse to make any predictions except to say that the country is not out of the ideological or the political woods yet.

Nonetheless, if America now baffles Europeans, they should prepare to become more baffled still. The country is changing and moving away from Europe. Historically, as my own story shows, immigration came first from Britain and Northern Europe. It shifts in the 1880s to Southern and Eastern Europe. Between 1881 and 1920 almost 24 million people, virtually all of them Europeans, sailed past the Statue of Liberty.* Meanwhile, Chinese and other Asians were used as laborers to build the railroads but were legally banned from becoming citizens for decades.

---

* A bit of poetic license here, as the Statue of Liberty was not dedicated until 1886.

Contrast this historic immigration with that of today: Between 2000 and 2005, a total of 5.7 million immigrants received legal permanent resident status in the United States. Forty-one percent of them were Hispanics from Mexico, Central and South America, almost half of those from Mexico alone. Another quarter of them were Asians; only 15 percent came from "Europe," broadly defined, with a good third of those European immigrants coming from Russia and former Soviet Union countries.[5]

America is also demographically destined to pull yet further away from Western Europe and increasingly to disregard European views and attitudes. European opinions – especially those of "old Europe" as Bush and Rumsfeld called it – will count for even less than they did at the time of the Iraq invasion. Just as the American population is on the march, the United States is itself moving southwards and westwards, toward Latin America and Asia. When it suits US corporate or State interests, Europe will continue to be treated as a partner (for example in the "Open-Skies Agreement" for air-travel or other free-trade arrangements); otherwise, Europe is nothing but a potential rival and must be kept in its place. So far, the European Commission and most European governments meekly submit, quite content with this scenario of subservience.

My view is that Europeans should be investing heavily in their own future as a geo-political entity and in their own infrastructural, educational, and intellectual base. Four hundred thousand European scientists are working in the United States and three-quarters of them have no intention of ever returning "home."[6] But Europe must also take the trans-Atlantic ideological challenge seriously and stop following the cultural lead of the United States. The present European Commission is undoubtedly the most neo-liberal in history. The European Constitution proposed a detailed blueprint for an irreversible, neo-liberal and militarized economy until it was defeated in the French and Dutch referendums in 2005. The so-called "Reform Treaty" that replaces it is virtually the same – don't trust me on this point but the Constitution's principal author, former French President Valery Giscard d'Estaing. He said of the new Treaty, "They made some cosmetic changes to make it easier to swallow." It is still neo-liberal, militaristic, and almost impossible to change. The French voters have chosen Nicolas Sarkozy, a Gallic version of Thatcher or Reagan for President. Other EU countries have taken the road to the right.

The political task for all those who oppose these trends, whether Americans or not, seems clear. We must combat this ideology and learn the lessons of the American right wing's "long march through the institutions." People and institutions with the means to do so should finance the production and dissemination of new and progressive ideas (along with many good old ones). Intellectuals and educators should be contributing to forging and spreading them; students should be studying them; citizens should be discussing them; everyone should be proud of them.

To paraphrase Marx and Engels, "Progressives of the world unite! You have nothing to lose but your cultural chains."

NOTES

Introduction: How the Secular and Religious Right Captured America

1 Eric Alterman, *When Presidents Lie*, Viking, New York, 2004, has a lot more to say on this topic.
2 Michael Kinsley (American editor of *Guardian Unlimited*, London), *Washington Post*, April 19, 2002
3 Gore Vidal was speaking on the BBC World Service on September 10, 2002 ("East Asia Today").
4 Chris Hedges, *American Fascists. The Christian Right and the War on America*, The Free Press, 2007

Chapter 1 Manufacturing Common Sense, or Cultural Hegemony for Beginners

This chapter began as a contribution to the Transnational Institute book called *Selling US Wars* edited by TNI Fellow Achin Vanaik, with a preface by Tariq Ali (Olive Branch Press, an imprint of Interlink Publishing Group, Northampton, Massachusetts). Here it has been greatly expanded and revised.

1 Mandelson made this declaration at a Party seminar in June 2002 and published his contribution shortly afterwards in *The Times*, June 10, 2002.

2 *Time Magazine* cover story of December 31, 1965.

3 Particularly, for example, Article 25 of the Universal Declaration of Human Rights of 1948.

4 Thus, "freedom of speech" does not include the right to shout "Fire!" in a crowded theater, as a famous US Supreme Court decision made clear.

5 Hurricane Katrina revealed the social and ecological consequences of the "economic freedom" to increase global warming and to leave the poor to their fate.

6 See chapters 3 and 4.

7 See my *Remettre l'OMC à sa place*, 1001 Nuits, Paris, 2001 where the former WTO director of the General Agreement on Trade in Services (GATS) is quoted to this effect. US companies were also instrumental in the provisions of the TRIPS (intellectual property) agreement.

8 John Micklethwait and Adrian Wooldridge, *The Right Nation: Conservative Power in America*, Penguin, 2004.

9 Micklethwait and Wooldridge, ibid., p. 10.

10 James Allen Smith, *The Idea Brokers*, The Free Press, New York, 1991; Jon Wiener, "Dollars for Neocon Scholars," *The Nation*, January 1, 1990.

11 Susan George, "How to Win the War of Ideas: Lessons from the Gramscian Right," *Dissent*, Summer 1997.

12 These remarks do not apply to TNI's American funders, particularly the Samuel Rubin Foundation which has shown admirable constancy in its commitments. It is, however, quite small compared to the neo-con giants.

13 Joyce took early retirement from Bradley in 2002, after fifteen years at the helm, in order to satisfy George Bush's and Karl Rove's request that he set up a new organization called Americans for Community, Faith-Centered Enterprise.

14 In his regular *Washington Post* column, June 8, 2001.

15 An extremely useful source on both Bradley and Olin is John J. Miller, "Strategic Investment in Ideas: How Two Foundations Reshaped America," brochure for *The Philanthropy Roundtable*, Washington, DC, 70 pp.

16 www.mediatransparency.org

17 I have used among other sources the site of People for the American Way (www.pfaw.org) for information about foundations: though now dated, their work remains extremely useful. Heavily footnoted, all references can be found on this site for those who want to pursue the study of US neo-cons, at least through the mid-1990s.

18 "Cheney's Guy," *US News and World Report*, May 29, 2006.

19 The most thorough source on Addison is Jane Mayer, "Letter from Washington: The Hidden Power," *The New Yorker*, March 7, 2006. On Cheney, Addington, and their circle, see Joan Didion, "Cheney: The Fatal Touch," *The New York Review of Books*, October 5, 2006.

20 Jane Mayer, "Letter from Washington": The source is Scott Horton, adjunct professor at Columbia Law School but also a distinguished human rights law defender.

21 Didion, "Cheney: The Fatal Touch."

22 Robert Kuttner, Comment: Philanthropy and Movements," *The American Prospect*, vol. 13, no. 13, July 15, 2002.

Chapter 2 Foreign Affairs

1 David Cay Johnston, "US multinationals shift their tax burden: profit taken in offshore havens rose 68% over three years, report finds," *New York Times* (quoting a study in *Tax Notes* and Commerce Department documents), September 13, 2004,

2 Justin Raimondo, "Norman's Narcissism: Podhoretz in love," a column on the site of antiwar.com, October 16, 2000

3 Norman Podhoretz, "World War IV: How it started, what it means and why we have to win," *Commentary*, September 2004. This immensely long piece – almost a book – is an excellent source for seeing the entire history of the post-war world from the neo-con viewpoint.

4 Joshua Muravchik, "Operation Comeback," *Foreign Policy*, November–December 2006.

5 Joshua Muravchik, "Bomb Iran: Diplomacy is doing nothing to stop the Iranian nuclear threat; a show of force is the only answer," *Los Angeles Times*, November 19, 2006

6 "Lieberman speech to AIPAC National Policy Conference"; press release from Senator Lieberman's office, March 12, 2007, http://lieberman.senate.gov

7 The initial Mearsheimer–Walt article "The Israeli Lobby" appeared in the *London Review of Books* in the March 23, 2006 issue; *Foreign Policy*'s piece is called "The War over Israel's Influence" with counter arguments from Aaron Friedberg, Dennis Ross, and Shlomo Ben-Ami, July–August 2006; the much longer Mearsheimer–Walt *Middle East Policy* article ("The Israel Lobby and US Foreign Policy," *MEP*, Vol. 13, no. 3 September 2006, pp. 29–87) is the one I refer to in following passages unless otherwise noted. Their book, also titled *The Israel Lobby*, was published by Farrar Strauss and Giroux in September 2007.

8 Jeffrey H. Birnbaum, "Washington's Power 25," *Fortune*, December 8,1997; Jeffrey H. Birnbaum and Russell Newell, "Fat and Happy in DC," *Fortune*, May 28, 2001; Richard Cohen, Peter Bell, "Congressional Insiders Poll," the *National Journal*, March 5, 2005.

9 See Mearsheimer & Walt's long and detailed notes 21, 22, and 23 in *MEP*, note 7.

10 "A Bad Influence?" *Foreign Policy*, March–April 2007, p. 66, my emphasis.

11 The critics, Aaron Friedberg, Dennis Ross and Shlomo

Ben-Ami are quoted from their rebuttals of Mearsheimer and Walt in *Foreign Policy*, as in note 7.

12 See "Who Wins in Iraq," a symposium of ten authors claiming victories for ten winners, *Foreign Policy*, March–April 2007.

13 Sheldon Rampton and John Stauber, *Weapons of Mass Deception: The Uses of Propaganda in Bush's War on Iraq*, Jeremy P. Tarcher/Penguin USA, New York, 2003.

14 Rampton and Stauber, ibid., chapter 1, "Branding America."

15 Ibid., p. 41.

16 Not all of these people signed all of the PNAC documents.

17 For an expansion on this theme, see my "Brief History of Neo-liberalism," at www.tni.org/george; *A Fate Worse than Debt* (Penguin, 1987), *Faith and Credit: The World Bank's Secular Empire* (with Fabrizio Sabelli, Penguin 1995) as well as chapters one and three of *Another World is Possible, If . . .* (Verso 2004).

18 I am grateful to *The Ecologist* for this handy compendium of Boltonisms: September 2005, p. 9. More detailed information in the well-researched paper by Tom Barry, "Bolton's Baggage," International Relations Center, www.irc-online.org, March 11, 2005.

19 "American ex-diplomats urge to block Bolton nomination to UN post," *USA Today*, Associated Press, March 28, 2005.

20 Phyllis Schlafly, "The impertinence of our so-called allies," Eagle Forum, June 25, 2003.

21 See the website of People for the American Way, www.pfaw.org .

22 See the excellent and copiously documented Special Report from the People for the American Way Foundation: "UN-dermined: The Right's Disdain for the

UN and International Treaties," n.d. (2nd half 2005); www.pfaw.org .

23 Karen Kwiatowski, US Army Lieutenant Colonel (Ret); "In Rumsfeld's Shop," *American Conservative*, 1 December 2003 and idem, "The New Pentagon Papers," www.slate.com, March 10, 2004

24 Seymour Hersh, "The Iran Plans," *The New Yorker*, April 17, 2006.;

25 David Hartridge, speaking at a symposium organized by the international law firm Clifford Chance in 1997 called "Opening Markets for Banking Worldwide." The proceedings are no longer on the website of the firm.

26 Europeans behave no better in any of these areas, particularly with Peter Mandelson in the position of Trade Commissioner, but this book is concerned primarily with American neo-liberalism.

Chapter 3 The American Religious Right and its Long March through the Institutions

1 Based on Tables 67, 68, 69 of the *Statistical Abstract of the United States 2004–05*, US Census Bureau, Washington DC; Table 73 in the 2007 edition. The most recent figures on religion date from 2001.

2 Bill Moyers, "Welcome to Doomsday," *New York Review of Books*, March 23, 2005.

3 Pew Forum on Religion and Public Life, survey by the Pew Research Center, August 2006.

4 Arthur Schlesinger, "Eyeless in Iraq," *New York Review of Books*, 23 October 2003

5 Garry Wills, "A Country Ruled by Faith;" *New York Review of Books*, November 16, 2006.

6 Ibid.

7 www.theocracywatch.org is a good site on all these ques-

tions, see also Americans United for the Separation of Church and State.

8 Frederick Clarkson, a series of four articles on "Christian Reconstructionism" in *The Public Eye* Magazine, vol. 8, no. 1, March–June 1994 quote in Part Four; see also Paul Krugman, "For God's Sake," *New York Times*, April 13, 2007.

9 The quotes from Gary North are from Walter Olson, *Reason*, November 1998 and reasononline www.reason.com/news/show/30789.html .

10 Pew Survey, op.cit.

11 David D. Kirkpatrick, "Club of most powerful gathers in strictest privacy," *New York Times*, August 28, 2004; I also found a partial list of attendees for one meeting in 1998 on line.

12 More on Pat Robertson on www.publiceye.org .

13 Reported by James D. Besser in *The Jewish Week*, November 11, 2006

14 Jim Naughton, "Follow the Money," a Special Report in *Washington Window*, the monthly magazine of the Episcopal Diocese of Washington DC, May 2006.

15 *New York Times*, June 18, 2004.

16 Craig Berkman, cited by Greg Goldin, "The fifteen percent solution: How the Christian right is building from below to take over from above," first published in *The Nation* in 1993, available on the site of theocracywatch.org.

17 Associated Press dispatch December 4, 2006

18 "SNAP to US Bishops: Stop International Movement of Pedophile Priests," SNAP press release, November 13, 2006

19 www.richardsipe.com/reports/sipe_report_2005.htm.

20 See Sipe's heartrending "Dialogues" on his site.

21 This information and much else in Garry Wills, "Fringe Government," *New York Review of Books*, October 6, 2005.

22 Wills, ibid., note 22.

23 Those who wish to pursue the topic seriously should look at the Fundamentalism Project at the University of Chicago which covers Christian, Jewish, Muslim, Hindu, Sikh, and Buddhist fundamentalisms in a series of volumes published between 1993 and 2004.

24 "September 11th and the mandate of the Church," October 8, 2003, www.focusonthefamily.org. Go to Focus on Social Issues, Political Islam.

25 Bill Moyers as in note 2 citing journalist Tom Harpur of the *Toronto Star*, n.d.

26 Michael C. Dorf, "The Justice Department's Change of Heart on Torture," on the FindLaw site, January 5, 2005.

27 Quoted on the site of the Christian Kos Community "Street Prophets:" "Abu Ghraib is the Hell House of the Christian Right," November 25, 2005.

28 Matthew J. Morgan, "The Origins of the New Terrorism," *Parameters* (the United States Military College quarterly), Spring 2004, citing Amir Taheri, *Holy Terror: The Inside Story of Islamic Terrorism*, London, Hutchinson, 1987, p. 192. Morgan, a Captain in the US Army, is part of the Military Intelligence Battalion later deployed to Afghanistan for Operation Enduring Freedom, Joint Task Force Intelligence Staff.

29 David Kibble, "The Attacks of 9/11: Evidence of a Clash of Religions?," *Parameters* (the United States Military College quarterly journal) Carlyle, PA, Autumn 2002. Kibble, a Lieutenant Commander in the British Royal Naval Reserve, Ret., also holds a degree in theology. Born-again Christians have tried to take over the Air Force Academy and exclude cadets who do not profess these religious views.

30 Nearly all the information about Hell Houses found on the page, or the references, of the Ontario Consultants on Religious Tolerance, or on http://beliefnet.com.

31 Les Eskridge of the Institute for the Study of American Evangelicals, *Rolling Stone*, January 28, 2004.

32 Quoted from George Monbiot's very useful summary, "Apocalypse Please," *Guardian*, April 20, 2004.

33 Joan Didion, "Mr Bush and the Divine," *New York Review of Books*, October 9, 2003.

34 See the CFOIC site.

35 Site of the Hagee ministries www.jhm.org.

36 Countercurrents.org posted November 6, 2006. It is likely that the mid-term elections, held the following day, threw cold water on any plans of this nature which Bush might have been nurturing.

37 James D. Besser, "ADL breaks with Pack on Church-State, *The Jewish Week*, November 11, 2005.

38 Zev Chafets, "The Rabbi who loved Evangelicals (and vice-versa)," *New York Times*, 24 July 2005.

39 Bill Moyers, "Welcome to Doomsday."

Chapter 4 Extinguishing the Enlightenment: The Assault on Knowledge

1 The definition comes from the internet encyclopedia Wikipedia.

2 The Galileo quote about heaven and the heavens is borrowed from John Gribben, *Deep Simplicity*, Penguin, 2005, p. 6.

3 ABC News Primetime Poll: Bible Stories, February 10, 2004: "Six in ten take Bible stories literally but don't blame Jews for death of Jesus."

4 "Christianity reborn," *The Economist*, December 19, 2006.

5 Kenneth Miller, a professor of biology at Brown University testified to this effect in the intelligent design case *Kitzmiller* et al. v. *Dover Area School Board* heard by Judge John E. Jones in Federal District Court, December 2005.

6 The ID debates have been going strong since the

Discovery Institute was founded in 1996. Those wishing to pursue the matter in depth will find dozens of articles from about 1996 to 2001 at the link. www.simonyi.ox.ac.uk/dawkins/WorldOfDawkins-archive/Catalano/box/behe.shtml#intro .

7 Taken from Richard Lewontin, "The Wars over Evolution," *New York Review of Books*, October 20, 2005.

8 Charles Darwin, quoted from the "Summary and Conclusion" of *The Descent of Man*; Behe's book *Darwin's Black Box: The Biochemical Challenge to Evolution*, is published by The Free Press, a division of Simon and Schuster, New York, 1996.

9 H. Allen Orr, "Darwin vs. Intelligent Design (Again)," a review of Michael Behe's book, as above, *The Boston Review* (MIT), December 1996–January 1997. I highly recommend this long, well-written, well-reasoned review which is a quick guide to dismantling all of the ID arguments.

10 Ronald Dworkin, "Three Questions for America," *New York Review of Books*, September 21, 2006.

11 See Mark Lombard, "Intelligent design belittles God, Vatican Director says," Catholic Online, January 30, 2006; Cardinal Schoenborn published his op-ed "Finding Design in Nature" in the *New York Times*, July 7, 2005. Schoenborn is known to be close to Benedict XVI and this may well be the present Pope's view. If so, Father Coyne was particularly courageous to speak out.

12 Celeste Biever, "The God Lab," *New Scientist*, December 16, 2006.

13 p. 43 of Judge Jones's opinion in *Kitzmiller* et al., as above.

14 Mike Holderness, "Enemy at the Gates," *New Scientist*, October 8, 2005.

15 See the *Beyond Belief* and the Science Network's websites and George Johnson, "A Free-for-all on Science and Religion"; the *New York Times*, November 21, 2006.

NOTES TO PAGES 185-209

16 Personal communication, January 15, 2007.

17 Bob Unruh, "Brave New Schools: Baptists' 'exit strategy' means get kids out of public schools," quoting Pastor Wiley Drake of California, the Rev. Albert Mohler, President of the Southern Baptist Theological Seminary and others in the WorldNetDaily, October 20, 2006. WorldNetDaily, a highly conservative news service and book/magazine publisher with clear ties to the religious right, has a daily readership of six to seven million.

18 Unruh, ibid., citing Rick Scarborough, author of a book titled *Liberalism Kills Kids*. This long piece includes many references and links to the Homeschool Movement.

19 Aside from the sites of exodus2000.org, homeschooling-familytofamily.org, and hslda.org, see the excellent special report in the *New Scientist*, Amanda Gefter, "Home-schooling special: Preach your children well," November 11, 2006.

20 Amanda Gefter in *New Scientist*.

21 See the Patrick Henry College website for the faith statement, the student handbook, etc.; also Hanna Rosin, "Annals of Education: God and Country," The *New Yorker*, June 27, 2005.

Chapter 5 *Lobbies, Corridors, and Seats of Power*

1 For the complete list, see LobbyWatch at the Center for Public Integrity, www.publicintegrity.org .

2 "Confidential Memorandum: Attack of American Free Enterprise System" 23 August 1971, TO: Mr Eugene B. Sydnor, Jr. US Chamber of Commerce FROM: Lewis F. Powell, Jr.

3 The goal of Reclaim.Democracy.org on whose site one can read the full text of the Powell Memo is "Restoring citizen authority over corporations." This organization shares my dim view of "progressive" organizations and

funders who focus only on "damage control, band-aids and short term results" whereas genuine systemic change is urgently needed.

4 US Department of Labor, Bureau of Labor Statistics, www.bls.gov, *Characteristics of Minimum Wage Workers 2005*, Tables 1–10.

5 Holly Sklar, "Imagine a Country: Life in the new millennium," CrossCurrents (Z Magazine Online); May 2003, vol. 16, no. 5.

6 Holly Sklar, "Minimum wage breaks no-raise record," Znet Commentary, December 29, 2006.

7 Sklar, "Imagine a Country."

8 The best official sources on skewed wealth in the United States of America are the Census Bureau and the Federal Reserve, notably Federal Reserve Board, *Survey of Consumer Finances (SCF)* which comes out every three years, the most recent covering 2001–4, published in February 2006. One can go directly to the *Chartbook* of the SCF or see: Brian Bucks, Arthur Kennickel, Kevin Moore, "Recent Changes in US Family Finance: Evidence from the 2001 and 2004 *Survey of Consumer Finances*," *Federal Reserve Bulletin*, vol. 92, February 2006. Excellent scholars on the subject are Edward N. Wolff (New York University), *Top Heavy: The Increasing Inequality of Wealth and What Can be Done About It*, New Press, New York, 2nd edition 2002 and G. William Domhoff, (University of California, Santa Cruz). See his website WhoRulesAmerica.net and his frequently updated book, also called *Who Rules America?* McGraw-Hill, latest edition 2006. Also Gerard Duménil and Dominique Levy, "Neoliberal income trends: Wealth, class and ownership in the USA," *New Left Review*, vol. 30 November–December 2004. An excellent long-term study based on federal income tax returns is Thomas Piketty and Emmanuel Saez, "Income

inequality in the United States 1913–98," *Quarterly Journal of Economics*, Vol. 118, I, 2003. In a more popular vein are several books by Kevin Phillips, a Republican, also sound on income gaps.

9 Doug Henwood, *Left Business Observer*, no. 114, December 2006, citing the work of Thomas Piketty and Emmanuel Saez based on US tax returns.

10 The OECD in Figures 2006–7, *OECD Observer 2006/ Supplement 1*.

11 All the funding figures are from the National Education Association, NEA Research, *Rankings and Estimates*, Report November 2006, various tables (129pp total).

12 Russell Berman, "New York Outpacing Other States in School Spending, US Data Show," *New York Sun*, April 4, 2006.

13 Speech by Secretary of Education Margaret Spellings to the "Celebration of Teaching and Learning Conference," March 23, 2007.

14 Information on the drawbacks of No Child Left Behind from National Education Association press releases "'No Child Left Behind funding plan shortchanges schools," July 14, 2004 and "Schools lack funding to comply with No Child Left Behind," March 29, 2006; Statement of Jack Jennings, President, Center on Education Policy before the Subcommittee on Labor, Health, and Human Services, Education and Related Agencies, US Senate Committee on Appropriations, March 14, 2007 and corresponding press release.

15 Bureau of Labor Statistics and Bureau of the Census, *Current Population Survey*, Table PINC-03, "Educational attainment – People 25 years and over, by total money earnings 2005."

16 For a critique of several books dealing with these problems and details on the quotes used (concerning CalTech

and the *New York Times* op-ed), see Andrew Delbanco, "Scandals of Higher Education,"*New York Review of Books*, March 29, 2007.

17 Jim VandeHei, "Businesses gain in GOP Takeover: Political allies push corporate agenda," *Washington Post*, March 27, 2005. 'GOP' stands for Grand Old Party – another way of naming the Republicans.

18 All data from official sites of the US House of Representatives and the US Senate.

19 The House of Representatives Committee on Education and Labor, Sub-Committee on Health, Employment, Labor and Pensions, Charles I. Cohen, Statement of the US Chamber of Commerce on the Employee Free Choice Act, February 8, 2007.

20 Factsheet on the Employee Free Choice Act, "Employer interference by the numbers" (relates to private-sector employers), AFL-CIO, n.d. all figures referenced in footnotes on the factsheet.

21 "The Thirteen Scariest People in America," Alternet, posted October 30, 2006, www.alternet.org/story/43586/.

22 "The Thirteen Scariest People in America"; *Old Trout Magazine* and AlterNet; October 30, 2006 and Sheldon Rampton and John Stauber, "Berman & Co.: 'Non-profit' Hustlers for the Food and Booze Biz," *PR Watch* , Vol. 8, No.1, first quarter 2001.

23 Fiona Harvey, reporting on the latest United Nations Intergovernmental Panel on Climate Change report in the *Financial Times*, April 7–8, 2007, p. 3.

24 George Monbiot, "The Real Climate Censorship," *Guardian*, April 10, 2007.

25 The full report *Smoke and Mirrors* is available on ucs@ucsusa.org 68 pp.

26 Statement of the participants in the World Conference on "The Changing Atmosphere: Implications for Global

Security," Toronto, June 30, 1988. See Jeremy Leggett's Introduction to the *Greenpeace Report*, cf. following note.

27 Jeremy Leggett, ed. *Global Warming: the Greenpeace Report*, Oxford University Press, 1990. My chapter was entitled "Managing the Global House: Redefining Economics in a Greenhouse World."

28 I have reconstructed the sequence from Chapter three of the Union of Concerned Scientists and Global Accountability Project report *Atmospheric Pressure: Political Interference in Federal Climate Science*, Chapter 3, Cambridge, Massachusetts, February 2007; the Greenpeace press release and the account of it published on the site of www.truthout.org ("Greenpeace obtains smoking-gun memo: White House/Exxon link," September 9, 2003) and other media accounts.

29 Union of Concerned Scientists and Government Accountability Project, *Atmosphere of Pressure*, Cambridge, Massachusetts, February 2007.

Conclusion: Why Undertake this Book?

1 In *Le Monde Diplomatique* and *Guardian Weekly*, August 1999.

2 Thomas F. Schaller, *Whistling Past Dixie. How Democrats Can Win without the South*, Simon and Schuster, New York, 2007.

3 Roger L. Ransom, *The Confederate States of America: What Might Have Been* , W. W. Norton, New York, 2006.

4 Paul Krugman, "Distract and Disenfranchise," *International Herald Tribune*, April 3, 2007

5 Calculated from the Department of Homeland Security, *2005 Yearbook of Immigration Statistics*, Table 2: "Persons obtaining legal permanent resident status by region and selected country of last residence 1820–2005."

6 John Blair, "Trans-Atlantic Brain Drain Worries Europe's Policy Makers," *Research-Technology Management* (Industrial Research Institute), March 1, 2004.

INDEX